French Film in Britain

FRENCH FILM IN BRITAIN

Sex, Art and Cinephilia

Lucy Mazdon and Catherine Wheatley

berghahn
NEW YORK • OXFORD
www.berghahnbooks.com

First published in 2013 by
Berghahn Books
www.berghahnbooks.com

©2013, 2021 Lucy Mazdon and Catherine Wheatley
First paperback edition published in 2021

All rights reserved. Except for the quotation of short passages for the purposes of criticism and review, no part of this book may be reproduced in any form or by any means, electronic or mechanical, including photocopying, recording, or any information storage and retrieval system now known or to be invented, without written permission of the publisher.

Library of Congress Cataloging-in-Publication Data

Mazdon, Lucy.
   French film in Britain : sex, art and cinephilia / Lucy Mazdon and Catherine Wheatley.
     p. cm.
  Includes index.
  ISBN 978-0-85745-350-1 (hardback : alk. paper) -- ISBN 978-0-85745-379-2 (ebook)
   1. Motion pictures, French--Great Britain. 2. Motion pictures--France--History--20th century. I. Wheatley, Catherine. II. Title.
  PN1993.5.F7M39 2013
  791.43094409'04--dc23

2012032898

British Library Cataloguing in Publication Data

A catalogue record for this book is available from the British Library

Printed in the United States on acid-free paper.

ISBN 978-0-85745-350-1 (hardback)
ISBN 978-1-80073-012-0 (paperback)
ISBN 978-0-85745-379-2 (ebook)

Contents

List of Illustrations	vii
Acknowledgements	ix
Introduction	1
1 The Advent of Sound: A Changing Film Culture (1925–1939)	17
2 Cinema Goes to War (1939–1950)	51
3 'Saucy and Naughty and Witty and Chic': Can French Films Fill the Gap? (1950–1959)	81
4 The French New Wave on British Shores (1959–1970)	105
5 'A New Low in French Films': Changing Perceptions of French Cinema (1970–1982)	141
6 Video Saved the French Film? (1982–2002)	175
Conclusion	211
Index	223

List of Illustrations

1. Poster advertising the re-release of *Les Enfants du Paradis* (Marcel Carné, 1945).   3
2. Poster advertising the re-release of *Les Enfants Terribles* (Jean-Pierre Melville, 1950).   4
3. Jean Dujardin and Bérénice Bejo in *The Artist* (Michel Hazanavicius, 2011).   12
4. *Zéro de Conduite* (Jean Vigo, 1933).   40
5. Mireille Balin, Jean Gabin and Lucas Gridoux in *Pépé le Moko* (Julien Duvivier, 1937).   45
6. A Peter Strausfeld poster advertising a re-release of *La Kermesse Héroïque* (Jacques Feyder, 1935) at Academy Cinema Two.   46
7. Poster advertising a 1940s release of Jean Renoir's *Partie de Campagne* (1936).   52
8. Poster advertising a post-war release of *Pépé le Moko* (Julien Duvivier, 1937) and *Paris 1900* (Nicole Vedres, 1947).   73
9. A Peter Strausfeld poster for a screening of René Barberis' *Ramuntcho* (1937) at The Academy.   76
10. Vittorio de Sica, John Ford and René Clair celebrate the opening of the NFT in October 1952.   85
11. A poster advertising a much later re-release of 1950s success *Les Diaboliques* (H.G. Clouzot, 1955).   96
12. British publicity poster for *The Wages of Fear* (H.G. Clouzot, 1953).   98
13. A Curzon poster for Marcel Camus' *Orfeu Negro*, which arrived on British shores already garlanded with prizes.   109
14. A UK poster for François Truffaut's *Les 400 Coups*, distributed by Kenneth Rive's Gala.   111

15. A UK poster for Truffaut's 1964 *La Peau douce*. The film was deemed a critical failure by the British Press, despite a typically racy advertising campaign. 122
16. Connoisseur's poster for Claude Chabrol's *Le Boucher*, the type of 'quality' film that the company's director William Pallanca felt should be subtitled but not dubbed. 150
17. UK poster for *La Nuit Américaine*, shown in both dubbed and subtitled versions as *Day for Night*. 153
18. Gala's poster for Louis Malle's *Le Souffle au Coeur*, translated by Rive as *Dearest Love*. 163
19. UK poster for *Betty Blue*, starring Béatrice Dalle. 191
20. UK poster for *Cyrano de Bergerac*, starring Gérard Depardieu. Twenty years after its release, it remains the second-biggest grossing French film at the UK box office. 204
21. *Tell No One* (Guillaume Canet, 2006). 213
22. *La Vie en Rose* (Oliver Dahan, 2007) 214
23. Jean Dujardin and Bérénice Bejo in *The Artist* (Michel Hazanavicius, 2011). 215
24. *Amélie* (Jean-Pierre Jeunet, 2001). 216

Acknowledgements

This book is the final product of four years research, funded by the Arts and Humanities Research Council. Our first debt is to them for awarding a grant to Lucy Mazdon, for her 'French Cinema in Britain' project.

We have been fortunate to benefit from the experience and advice of archival experts and librarians. We would like to express our gratitude to the staff at the BFI library, special collections and stills department, at the Bibliothèque de film in Paris and at the viewing department of the *Centre national de la cinématographie*.

A number of other individuals and organisations have benefitted the production of this work in various manners. Richard Napper of Curzon Cinemas, Caroline Aymer of Unifrance, Alex Stolz of the now-defunct UK Film Council, Sandra Hebron, former Director of the London Film Festival, and Robert Beeson of New Wave films all kindly agreed to interviews, and were generous with their time and their knowledge. Our fellow researchers Geoffrey Nowell-Smith and Christophe Dupin were gracious enough to share with us archival findings and a wonderful interview with Penelope Houston.

An early event in the lifespan of the project was a major conference on Franco-British cinematic relations held at the University of Southampton in 2007. We would like to thank all those who participated in that conference for their enthusiasm and inspiration. Thanks must also go to colleagues and students in Film Studies at the University of Southampton whose encouragement and interest has been much appreciated, as well as to the staff of the various universities who invited us to share our research with them, and who offered fascinating and very useful feedback.

Last, but far from least, our thanks go to the team at Berghahn, and in particular to Mark Stanton for his editorial support and guidance: having joined the project early on, he has expertly steered it through to production.

Introduction

In Gilbert Adair's 1930s-set Agatha Christie pastiche of 2007, *A Mysterious Affair of Style*, a visit to a film set provokes a discussion about the 'special' nature of French cinema. Philippe Françaix, a French film critic, claims that in his experience the English 'like to watch nothing but foreign films' (Adair 2007: 112). Evadne Mount, bestselling whodunit author and amateur sleuth, protests, 'Why Monsieur Françaix, only a very few foreign films open in London, mostly at a cinema called the Academy. And what a godsend it is for us devotees of the Seventh Art' (112). Much to Mount's astonishment, Françaix points out that he was referring to the 'films of Ollywood' (112). 'It's a funny thing,' states Mount. 'We somehow don't really think of them as foreign' (113). The limited appeal of French cinema is further underlined when both Françaix and Mount express surprise at plodding police officer Trubshawe's admission that he had once seen a French film. The film in question was *The Dames of the Bois de Boulogne* (*sic*) which Trubshawe confesses had been something of a disappointment as he was 'expecting something a bit ruder, a bit naughtier – you know, ladies of the night and all that' (113).

While this is of course a light-hearted, fictional definition of French film, it does provide a very accurate summary of dominant perceptions of the Gallic cinematic product in Britain, perceptions established in the early decades of the twentieth century and still prevalent today. French films are 'a special taste', they have a limited presence and are not typically destined for the general cinema-going public (such surprise at Trubshawe's brush with Bresson!). In Britain French films are seen as foreign, unlike the products of Hollywood which, thanks to their sheer ubiquity and common language, are perceived as a part of the domestic culture. French films might be worth a look for their 'raciness', a naughtiness rarely found in British and American movies. Yet despite enticing titles (those Dames of the Bois de Boulogne), the expected raciness often fails to materialise and the viewer in search of titillation is left to contend with a rather challenging 'foreign' film.

This emphasis on difference is not of course limited to fiction. In an article in the *Observer* in August 2010, Henry Porter laments the demise of the UK Film Council and suggests that this says much about the general disregard for the importance of cinema which typifies British cultural life (Porter 2010). In contrast he claims that French cinema is experiencing a 'golden age' with a wide selection of 'quality' films enabled by a supportive film-going public and State funding system. He concludes: 'French films are made for grown-ups and, because of the unabashed interest in their own society and their own stories, often have as much integrity as they do charm. The French accept that cinema is more than entertainment, a revenue earner and an employment generator: it is culture' (Porter 2010). In other words, Porter draws a clear line between French and British film culture, emphasising the superiority but also the sheer difference of the Gallic product. The article closes with a list of 'French classics': *La Règle du jeu*; *Les Enfants du Paradis*; *A bout de souffle*; *Jules et Jim*; *Le Mépris* and *Jean de Florette*, all films which, as we shall discover, have been used to form a 'canon' of French cinematic excellence for British audiences.

That British audiences should continue to perceive French cinema in such specific ways is perhaps surprising given recent developments in French film-making and cinema-going. In an article in the *Guardian* newspaper of 29 January 2007, Angelique Chrisafis describes the demise of the *cinéphile* and the art-house cinema in contemporary France:

> The nation that created the New Wave and elevated film-makers such as Godard and Truffaut to god-like status, can no longer bear to sit through anything that smacks of seriousness or pretension. So great has the public's aversion to art house cinema become that one distributor has warned that the very French species of the cinéphile – the discerning movie-buff who ignores marketing hype and seeks out intellectual masterpieces – is becoming extinct.
> (Chrisafis 2007)

While the recent decline in France's art-house audience is undeniable, Chrisafis' perception of a long history of French cinephilia and love for all things 'artistic' masks an equally long and arguably more important history of popular film consumption. As she herself points out, the current decline in art-house audiences is matched by the recent success of 'France's low-brow commercial films'. Indeed cinema audiences in France have continued to grow but the films they choose to watch are 'not broody epics but rom-coms and a new crop of slapstick'. Yet even the most cursory glance at French box-office takings of the last fifty years will reveal that this state of affairs is nothing new. Comic films dominate the list of the best-selling French films and the films of Godard, Truffaut and other New Wave luminaries are nowhere to be seen.

1. Poster advertising the re-release of *Les Enfants du Paradis* (Marcel Carné, 1945).
Image courtesy of the BFI stills department.

2. Poster advertising the re-release of *Les Enfants Terribles* (Jean-Pierre Melville, 1950).
Image courtesy of the BFI stills department.

So rather than provide an accurate picture of contemporary French film-going, what Chrisafis' account instead suggests is a picture of French cinema dominant outside France, a picture constructed with the middle-class, middle-brow British *Guardian* reader very much in mind. Yes, art-house cinemas have survived and even thrived in France largely due to various forms of state support and there is a long tradition of taking film seriously. However, there has also been, and continues to be, a thriving popular cinematic culture and a vast audience for movies far removed from the experimentation of Godard et al. Somehow this culture and these movies either disappear or become something other as French cinema crosses the Channel.

This book then emerges from a curiosity and an unease at the very limited ways in which French cinema is described and discussed in Britain, both at the level of popular criticism and within more serious academic study. In a British market long dominated by Hollywood, French films are consistently the most widely distributed non-English-language work apart from Bollywood cinema. However, French cinema appears to undergo a transformation as it reaches Britain, becoming something quite different to that experienced by audiences at home. Films which in France have been distributed, exhibited and viewed according to their genre, the presence of particular stars, the identity of the director and so on are to a great extent positioned within the UK market as *French* films. Moreover, those films which actually make the journey to British screens constitute a very limited group defined, to a great extent, by distributors' expectations of British tastes which are themselves shaped by longstanding preconceptions of British resistance to the 'foreign'. It is worth noting that Unifrance, the French government-funded agency established to promote domestic cinema overseas, is far less active in Britain than in other European countries as it is perceived as barren territory for French box-office success.

What this book thus sets out to do is to analyse how and why this process of transformation takes place and to what extent it curtails French cinema's plural identities via a study of the distribution, exhibition, promotion and reception of French cinema in Britain. By moving beyond accounts of French cinema as it is experienced and articulated within France and engaging instead with a detailed historical study of the dissemination of French cinema in Britain we aim to problematise dominant Anglophone and French understandings of what constitutes 'French' cinema and construct a clear picture of the various transformations which occur as films travel between these two cultures.

Although the filmic text can never of course be entirely 'up for grabs', the processes of travel and cross-cultural re-contextualisation and reception which take place as a film moves from France to Britain have a significant impact upon that film and potential modes of reception, a process which is often rendered invisible in the various discourses which surround the film. Removed from its initial context of production and relocated and re-presented to new audiences with very different expectations of this 'foreign' cinema, the imported film becomes something 'other' subject to new interpretive strategies. This is perhaps particularly true of non-English-language cinema within the UK. The dominance of American and, to a lesser extent, British film, the limited space for non-English-language works and the subtitling or dubbing of the imported films means an even greater 'othering' of these works and an extension of the process of transformation or indeed 'remaking' which, as this book argues, is central to the cross-channel journey of French cinema.

This 'remaking' is often made clearly visible at the level of film titling. As we reveal in the chapters that follow, while some films retain their French titles for British release and some are translated literally, others are given English versions which differ wildly from the French original and are often chosen to entice audiences with suggestions of daring material not necessarily visible in the film itself (recall once again Trubshawe's excitement at the thought of those Dames from the Bois de Boulogne!).[1] And yet the impact of this re- or dis-location is either ignored entirely (typically in British academic accounts of French cinema which assume an educated readership and disavow the fact that the majority of those readers will only have access to this cinema in a 'foreign' context) or, as in the case of popular criticism, simply accepted as somehow a key part of the identity of 'foreign' cinema, as if all French or Italian or Spanish films were subtitled and shown in specialised cinemas from the out-set. This of course raises a number of interesting questions in terms of the discourses of 'transnationalism' or 'global cinema' so central to both recent academic work on film history and the contemporary film industry. While the importing of French cinema to the United Kingdom is indubitably an element of transnational exchange, the modes of distribution, exhibition and reception accorded to these films in many ways curtail the hybridity which this cross-channel exchange may at first seem to engender. French language movies, when they come to Britain, become 'French cinema' (or, in earlier decades, 'Continental' cinema), a limited and highly constrained body of work which is in fact seen to represent, however erroneously, a 'national' cinema and a 'national' culture.[2]

The discourses and decisions which construct 'French cinema' in and for the British market – distribution, exhibition, critical responses, dubbing and/or subtitling – are not of course the result of happenstance. As we will demonstrate, they are embedded within and shaped by specific historical contexts and industry paradigms. The following chapters will thus analyse, through the study of these discourses, the varying ways in which French cinema has been located and perceived in the British context in the last eight decades. The organisation of our analysis into specific historical periods enables a study of French cinema in Britain which fully acknowledges the impact of socio-cultural context on this presence. That said, we are of course aware of the somewhat artificial nature of the division into decades. While this is without doubt a useful heuristic tool, it is vital to acknowledge the fluid nature of historical divisions and the continuities which mark relationships between decades as well as the differences. So while the following chapters will trace the shifts in the distribution, exhibition and reception of French cinema in Britain in the 1930s, 1940s, 1950s, 1960s, 1970s, 1980s and 1990s, it will also set out to stress the similarities and continuities which each period shares.

The advent of sound in the late 1920s had a profound impact on transnational cinematic exchange: whereas silent French films had travelled to Britain and for the most part found a ready commercial market, sound films with their French dialogue created a new barrier to exportability. As a result, attempts to create a space for 'Continental' films in Britain in the 1930s were bound up with debates about the aesthetic limitations and/or potential of sound film and the establishment of a serious film culture. The outbreak of war in the 1940s and its impact on cinema both in France and Britain meant a shortage of the Gallic product which posed a number of problems for the 'Continental' distributors and exhibitors. In the 1950s and again in the 1970s, the British distribution of French film was deeply influenced by debates about censorship and certification and foreign cinema's potential for pushing the boundaries of what might be deemed morally acceptable and cinematically appealing. While the 1950s proved to be a 'golden age' for French cinema in Britain, the 1970s was generally perceived to mark an all-time low. The 1960s saw the arrival of the French New Wave on British shores. The subsequent canonisation of these films might suggest that this would also be a high spot for the British exhibition of French cinema, yet the reality was in fact rather different as distributors and exhibitors struggled to balance commercial success with critical standing. Changes to film and television culture in the 1980s and onwards, in particular the advent of video and later DVD technology, would also have a significant impact on the availability of and audiences for French cinema in the UK, changing once again the landscape for this particular form of cross-channel exchange. In other words, as the chapters which follow reveal, those longstanding definitions of French cinema, which at first glance may seem entirely self-evident to the average British film-goer, are the result of complex debates and decisions themselves rooted within specific historical and cultural contexts.

Given this book's own position within British academic discourse, it is important to note the significant role played by such discourse in the construction of British articulations of 'French cinema'. The study of French cinema in the United Kingdom has long been firmly established within the discipline of French Studies. While approaches to French film have been rich and varied, the vast majority repose upon an unquestioned notion of what constitutes French cinema or indeed France: 'France' is metropolitan France and 'French cinema' is the films of that nation. Particularly problematic from this study's point of view is the failure of the majority of these works to acknowledge the transformation experienced by 'French cinema' as it moves beyond France that we describe above. Written essentially for an Anglophone readership, these works base their arguments upon a 'French cinema' available only to domestic audiences and a limited number of bilingual readers with the wherewithal to see and understand untranslated films never actually exported to the United Kingdom. In other words there is a gap between the 'French cinema' much academic writing describes for its readers and the 'French cinema' many of those readers will have actually experienced. The failure to acknowledge that gap is a thoroughly homogenising gesture which denies the process of transformation or remaking undertaken by films as they move across national borders and into new viewing contexts. In a strongly worded discussion of 'French Studies' Bill Marshall describes this focus on the 'centre', on metropolitan France, as a form of 'officialising' and claims that this, coupled with the automatic prestige anything in France seems to take on in Anglo-Saxon countries, bedevils 'French' culture (Marshall 1999: 263):

> French culture is too important to be left to the French, nothing is 'betrayed', quite the contrary, by teaching it in English, seeing it from the outside, feeling the *va-et-vient* as we journey through cultures and languages. The most interesting French people working in 'French' are the exiles, those who left to avoid military service, to escape the appalling sexual politics or the immobilism of the university system, not those for whom French or France are something fixed and finished. 'French' and 'France' need to be articulated with what they are not, with the European and even Atlantic context, and beyond.
> (Marshall 1999: 263)

It is just such a deterritorialisation that is described in this book. However, while it does indeed reveal another 'French cinema', a 'French cinema' not identical to that experienced within metropolitan France, it would be foolhardy to perceive this shift in terms of the plurality envisaged by Marshall: as we have discussed, French cinema's journey to British shores is largely subject to various forms of curtailment (a limited selection of films shown and consumed in very specific contexts). Nevertheless, via an historical study of the discourses and practices which have shaped that journey and the new identities acquired by 'French cinema' in the British context, this book unpacks hegemonic notions of 'Frenchness', revealing the shifts that such constructions experience as they move to new contexts and new modes of consumption.

The book also plays a role in deterritorialising British film culture as it reveals the roles truly 'foreign' films (as opposed to the assimilated Hollywood product) have played in its formation. Indeed, as we discussed in our earlier book, *Je t'aime, moi non plus: Franco-British Cinematic Relations* (Mazdon and Wheatley 2010), that particular *va-et-vient* between French and British cinemas has been far more significant than histories of the respective 'national' industries have acknowledged. Exchanges at the level of production, exhibition and distribution, reception, representation and personnel have helped to shape these two film cultures so often described, as Porter reveals in his aforementioned *Observer* article, as polar opposites. In many ways this book is much more a study of British film culture and the ways in which it has resisted, embraced, exploited or assimilated the French product than it is a history of French cinema. And yet it is important that we stress the limitations of the British film culture or indeed the 'Britain' we are describing here, for, as our history reveals, the presence of French film in the United Kingdom has to a great extent been restricted to the nation's major cities and at certain moments and, in the case of certain films, it has struggled to move beyond London. So to some extent the 'Britain' we describe here is essentially an English, indeed London based, construction and thus a very partial and arguably problematic take on national identity. Our study does reveal the presence of French film in Wales, Scotland and Northern Ireland, and these particular relationships and the ways in which they differ from English and/or London attitudes to the cross-channel product certainly merit further study. Nevertheless, the research which forms the basis of our narrative has predominantly told the story of a middle class, metropolitan Englishness and its responses to French film. This is clearly significant and says much about the type of space and audience created for French film in this country, of the expectations as to what 'kind' of people would be interested in these films. However, an understanding of these limitations, of the particular nature of the 'Britain' we articulate here, should not be ignored.

All of this reminds us then of the instability of any notion of a 'national' cinema. That which may be constructed and marketed as 'French' for a domestic audience is not identical to that which will be sold as 'French' elsewhere. Moreover, the specificities of region and class for example, readily available to audiences in Paris, will typically be subsumed within a generalised 'Frenchness' by audiences in London, a 'Frenchness' which seems to hold great appeal for these audiences as evidenced by the overwhelming British success of films such as *Jean de Florette* (1986) and *Amélie* (2001) with their loving recreations of recognisable (and yet highly artificial) French land and cityscapes. There is no single 'French' cinema but rather a whole series of French cinemas and yet the journey to the British context invariably curtails that plurality and contains French-language movies within a very limiting set of categories and expectations. Further problematising this process is of course the overweening presence of Hollywood cinema in the British market. As fictional film critic Philippe Françaix notes, the British don't regard the films of Hollywood as foreign. And this of course has serious implications for those films which *are* perceived as foreign (essentially films with non-English-language dialogue). The dominance of the Hollywood product automatically limits space for other types of cinema while its absolute assimilation within British culture, its status as the cinematic 'norm' for the vast majority of British filmgoers, further 'others' those 'truly' foreign films, inevitably limiting their chances of box-office success.

Hollywood's prominence in British film culture reminds us of the absolute centrality of language to any attempt to understand the place of French cinema in Britain.[3] If American films are not perceived as foreign in Britain this is of course essentially due to a (mostly) shared language. As Joachim Lembach points out, 'For UK audiences this means that they are in the enviable position that the mainstream Hollywood product, which for them holds the same attraction as for any other audience in the world, is available to them in the original version, and that it looks no different from the domestic product they sometimes find at the cinema, but above all on television' (Lembach 2003: 49). The situation is of course entirely different in other European countries where consumption of American cinema means viewing the films in either dubbed or subtitled versions. This has meant that translated films are an accepted part of French, German or Italian film cultures and the concessions made to authenticity (through dubbing) or viewing ease (subtitling) are similarly afforded to films from a whole variety of other countries (50). That non-English-language cinema has, for so many years, had such a limited presence in Britain is often attributed to insularity and hostility to the foreign. As this book will reveal, this has played and indeed continues to play a role in defining French cinema's place in the United Kingdom: recall again the French industry's own limited interest in the British market. It is worth noting that for the most part it is foreign films that are able to disguise their foreignness which best perform at the British box office. These include animated films (*Igor*, 2008), English language co-productions such as *Taken* (2008) and the documentary *March of the Penguins* (2005) which, through the addition of an American voice-over narrative, effaced all trace of Frenchness. It is also worth underlining the box-office success of a very particular group of non-English-language films, subtitled American films such as *The Passion of the Christ* (2004), *Apocalypto* (2006) and *Inglourious Basterds* (2009). That these 'foreign language' films should achieve credible box-office results in the UK to a great extent reinforces suspicions about British audiences' resistance to the foreign. Here the subtitles and the foreign language are made palatable by the presence of familiar and, for the most part, American stars: the films may not be in English and yet they are very patently not 'foreign'.

As I write this Introduction, a French film is enjoying unprecedented success at the British box office, so far grossing around £8,000,000 and almost matching French box-office takings. This film is of course Michel Hazanavicius' *The Artist*, a black-and-white, silent homage to the great works of early American cinema. In addition to its substantial international box office, the film won seven BAFTAs and five Oscars in 2012, another unprecedented success for a French movie. While it is refreshing to see a French film achieving such success both in the U.K. and the U.S., it should perhaps best be described as the exception which proves the rule. Its gentle humour, loving recreation of 1920s/1930s Hollywood and romantic narrative echo that other nostalgic French crowd-pleaser, *Amélie* (2001), and its appeal to middle-brow British audiences with a taste for 'quality' French cinema. However, by effacing its very Frenchness, both at the level of narrative and in particular language itself, *The Artist* managed to reach well beyond the typical audience for 'foreign' cinema thus underlining the absolute centrality of language to the British reception of French film. While tales of spectators walking out of screenings of *The Artist* upon realisation that it was a silent film suggest some resistance to its lack of dialogue, its box-office takings so far reveal that most British cinema-goers would much rather see a silent film than a film in French.

Particularly important is what Lembach condemns as 'the cultural and intellectual snobbery at the heart of a highly polarised film culture [which] for decades has contributed to preventing mainstream non-English-language films from becoming available to wider audiences in well-dubbed versions' (50). As Chapter One reveals, the re-creation of a place for 'Continental' cinema in Britain after the advent of sound was largely the work of a small group of somewhat 'highbrow' film lovers. Their efforts, via a private members club dubbed the Film Society and specialised cinemas such as London's The Academy which acted as both distributor and exhibitor, were, as we shall see, impressive and played a vital role in making the 1930s something of a golden age for French cinema in Britain. However, their highbrow tastes meant that early experiments in dubbed cinema were met with distaste as they saw the process as an attack on cinematic art. Writing in 1947, Julia Wolf, a pioneer in dubbing techniques, attributed the limited box-office success of the foreign language film in Britain to the decision to subtitle most releases (Wolf 1947: 89). She argued for the dubbing of films not considered suitable for the specialised cinemas and thus an extension of foreign cinema beyond the rather rarefied, and mostly London based, venues in which it then found a home. Yet over sixty years later, the prejudice and the obstacles identified by Wolf to all intents and purposes remain in place as the vast majority of foreign-language films are released in subtitled versions to essentially

3. Jean Dujardin and Bérénice Bejo in *The Artist* (Michel Hazanavicius, 2011). Image courtesy of the BFI stills department.

'specialised' audiences and those few films which are released in dubbed prints frequently meet with quite lukewarm audience response.

A brief exit poll survey carried out on behalf of Momentum Pictures and the now defunct U.K. Film Council on Saturday 13 March 2010 sheds some interesting light on audiences for dubbed and subtitled films.[4] The film in question was *The Girl with the Dragon Tattoo*, a Swedish film based on Stieg Larsson's best-selling Millennium trilogy. The film was shown at the Curzon in London's Mayfair (a cinema which has a long history of screening foreign film), the Odeon Printworks in Manchester and the Vue Cinema in Hull. In London only the subtitled version was shown, in Hull only the dubbed print and in Manchester both versions were screened. The poll's results revealed that the dubbed version attracted more mainstream cinema-goers, those more likely to have seen recent box-office hits such as James Cameron's *Avatar*. The subtitled audience, especially in London, showed a much stronger preference for foreign/art-house films (foreign and English language) and were significantly more likely (65 per cent versus 34 per cent) to watch foreign films 'a lot' or 'occasionally'. Furthermore, a greater proportion of the subtitled audience (22 per cent versus 4 per cent for dubbed) had planned for more than a week to watch the film. In other words, the audience for the subtitled film revealed themselves as more selective in their cinematic choices than the audience for the dubbed print who were far more spontaneous. Those seeing the subtitled version of the film were also significantly more likely (45 per cent versus 26 per cent) to rate the film 'excellent' than those seeing the dubbed print.

This was perhaps partly due to the film itself. Although an action-packed thriller, the film does not entirely conform to Hollywood standards in terms of narrative, genre and aesthetic and features Scandinavian actors largely unfamiliar to most British film-goers. As such, those seeing the film in the dubbed version, and thus expecting something very close to or even identical to the products of Hollywood (an expectation largely encouraged by the film's Hollywood-style trailer which elides all trace of foreignness), may well have been disappointed. However, it is likely that their reduced enthusiasm for the film was also provoked by the dubbing itself. One in six respondents mentioned that the dubbing was low quality and around half of those watching the dubbed version would have preferred to see the subtitled version as opposed to only 14 per cent of the subtitled audience expressing preference for the dubbed film.

The report concludes that dubbed prints are more effective in attracting a mainstream audience for foreign film. Interestingly, ratings for the dubbed print were higher in Manchester where audiences were offered a choice and the survey determines that giving such choice is key: 'While it may not be feasible to secure multiple screens to show both the subtitled and dubbed versions at the same cinema across multiple cities, offering each version at different sites within a defined catchment area and communicating this could attract wider audiences.' To a great extent this echoes Lembach's conclusion that offering good quality dubbed prints of foreign films to British audiences would help it to escape from the specialised circuit in which it has, with some notable exceptions, been situated in Britain since the early 1930s.[5]

Without doubt more choice would seem to be a positive thing, particularly when we consider the limiting impact that distribution within the British market tends to have on French cinema. And yet, as this book will reveal, the likelihood of such choice becoming widely available is far from certain. Distribution and exhibition patterns for French cinema in the United Kingdom, along with decisions over translation, have of course experienced some degree of change in the decades since sound technology rendered foreign cinema's journey to Britain so perilous. However, as our study reveals, expectations and agendas established as early as the late 1920s (French cinema as a quality product destined for a specialised audience) have essentially remained in place and continue to do so to this day. Indeed, the UK Film Council's own definition of foreign cinema as 'specialised' is worth noting here, suggesting the somewhat disingenuous nature of its call for more choice in the survey described above. This account of the distribution, exhibition and reception of French cinema in Britain is a story of twentieth-century British film culture and the spaces it created for and its responses to the 'foreign' and to a great extent this is the story of a film culture dominated absolutely by English-language cinema (notably Hollywood) which left little space for a taste for alternative fare. Yet it is also the story of cinephilia, a love for film and in particular a love for the films of the 'continent'. This is to some degree the story of a relatively small group of individuals who at different junctures and in different ways have fought to bring the films they perceived as important, moving, valuable and enjoyable to British audiences: Iris Barry, Elsie Cohen, Ivor Montagu, Julia Wolf, Olwen Vaughan, Jan Dawson, Penelope Houston, Romaine Hart and Andi Engels to name but a few. These pioneering and often colourful individuals played a crucial and frequently under-recognised role in British film culture through their sourcing and exhibition of foreign films. And yet in their love for the 'high-brow' they were also guilty of the 'specialisation' of foreign film which to a great extent continues to bedevil its chances of mainstream success to this day.

Notes

1. Titles which are translated for a film's initial release within the U.K. are sometimes discarded in favour of the French title for subsequent re-releases,

perhaps in an attempt to reposition the film as a culturally valuable work. As much as possible we have attempted to detail such changes in the text. All filmographies will include French titles and any English release title.
2. French and other European films were commonly described as 'Continentals' in the 1930s, 1940s and 1950s. As Joachim Lembach remarks (Lembach 2003: 20), by the 1960s the term was rather ironically extended to independently made English-language films which, like their foreign counterparts, were considered specialised.
3. It is worth noting those 'French' films made in English (most famously perhaps Besson's *The Fifth Element*) are not subject to the same distribution and exhibition strategies and constraints accorded to French language films.
4. See http://www.ukfilmcouncil.org.uk/media/pdf/i/2/Subtitling_versus_Dubbing_case_study_-_The_Girl_with_the_Dragon_Tattoo.pdf (accessed 9 May 2011).
5. The release in 2011 of an American remake of *The Girl with the Dragon Tattoo* is a fate typical for non-English-language films which have found success in their country of origin yet have been unable to break beyond the confines of the specialised circuits in the U.S. and the U.K.

Bibliography

Adair, G. 2007. *A Mysterious Affair of Style*. London: Faber and Faber.
Chrisafis, A. 2007. *The Guardian*, 29 January.
Lembach, J. 2003. *The Standing of the German Cinema in Great Britain After 1945*. New York: The Edwin Mellen Press.
Marshall, B. 1999. 'Minor Leapfrogs', *French Cultural Studies* 10(255): 255–64.
Mazdon, L. and Wheatley, C. 2010. *Je t'aime, moi non plus: Franco-British Cinematic Relations*. Oxford: Berghahn Books.
Porter, H. 2010. 'French Films Glow with Confidence and Culture. Ours Should Do the Same', *The Observer*, 8 August.
Wolf, J. 1947. 'The Continental Film in Britain', *Penguin Film Review* 4: 89–94.

Filmography

Artiste, L' / *The Artist* (2011, Michel Hazanavicius)
Avatar (2010, James Cameron)
A bout de souffle / *Breathless* (1960, Jean-Luc Godard)
Apocalypto (2006, Mel Gibson)
Cinquième élément, Le / *The Fifth Element* (1997, Luc Besson)
Dames du Bois de Boulogne, Les (1945, Robert Bresson)
Enfants du Paradis, Les / *Children of Paradise* (1945, Marcel Carné)
Fabuleux destin d'Amélie Poulain, Le / *Amélie* (2001, Jean-Pierre Jeunet)
Girl with the Dragon Tattoo, The (2011, David Fincher)
Igor (2008, Anthony Leondis)
Inglourious Basterds (2009, Quentin Tarantino)
Jean de Florette (1986, Claude Berri)
Jules et Jim / *Jules and Jim* (1962, François Truffaut)

Män som hatar kvinnar / The Girl with the Dragon Tattoo (2009, Niels Arden Oplev)
Marche de l'empereur, La / The March of the Penguins (2005, Luc Jacquet)
Mépris, Le / Contempt (1963, Jean-Luc Godard)
Passion of the Christ, The (2004, Mel Gibson)
Règle du jeu, La / The Rules of the Game (1939, Jean Renoir)
Taken (2008, Pierre Morel)

1

THE ADVENT OF SOUND

A Changing Film Culture (1925–1939)

The moving picture had first been demonstrated in London by the Lumière brothers in 1896 – a Franco-British exchange worth noting given the focus of our study here. What started as little more than a technical marvel gradually became the focus of a working film industry as the 1900s progressed. Key developments such as the 1907 opening of the Balham Empire, the first British theatre devoted entirely to film shows; the 1909 Cinematograph Films Act giving local authorities the power to license cinemas and the formalisation of censorship via the founding of the British Board of Film Censors (BBFC) in 1912; the establishment of the Kinematograph Renters' Society in 1915 and the creation of the British National Film League for the protection and development of the British Film Industry in 1921 all bear witness to the growing importance of the moving picture as both industry and entertainment. As John Sedgwick and Michael Pokorny reveal, by the 1930s 'film going was the dominant paid-for leisure activity [in the U.S. and Britain], with revenue from the box-office of the two countries constituting two-thirds and four-fifths, respectively, of all entertainment expenditure. It was, as A.J.P. Taylor wrote, "the essential social habit of the age ... [which] slaughtered all competitors"' (Sedgwick and Pokorny 2005: 79). Recalling her film-going of the 1930s in a special edition of *Film* in 1975, then film critic of *The Daily Mail* Margaret Hinxman remarked, 'In my young day we didn't talk about film appreciation. You just liked going to the cinema. The man who didn't go once a week was a rarity, as dubious as the holier-than-thou character nowadays who won't admit to owning a Television set' (Hinxman 1975: 39). Hinxman also described the sheer number of films on offer, the frequent changes of programme and the questionable quality of many of the films:

> Many of the cinemas changed their programmes twice a week and everyone had a Sunday programme of old films. On Sundays, my brother, sister, mother

and I would walk through Beckenham Park to the Regal, feeling we had given a nod to God on the way before incarcerating ourselves in that lovely darkness. Of course seventy five per cent of it was rubbish, just as seventy five per cent of anything is rubbish.

(Hinxman 1975: 39)

However, she continues, 'But it was in those local cinemas, where you crunched on peanut shells and orange peel between each row that I first saw Fritz Lang's *M*, *Carnet de Bal*, *Le Jour se Lève* (all sub-titled) as well as the best of Howard Hawks, von Sternberg, John Ford and Hitchcock and such rarities as *We From Kronstadt*' (39).

This dual recollection of cinema's sheer presence, of peanuts and popular films set alongside works now perceived as classics, provides a useful snapshot of the British cinema-going of the 1930s. Film, particularly the new 'talkies', became a dominant entertainment form and yet a space was also created for more 'specialised' work, including of course the cinema of France. As Vincent Porter notes, 'The exhibition of French films in Great Britain expanded dramatically during the 1930s and by the outbreak of the Second World War a Francophile cinemagoer living in London could have seen approximately 110 feature films, and some twenty shorts and documentaries' (Porter 2010: 19). It is important to underline the London bias of this exhibition – film lovers in many parts of the country had no access to French films at all. Nevertheless, the 1930s are a period in which French cinema enjoyed a presence within the British cultural landscape which it has struggled to regain in subsequent decades and this within a context of enthusiastic consumption of British, and more particularly Hollywood, film. What enabled the creation of this place for French film and what impact was it to have on British attitudes towards and articulations of the cross-channel cinematic product?

Beginning to Take Film Seriously

In the early days of the medium most commentators did not fully acknowledge the artistic potential of film. There was a very clear fascination with the technical aspects of cinema, particularly in the early years of the century. Film's educational impact was also considered highly significant, with early newspaper reviews focusing heavily on the pedagogical aspects of the 'kinema'. The first edition of *Sight and Sound*, published in Spring 1932, was very clear in its remit, stating: 'The present publication of *Sight and Sound* is a direct consequence of the enthusiasm aroused by the two Exhibitions of Mechanical Aids to Learning in 1930 and 1931 [. . .] Its purpose is to provide a permanent channel of communication between the producers of these instruments and all those who, in the educational world taken at its widest, are interested in their possible application to cultural ends' (Anon. 1932b: 3). Caroline Lejeune, then film critic on *The Observer*, continued this pedagogical and improving tone with a column entitled 'Films You Ought to See' (ibid.: 25). The prominence of the documentary movement in the 1920s and on into the 1930s, and the 1932 publication of the 'The Cinema in National Life', a report by the Commission on Educational and Cultural Films, also bear witness to this widespread pedagogical focus. The latter report was to a great extent the catalyst for the establishment of the British Film Institute in 1933 and the National Film Library in 1935, and here again we can see a real concern for the educational potential of film. Early writings on film thus played a role in educating the British public *about* film – Caroline Lejeune's *Sight and Sound* column like her *Observer* reviews meticulously list the merits and weaknesses of her chosen films – while at the same time demonstrating film's use value in education itself. This is significant when it comes to foreign-language films, as a key aspect of the appeal of the early Continental talkies was their instructional potential. Also writing in *Sight and Sound* in 1932, Elsie Cohen, programmer of the Academy cinema and, as we shall see, a pioneer in the distribution and exhibition of 'foreign' film in Britain, describes the recent introduction of the 'Continental dialogue film' to English cinemas. While focusing in particular on the work of the Academy (of which more later) and on a number of key films, Cohen concludes her piece by remarking, 'The greatest interest is taken by language teachers in these foreign dialogue films and groups of students visit the Academy in parties, special terms being arranged on such occasions' (Cohen 1932/33: 113).

Cinema's commercial power was not of course ignored. The growing popularity of the medium led to much interest in its money-spinning potential and to a great extent this obscured or overrode any serious recognition of its artistic power. As Jamie Sexton notes, 'The domination of the commercial imperative was reflected in trade papers that mainly focused on film from a commercial angle. In newspapers, coverage of film was extremely limited and was overwhelmed by space devoted to other arts. While this was slowly beginning to change in the late 1910s and early 1920s, coverage was still not substantial. In the trade press cinema was still often treated as a business' (Sexton 2008: 13). Hollywood movies, and to a lesser extent British films, by dint of their very popularity were the main focus of the trade papers. The American films shown were not an undifferentiated mass as the industry attempted to appeal to different audience groups. Nevertheless, from the point of view of those relatively rare commentators with a real interest in cinema as art, Hollywood represented mass production and a general lack of intelligence (47) while the trades' overweening focus on commercial cinema enabled and entrenched its dominance of the newly developing cinematic language. Writing in

The Evening Standard in 1925, Hugh Miller, a co-founder of the Film Society, which as we shall see played a major role in bringing 'quality' cinema to London audiences, opined, 'The maker of pictures in America reduces the public's intelligence to the least common denominator. The whole business rests on a foundation of spurious values. Most of the genuine talent goes unrecognised. It is a business first and an art a very long time afterwards' (Miller 1925).

Resistance to the entrenchment of the commercial cinema was to play a great part in the rise of a British art-film culture. By the early 1920s a range of weekly newspapers and other publications included film comment based on an understanding of film as both entertainment and art. Seminal figures such as Walter Mycroft at *The London Evening Standard* (1922–27) and Ivor Montagu at *The Observer* (1925–26) provided a counter voice to the previously described interest in film as education and business by paying attention to the aesthetic power of the medium. While Caroline Lejeune has been much decried for her rather limited and middle-class taste, her early writings in *The Manchester Guardian* (1921–28) and subsequently *The Observer* (1928–60) were to play an equally important role in this process. Particularly influential was Iris Barry, the most widely read British critic of the 1920s. Barry began writing for *The Spectator* and *Vogue* in 1924. However, it was her tenure at *The Daily Mail* from 1925 to 1930 which brought her to a wide readership. Her detailed and passionate accounts of both Hollywood films and the 'Continentals' emphasised her role as advocate for the sheer pleasure of cinema as both entertainment and art. In 1926 Barry published *Let's Go to the Pictures*, a book-length affirmation of cinema's intellectual and aesthetic ambition and entertainment value, claiming that 'going to the pictures is nothing to be ashamed of' (Barry 1972: viii). Hers was not the only book devoted to the serious study of cinema to emerge in the period. Montagu's translation of Pudovkin's work on film technique and Paul Rotha's magisterial *The Film Till Now*, both published in 1930, joined Barry's volume in the construction of a British cultural discourse which took film seriously.

Very significant in the development of this discourse was the journal *Close Up* which was first published in July 1927 and ran until December 1933. The journal was published by a group of collaborators who went under the collective name of the POOL enterprise: Kenneth Macpherson, Bryher (Annie Winifred Ellerman) and H.D. (Hilda Doolittle). All came from a literary background, and alongside *Close Up* they published a number of books on literature, film criticism and memoirs and made four films (Sexton 2008: 37). As Anne Friedberg reveals:

> From the beginning of its publication, the writers for *Close Up* were determined to transform the cultural topography of the cinema and its future. To

do so, they were invested in the power of writing *about* film, enlisting it as a discursive midwife to aid in the development of the cinema's potential. [. . .] *Close Up* became the model for a certain type of writing about film – writing that was theoretically astute, politically incisive, critical of films that were simply 'entertainment'. For six and a half years, *Close Up* maintained a forum for a broad variety of ideas about the cinema; it never advocated a single direction of development, but rather posed alternatives to existing modes of production, consumption and film style.

(Friedberg 1998: 3)

Close Up became a focal point for all those interested in avant-garde cinema or film as art and its role in constructing a British art-film culture has been well documented. However, what is of particular interest here is the journal's internationalism. Macpherson and Bryher lived in Territet, Switzerland, and this is where most of the magazine was edited. While articles were published in English, correspondents were based in Moscow, Paris, Berlin, Geneva, London, New York and Los Angeles, thus aspiring 'to do for English-language film writing and for the dissemination of film theory what the silent cinema did for the spectator: transcend the boundaries of language and nation. The writing in *Close Up* created a mobile discursive forum, a diffused salon' (ibid.: 10). The journal was to play a vital role in opening a serious debate within Britain about film art (constructed as thoroughly international) and in supporting the British dissemination of films that were not part of the dominant commercial mode (for the most part non-English-language films). The journal's original paper wrappers proclaimed, 'WE WANT BETTER FILMS!!!', 'The Only Magazine Devoted to Films As An Art – Interesting and Exclusive Illustrations – THEORY AND ANALYSIS – NO GOSSIP' (ibid.: 3). And in his opening essay in the first edition of the journal, Kenneth Macpherson declared presciently, 'Fifty odd years hasn't done so badly in getting an art into the world that fifty more will probably turn into THE art, but now, after somewhat magnificent growth, one feels here is its critical age' (Macpherson 1927: 36).

The very newness of this British art film culture in the 1920s and early 1930s reminds us that what constituted 'art' film was far from clear cut. In attempting to construct a serious discourse about cinema, a discourse which took cinema seriously, Macpherson, Mycroft, Barry et al. were also instrumental in making choices and decisions which would define certain films as 'art' or 'specialised' for a much wider audience. As Jamie Sexton has noted, 'During the inter-war period fixed conceptual divisions between types of film production did not exist' (Sexton 2008: 4). Film art could thus be found, and indeed often was, within commercial, narrative feature films. What constituted 'art' was to a large degree up for grabs. A relatively small group of cinephiles could set the parameters of 'progressive' or 'artistic' cinema according to their own tastes and strategies for exhibition and dissemination. And it was these strategies that played a particularly crucial role in constructing a body of 'serious' film, to a great extent above and beyond the quality of the films themselves.

René Clair, whose films enjoyed significant success in the British market, remarked in an interview with Caroline Lejeune in 1939, 'Make no mistake about the French cinema. The ordinary, bread-and-butter French picture is just the same as ever. We have as many bad films in France as you have in England, only you people don't see them. The vogue for French films abroad is largely mere exoticism. You admire French films as we in Paris admire the big Hollywood production. They are foreign and interesting' (Lejeune 1939). Clair was speaking at the end of the decade when the presence of French films in Britain and the type of films shown had undergone a number of shifts and alterations; French films selected for British exhibition in the late 1920s were indeed seen by many cinephiles as 'foreign' and 'interesting'; however their appeal also lay in their ability to offer pleasures very different to those handed out by Hollywood. Nevertheless, his remarks are pertinent as he stresses the absolute importance of exhibition in the foreign consumption of films. New venues for showing Continental films in London in the late 1920s and the 1930s did give rise to the mini-boom described by Porter above. However, as we shall go on to discuss, it also set in place a particular perception of French cinema which has to a great extent remained in place to this day. As Clair remarked in an earlier interview, published in fan magazine *Picturegoer* in 1934, 'Of course, my films have never really known a typical English audience, because they have only been shown so far at certain London kinemas which cater for a special type of audience' (Moore 1934: 21).

The Advent of Sound

Debates about film art and attempts to construct a serious film culture were to meet a very important challenge at the end of the 1920s with the advent of sound cinema. In contrast to France for example which was slow to convert cinemas to sound technology, United Kingdom exhibitors wired quickly with 22 per cent in 1929 and 63 per cent by the end of 1930 (Gomery 1980: 82). While this was a great boon to commercial distributors and exhibitors, in particular those selling the new Hollywood 'talkies', it posed a number of problems for those with a vested interest in non-English-language cinema and cinephiles dedicated to serious film culture. For many among the latter, sound was initially perceived as anathema to film as art. In their eyes the new technology further embedded Hollywood's domination of European markets and worked against the 'pure' film language and internationalist film culture advocated in particular by *Close Up*. As James Donald points out, the issue was not sound as such – films had always had sound via a musical accompaniment, a lecturer commenting on the film or the general hubbub of the movie theatre (Donald 1998: 79). The problem was synchronised speech, an emphasis on language which 'would inevitably be bought at the expense of the inner speech that was supposedly invoked and conveyed by the art of silent montage' (79). Writing in April 1929, Ernest Betts argues:

> The real anti-talkie argument is that speech attacks the film's peculiar and individual function, which is to imitate life in flowing forms of light and shade to a rhythmic pattern. That may sound a piece of abstract nonsense, but it is not so when we see Chaplin or Emil Jannings or any other great pantomimic artist. Put speech into films, and you will get speech plus film but you will not get film.
>
> (Betts 1929: 90)

Attitudes did adapt as critics and commentators began to accept that sound film could in fact offer new forms of creativity, new forms of expression. The advent of sound technology was however far more intractable for foreign-language film. Synchronised speech meant synchronised national language and thus the apparent internationalism of silent film was destroyed. French silent films had found a ready commercial market in Britain. Indeed the majority of Clair's silent films of the 1920s and early sound films of the beginning of the 1930s had been released in Britain within months of their French release, to some extent giving the lie to his previously quoted claims about the specialised nature of his films' British reception. In 1931 the Rialto cinema, a specialised theatre in London, showed *Sous les toits de Paris* (1930) without any form of translation to 'packed houses for months' (Thomas 1939: 29) and then swiftly followed this success with *Le Million* (1931). However, to some degree these films were the exception which proved the rule. Their popularity, in spite of their non-translated dialogue, was almost certainly due to the very limited use of dialogue in *Sous les toits*, *Le Million*'s status as a musical (songs in French were arguably more accessible, if not comprehensible, to an English audience than straightforward dialogue) and the presence in both films of popular star Annabella. An article in *The Times* discussing an earlier showing of *Sous les toits* at London's Alhambra in 1930 remarks, 'M. Clair is justified in claiming that the film can be perfectly understood by people with no knowledge of French. His method makes far greater use of visual imagery than is common' (Anon. 1930b). Nevertheless, writing in *Sight and Sound* in 1939, Yvonne Thomas maps out the popularity of the Continental 'silents', 'During the long period of silent films Continentals were in great demand over here, and were shown regularly at nearly every cinema. [. . .] The only bother with Continentals in those days was, that from an English audience's point of view, they were far too long. They invariably had to be cut to meet our own requirements, but these cuts could usually be made without detracting from the story' (Thomas 1939: 28).

Thomas' positing of 'national' taste is striking here. The exportability of silent cinema and the cosmopolitan film culture it seemed to enable have tended to the truism that prior to the advent of sound, national identity in film was of little or no importance. And yet here we have Thomas, writing in 1939, claiming that British audiences of the 1920s did 'not like a film – unless it is very exceptional – that runs for more than one hour and a half, whereas the rest of Europe seems to revel in entertainment lasting at least two hours or more' (ibid.: 28). In a comment which seems to underwrite long-standing French perceptions of British philistinism, she claims that cuts to the films 'merely meant that a lot of unnecessary action was removed, with the result that the real point of the story was arrived at sooner' (28). National identity *did* then matter in the days of silent cinema, perhaps not to the general cinema-going public but certainly to many critics. From a purely practical or commercial point of view it did not hinder export as inter-titles were easily translated and language was not a barrier. However, in terms of responses to the films, national identity could and often did play a significant role – critics identified and recognised films as French, Italian, German and so on. Thus national identity as a crucial marker pre-existed the advent of sound film and fed into its distribution and reception in the United Kingdom. Listen to Iris Barry writing in 1926:

> We are always being told that the cinema is international: like music or eggs. It is true that films are no respecters of frontiers. You may see Harold Lloyd in Pekin [sic], Sydney, Salzburg, Paris or South America; Emil Jannings in Tokio [sic] or Atlanta. But films are not international. There is no mistaking an English film for an American one, or an American film for a German, and Swedish films are easily detectable, though few and far between. Shall I say that American films are slick and speedy, English films pedestrian, German films ponderous, Swedish films severe, French films blustering? Even when an American film is made in Italy it remains American, or when it is made in the States with a German director, French photographer and a Babel of actors, it is always an American film. [. . .] Was *Madame Sans Gêne* a French film, though it was made in France with a French marquise (by marriage) as the famous washer lady? Not a bit!
>
> (Barry 1926 [1972] : 239)

Barry, like many of her fellow critics and cinephiles, may have strived for an international film culture yet she recognised the thoroughly national specificities of individual films. In similar vein, Paul Rotha maps out the national characteristics of cinemas in *The Film Till Now*, describing nationalities as connected but essentially distinct entities with their own themes and motifs which would be expressed in film. His account of French cinema is typical of this approach. Rotha criticises the French *cinéastes*' tendency to admire the cinema of other countries to the detriment of domestic productions, remarking in particular on their admiration for Hollywood and their 'constant craving after the metallic glitter of the movie' (Rotha 1930: 294). Salvation, argues Rotha, lies with, 'a few directors who have sufficient independence and are sane-headed enough to stand above this adolescent attitude of self-condemnation, such as René Clair and Jean Epstein, and it is to these men that we must look for the future of the French cinema in its purified form' (295). This is a crucial paradox in Rotha's argument: he stresses the value of the independent vision of key artists and yet believes that this would have no substance if it did not contribute to or extend a national cinematic 'spirit'. In France in particular, this 'national' spirit, indeed 'nearly every film of interest' has been the product 'of an individualistic artist mind' and Rotha sees this as the logical outcome of the 'painter's studio so inherent in French tradition' (295). The principal characteristic of the French cinema, he argues, is the 'single-minded production with the director or the cameraman, as the case may be, as the sole *metteur-en-scène*' (297).[1] He criticises French producers for their failure to realise and invest in the 'artist-mind' of the genius and claims that French cinema should give up attempts to ape the American product: 'The market for the French "artist" production must necessarily remain limited, for the French have not any idea of the entertainment of the masses. [. . .] The French cinema as a whole is incapable of competing with the vast commercial product of Hollywood, and no amount of "quota" regulations will make it possible' (298–99). Rotha goes on to describe what he sees as the defining traits of French film: a focus on the 'pictorial' often at the expense of any real feeling for the movement of 'acting material'; a leaning towards the decorative, artificially created environment which he sees as 'non-cinematic in its semi-theatrical artistry' (301). He singles out a number of directors for particular attention and praise. These include Jean Renoir, Jean Epstein, Abel Gance, the Danish Carl Dreyer, then working in France, the Belgian Jacques Feyder who had also made a number of films in France at this stage, Marcel L'Herbier, Alberto Cavalcanti and René Clair. It is notable that he praises Clair for his 'quality of employing movement of material which is absent from the work of most French directors. He has learnt freely from the American cinema, from Mack Sennett and from Lloyd, but his idol, of course, is Chaplin' (303). In other words, Rotha praises Clair for the very imitation he has earlier decried, going on to say that he has used this imitation to make films, *Un Chapeau de Paille d'Italie* (1928) and *Les Deux Timides* (1928), which are 'more completely French in feeling than any other productions' (304).

Rotha concludes on a cautious note:

> From this, some slight estimate of the significance of the French cinema may be gained. That it is important is very clear, despite the efforts of the *cineaste* and the cine-journalist to prove the contrary. Of the future of the French cinema it is impossible to write, for each step will depend on the precarious position of the dialogue film. Various experiments are being made with sound reproduction in France, but at the time of writing, no serious realisation has been seen, although several full-length dialogue films are said to have been completed.
>
> (Rotha 1930: 312).

What is certain is that Rotha's particular take on French cinema (and indeed on cinema more widely) anticipates attitudes towards and expectations of French cinema in Britain which to a great extent remain in place to this day. The arrival of sound crystallised the distinctions between different national cinemas, moving them beyond critical recognition of 'national' cinematic traits to very tangible evidence of origin witnessed primarily at the level of language. This posed huge problems for the British exhibition of French and other non-English-language sound cinema and to a great extent both the problem (the foreign language) and the eventual solution (dubbed and subtitled prints) have continued to confine the space and audience for French cinema in Britain to varying degrees. However, Rotha's description of French cinema, which is largely based on his knowledge of silent film, joined forces with the writings of like-minded cinephiles and critics to provide a set of definitions and expectations which have influenced, or dare I say it plagued, the British distribution of French film ever since: French cinema is not a cinema of or for the 'masses' and should not aspire to the audiences flocking to the latest products of Hollywood or Britain. Its value lies in its difference; French cinema is distinctively 'French' and this is an identity to which it should aspire but the 'French' cinema which merits showing in Britain is the work of a handful of directors, a carefully selected 'canon'.

Babel Comes to the Movies: Finding a Solution to Sound

Let us return then to the advent of sound and the problems it posed for the distributors of non-English-language cinema in Britain. The question of how to translate films for the export market vexed producers and distributors in both Europe and the United States at the close of the 1920s. Three solutions were arrived at: dubbing, subtitling, and the shooting of multi-language versions. The latter tends now to be perceived as a rather costly failure, although it was, as we shall discover, briefly revived in the 1970s. As Ginette Vincendeau remarks, 'in terms of an aesthetic history of world cinema, or of the national cinemas concerned, multi-language films, and particularly those produced by Paramount in Paris, are considered worthless – the universally recognised exceptions (*Marius, The Threepenny Opera*) being attributed entirely to the talent of their (European) *auteur*' (Vincendeau 1998: 24). Apart from the cost of this process, the multi-language version failed as it essentially reduced the film to story alone, assuming that it would appeal to new audiences once re-shot in the target language and forgetting that 'a national cinema is defined principally by its degree of intertextuality with the culture of its country, and in particular with its dominant narrative patterns' (39). As Rotha revealed, many of those with a taste for French films based that taste on the films' very Frenchness. Multi-language versions, rather like that linked phenomenon the cinematic remake, led to films which were not French or German or even American enough and so they failed to appeal.

The second solution, dubbing, was not a great deal more successful. Writing again in 1939, Yvonne Thomas opines:

> Later, a new method of presenting Continental films to the public was tried, and that was by using one cast, either German or French, and 'doubling' the voices of the original artists in the other languages. It was a sort of compromise on the former 'trilingual' [multi-language version] idea. This method saved cost of production considerably, but even so, three separate casts of artists had to be engaged. Again, there was the difficulty of 'matching' the doubling voices to those of the original artists. If this was not perfectly done, the effect was ridiculous, for one saw a definite personality on the screen, and heard a voice that was entirely opposed to it.
>
> (Thomas 1939: 29)

The third solution was of course subtitling and it was this which quickly became, and has remained, the norm for the British exhibition of non-English-language cinema. This was far from straightforward as the technology was in its infancy and the costs of subtitling added to import and other duties could easily cost an exhibitor hundreds of pounds before the film even opened (Porter 2010: 20). Recalling his early days programming the Film Society, Thorold Dickinson outlined some early solutions:

> We started by printing a synopsis of the story on translucent paper which the audience read by holding up their copies to the light from the screen. Then we began inserting between sequences in the film roll-up titles summarising the facts that had gone before and hinting at those to come. This is how we presented *Maedchen in Uniform* to an audience peppered with ladies in tweeds and monocles.
>
> (Dickinson 1975: 8)

Nevertheless, the art of subtitling developed quickly led by key figures such as Julia Wolf, who subtitled every foreign film at specialist cinema

The Curzon from its opening in 1934 to its closure due to bombing in the Second World War, and Mai Harris who began working with Elsie Cohen at The Academy in the early 1930s and went on to run her own highly successful subtitling and editing company.

Subtitling was then adopted as the most cost-effective solution to linguistic difference but also as it enabled the retention of difference that was such a significant part of the Continentals' appeal to many British cinema-goers. A striking example of this focus on 'difference' is provided by an article in *Kinematograph Weekly* of 12 June 1930 detailing a Bristol exhibitor's screening of and publicity for early French 'talkie' *Le Collier de la Reine* (*The Queen's Necklace*, 1929):

> The front of the house was dressed with a large red, white and blue banner on which, from corner to corner, was painted a necklace with the title 'The Queen's Necklace' right across it, with in one corner the words 'French talkie' and in the other 'English Subtitles'. From the roof of the house a large Union Jack was flown flanked by two French Tri-colours, with strings of bunting running down to the top of the canopy round the front of which hung English and French flags. There were similar banners at the top of the annexe and it was stated that the film had been banned in London.
>
> (Anon. 1930a)

The cinema (the King's Theatre) distributed 5,000 bead necklaces in small envelopes bearing the words, 'This is the King's Necklace. Come next week to see and hear "The Queen's Necklace" at the King's. The Anglo-French film that all can understand. The film that London banned' (ibid.). Local papers discussed the film's problems with the London censor and Kenneth Duffy, the exhibitor, took out special advertising with French headings in the Saturday evening papers and arranged a special 'tie-up' for the book of the film with Woolworth's. The result of the publicity was that many people 'who were not ordinary picture goers' attended the film, a fact which was remarked upon by 'the *Daily Mail* film critic who came specially from London. [. . .] Members of the crews of the French and English warships which were in Bristol visited the house to see the film, and Mr Duffy also received a personal letter of congratulation and best wishes from the French Ambassador' (ibid.).

This account of a particular instance in the exhibition and marketing of French cinema in Britain at the start of the 1930s is extremely revealing as it demonstrates the early implementation of methods and expectations which to varying degrees have continued ever since. The campaign stresses the film's Frenchness (note the French-language newspaper advertisements and fluttering tricolours) and as such markets the film for a specialised audience with a taste for foreign cinema. In other words it stresses the film's difference from other, more mainstream (read English-language) fare. However, it simultaneously underlines the film's accessibility – it is subtitled and is an Anglo-French production 'that all can understand'. In this way it sets out to sell the film to a much broader public who may well not normally attend the Continental picture, a practice which prefigures contemporary effacement of foreign language in trailers for non-English films.

Moreover the publicity makes much of the fact that the film had been banned by the censor and had not been screened in London. This underlining of the rather risqué nature of French cinema is a practice which was to become highly significant in the British exhibition of the cross-channel product. Finally, it is perhaps worth noting the sheer intensity of this publicity campaign. Clearly Mr Duffy of the King's Theatre was well aware that without broad and visible marketing this film, despite its apparent accessibility, would have little hope of reaching out beyond a very limited audience.

French Talkies on British Screens

As sound cinema took hold in Britain, the relatively healthy presence of the 'Continental' silents gave way to the initial precarity of the foreign talkies. As Vincent Porter notes, by 1930 virtually the only commercial cinema regularly screening continental films was the Avenue Pavilion on London's Shaftesbury Avenue (Porter 2010: 20). For a period of about eighteen months the cinema's owners, Gaumont British Picture Corporation, allowed its then owner Stuart Davis to show American, German and Swedish classics. Davis then went on to programme a season of French films (praised by Rotha in *The Film Till Now*) including *Finis Terrae*, *Un Chapeau de Paille d'Italie*, *Les Deux timides*, *En Rade*, *Rien que les heures*, *La Chute de la Maison Usher* and *Thérèse Raquin* which proved a huge success and went on to obtain many provincial bookings (20). Despite this success Gaumont chose to convert the Avenue into a newsreel cinema and London was left without a commercial venue for continental films. Moreover, the provincial success of *Thérèse Raquin* was not representative of prevailing conditions as provision outside London was even more meagre:

> Cinemagoers living outside London normally had to rely on their local film society in order to see a French film. [...] Distributors of continental films who tried to obtain commercial bookings by means of trade shows, dinner parties and other inducements, achieved only meagre and ephemeral results. The only continental films which were distributed outside London in dubbed versions were *Paris Méditerranée*, which was exhibited as *Into the Blue*, and *Le Roman d'un tricheur*, which was shown in the London suburbs during January 1939 as *The Cheat*, with a voice-over by Norman Shelley.
>
> (Porter 2010: 23)

There were a number of reasons for the limited presence of the Continentals at this stage. Clearly the transition to sound was indeed part of the problem as distributors and exhibitors struggled to find a solution to foreign dialogue. Writing in *Sight and Sound* in 1934 Eric Hakim, owner of a number of cinemas including the Academy, attributed the dearth of foreign films to prevailing conditions in the British film industry, notably the Cinematograph Films' Act of 1927 which in an attempt to stave off American competition had introduced a quota mandating a minimum allotment of screen time to British production:

> There is frequently talk of a shortage of unusual films when what is actually meant is a scarcity of such films available for British exhibition. This is directly due to the Films Act provision demanding the registration of each film by a renting concern. Every registration increases the renter's British quota obligation and it will be readily seen that it is bad business for a renter to register an 'unusual' film, for which he may expect perhaps only six bookings on a single copy, rather than a commercial film which may demand thirty copies and secure 1,000 bookings. The Quota obligation, in the case of an unusual film may be easily, in a strictly cash sense, from one hundred to five hundred times greater in the one case than in the other.
>
> (Hakim 1934: 12)

Writing a little later that year, Kenneth A. Nyman continues Hakim's argument:

> Films go through the censor and are 'trade' shown then usually become registered and available. A few do not but the importance of these few is in inverse proportion to their number: these are 'unusual' and 'foreign' films whose market is comparatively limited. Renters are not anxious to be involved in the heavy initial costs of registration, printing and distribution of copies and the cost of acquisition of British quota films to conform with the Act, because the market is limited to those towns (Liverpool, Leeds, London) where the population is big enough to support a 'specialist' cinema and to such cultural centres as Oxford and Cambridge. [. . .] Thus only a very few of these 'unusual' films theoretically available are ever shown – these being the few that appear to have sufficient chances of commercial success for the renters to get a monetary return for their exploitation.
>
> (Nyman 1934: 51)

Nyman goes on to echo Hakim's calls for the modification of the Quota Act 'in respect of these "unusual" films (mostly French and pre-Nazi German and some Japanese and Russian)', concluding:

> After all, this is the very type of film of which we want to encourage increased production and exhibition in order to give the public that 'something different' which they insistently demand and at the same time to raise the standard

of artistic quality of film product in general. (The fact that 'artistic quality' may mean different things to different people does not alter the point of this important plea.)

(Nyman 1934)

So it would seem that the decline in the British presence of foreign, including French, films during the late 1920s had rather more to do with the industry's attempt to bolster domestic production than the oft-cited advent of sound. This is somewhat paradoxical given that the quotas which made the British exhibition of continental cinema so risky were devised to limit the power of the very Hollywood films which are typically perceived as the reason for the enduringly limited space accorded to non-English-language cinema in the British market. Yet despite this rather disabling industrial context, the 1930s does become a golden moment in the British distribution of French cinema, a period during which some cinema-goers (and the limited nature of that potential audience is important) had access to a range of French films which arguably was not matched until the advent of DVD in the 1990s.

There existed two main outlets for the showing of French and other non-English-language films throughout the 1930s: the London-based Film Society established in 1925 and its regional off-shoots, and the specialised cinemas. As Vincent Porter has convincingly demonstrated, these institutions were highly proactive in the sourcing and exhibition of French cinema and in that sense were largely responsible for this 'golden moment'. However, the very specialised nature of these institutions – members-only film societies, Continental cinemas – led to a hiving off of French cinema from the commercial mainstream and in turn to perceptions of French film as 'special', 'different', 'challenging'; perceptions which still hold sway today. This was a danger remarked upon by some commentators at the time. Eric Hakim for example, in the course of his critique of the Quota Act, argues that the growth in film societies risks marginalising 'unusual' films, claiming that, 'there is a public for high class films (even films in foreign languages, and even silent films) which the trade hastily labels "uncommercial"' (Hakim 1934: 11). Arguably Hakim's attempts to prove that commercial potential through his own cinemas, notably the Academy, only contributed to the marginalisation he deplored. Yes, they were successful in showing a broad range of 'unusual' films and many of these films were sell-out success stories. However, the cinemas were quickly perceived and labelled as 'specialised' or 'Continental' picture houses and thus their programmes were set apart from the mainstream and their audiences potentially restricted.

That French cinema was included amongst these 'specialised' films is in many ways surprising given that French film was not held in great esteem in the latter half of the 1920s. In *Let's Go to the Movies* Iris Barry declares, 'France, alas, once a pioneer, is – like England until quite lately – in a rut. Her picture-makers are still working in an outworn mode, her actors still fling themselves about or stand stock-still like people in stage melodramas. Her photography is unsympathetic' (Barry 1926 [1972] : 243). Like Rotha in *The Film Till Now*, Barry sees French cinema as overly 'stagy', far too dependent on theatrical conventions. She claims that true cinematic art and experimentation came from the early films of Hollywood and from Germany, whose films showed 'a remarkable "feeling for the cinema"' (Barry 1926 [1972] : 246–51). Writing in *Sight and Sound* in 1932–33, Elsie Cohen describes the recent cinema programmes and singles out the films she sees as particularly 'important' and valuable. The films she cites are almost all German (*Westfront 1918*, *Kameradschaft* and *Maedchen in Uniform*, for example) and she gives a nod of approval to the Russian film-makers Pudovkin and Eisenstein. Only a few are French (such as *David Golder*), and perhaps not unsurprisingly René Clair's *A Nous la liberté* and 'new comedy *The Fourteenth of July*' are given special mention (Cohen 1932/33: 113). Cohen suggests the sheer diversity of films on offer at the Academy and to a lesser extent elsewhere by the early 1930s, a diversity which as we shall see is far less visible in later decades. However, it is striking that French cinema, the very cinema which later became the absolute staple of British specialist exhibition, which indeed comes to epitomise quality art cinema, is not at this stage deemed of particular interest in marked contrast to the films of Germany and Russia.

It is worth noting that although many of the experimental films shown were from France, in terms of full-length features the first three seasons of the Film Society were dominated by German productions with Russia taking a significant role in subsequent programmes. In other words, in the late 1920s and early 1930s it was German films which held the role later assumed by French cinema. Sabine Hake has pointed out that the films of Weimar Germany were international in scope and aimed 'to create a quality product and attract middle-class audiences to the cinema' (Hake 1993: 113). Jamie Sexton posits that since the Film Society members 'were looking for an alternative to commercial cinema, they were likely to look outside Hollywood to locate a cinema that could serve as a paradigm of artistic excellence' (Sexton 2008: 21). The big-budget, prestige Weimar productions served just that purpose and thus for a brief period in the late 1920s and very early 1930s became the gold standard of quality, art cinema, a role which, as we shall see, was later to go to, and indeed remain, with French cinema.

So what brought about that change? What was it that meant that the period 'between 1934 and the start of the War [. . .] saw the great revival of the French cinema which in England particularly has left to this day the legend that French films are superior to all others' (Robinson 1963: 240). Of course to a great extent this shift was due to cinematic and broader political developments in the various countries concerned. The rise of Nazism in Germany and Stalinism in the USSR led to the gradual decline of German and Russian films on the specialist circuit as they were perceived as either aesthetically uninteresting or politically beyond the pale. In contrast, French film production embarked on what has later been described as a 'golden age'. French film-makers embraced the sound technology they had at first resisted and began to produce films which could rival their silent predecessors in terms of both commercial and critical success. Production rose from around ninety-four films in 1930 to 158 in 1933, gradually stabilising at between 100 and 120 films throughout the rest of the decade. Stars such as Jean Gabin, Arletty, Raimu and Annabella proved popular with domestic audiences and many of the major box-office hits of the decade were French. The industry itself did not achieve economic or industrial stability: indeed it remained technically impoverished and decentralised, with around seventy independent producers making one or two films a year. However, in spite of, or perhaps even due to, this industrial instability, French film-makers enjoyed an artistic freedom not always available to those working in the Hollywood studio system: the piece-meal nature of the industry enabled diversification in access to capital and distribution while the absence of an overarching censorship mechanism accorded them a greater degree of 'moral' liberty than their Hollywood counterparts.

Pioneers and Aficionados

All of this is of course important. However, if our aim is to determine what led to the great esteem accorded to French cinema in Britain in the 1930s we must turn our attention to British exhibition. The specific strategies adopted for the British exhibition of French film played a vital role in constructing the perceptions and expectations previously outlined. As I have suggested, there existed two main outlets for the British sourcing and screening of non-English-language cinema at this juncture: the Film Society and its provincial off-shoots, and the specialised or 'Continental' cinemas. We will look more closely at these different institutions in a moment. However, before so doing I think it is important to stress the relatively small coterie of individuals behind these endeavours: a group of cinephiles, critics and film-makers who believed firmly in the importance of cinema and were not content with the offerings of the commercial circuits alone. Figures such as Ivor Montagu, Thorold Dickinson, Iris Barry and Elsie Cohen were film aficionados and their pioneering attempts to bring the best of continental production to the Film Society and/or the specialised cinemas were essentially so that they themselves could enjoy these films and share their preferences with like-minded individuals. In other words, the tastes and choices of a small group of cinematic pioneers who acted as both distributors and exhibitors would to a great extent determine what was shown to British audiences and thus go on to play a vital role in constructing dominant notions of what constituted 'quality' cinema. French cinema in Britain in the 1930s was not broadly defined: it was selected by a limited number of individuals according to their own personal tastes and it was shown in a restricted circuit of exhibition venues. In this it was to set firmly in place the pattern for future years.

The Film Society

The first screening of the Film Society took place on Sunday 25 October 1925 at the New Gallery Kinema in London's Regent Street and was attended by 1,400 people. The idea for such a society had come from film-maker and writer Ivor Montagu and actor Hugh Miller. They were keen to establish a film society which, like the Stage Society founded in 1899, would show work which either for reasons of censorship or because it would be considered uncommercial would not otherwise be performed (Samson 1986: 306). As Samson notes, the idea took shape during a dinner party at Iris Barry's house, reminding us once again of the highly 'cliquey' (and, it must be noted, upper-middle class) nature of these endeavours. Barry invited Montagu and Miller along with Adrian Brunel, film director at Gainsborough Pictures, Walter Mycroft, the sculptor Frank Dobson and Sidney Bernstein, film exhibitor and future Chairman of Granada Television (306). Montagu became Chairman of this group, the Film Society's first council, and Miss J.M. Harvey became secretary and the Society's key administrator. Those on the council were very clear in their ambition to 'take cinema seriously'. In this it has been argued, by David Robinson for example, that they were greatly influenced by developments on the continent (Montagu's visit to the Berlin film studios of course and Louis Delluc's *ciné-club* movement in France). However, it is notable that in her comments on Robinson's unpublished 1963 history of the Film Society, Iris Barry vehemently rejects this influence. Commenting on Robinson's claim that inspiration for the Film Society came from Germany, Barry declares, 'This is untrue. The inspiration came from a desire to see films not otherwise visible or visible only in mutilated form' (Barry 1963). Here again, the centrality of the founders' personal tastes and love for cinema is made very clear.

These aims and ambitions were spelt out in the Society's first statement of purpose which appeared in the first programme:

> The Society is under no illusions. It is well aware that *Caligaris* do not grow on raspberry bushes and that it cannot, in a season, expect to provide its members

with an unbroken succession of masterpieces. It will be sufficient if it can show a group of films which are in some degree interesting, which represent the work which has been done, or is being done experimentally, in various parts of the world. It is in the nature of such films that they are (it is said) commercially unsuitable for this country, and that is why they become the especial province of the Film Society.
(Council of the London Film Society 1972, *Film Society Programmes*: Programme One)

A further statement in Programme Eight continues:

The Film Society was founded in order that work of interest in the study of cinematography, and yet not easily accessible, might be made available to its members. During season 1925–26, it has shown thirty nine films. Twenty of these (thirteen French, six German, one Japanese) had not before, and have not since, been shown publicly in this country.
(ibid.: Programme Eight)

So the Society's Council sought out films that would otherwise not be shown in Britain, films which were apart from the mainstream and as such may have been relatively few and far between, and they showed them to like-minded people who would share their interest and, it was hoped, their tastes. Members who did not comply with the Society's expectations were reprimanded – both Programmes Fifteen and Eighteen noted that there had been complaints about audible comments and conversations during performances. The Society thus aimed to educate those who attended its screenings, to impart a taste for 'work of interest' in cinematography and to teach them, via its programmes and its lectures and discussions, how to understand and even how to watch its films. In this sense it continued the important contemporary focus on film and education described earlier and, as Jamie Sexton remarks, in one sense it was a kind of film school where 'the art of film was not only appreciated, but also studied' (Sexton 2008: 15).

The Film Society did demonstrate a very real curiosity about cinema – its early focus on the French avant-garde, including regular screenings of the work of Man Ray for example, is testimony to this. It provided a vital alternative to the commercial circuits, actively seeking out (often by Council members' trips to the Continent to acquire prints) these 'special' films and going against the prevailing wind in terms of aesthetic and indeed moral attitudes towards cinema. Programme Thirty-Eight for example shows *The Seashell and the Clergyman*, Germaine Dulac's surrealist film of 1928, noting that the film had been rejected by the BBFC with 'the infamous comment that "it is so cryptic as to be almost meaningless. If there is a meaning, it is doubtless objectionable"' (ibid.: Programme Thirty-Eight). However, this sense of going against the grain from a cinematic point of view is only part of the story. As Jamie Sexton suggests, 'the Society was not an alternative space that attempted to negate the commercial cinema: rather, such a space was created in order to feed into the industry, as well as to encourage practices that did not adhere to the requirements of commercial cinema' (ibid.: 15). This attempt to shape film production is witnessed in the Society's offer of cut-price membership to those working in the film industry and in many ways does, as Sexton suggests, position it as a 'different' part of the broader British cinema rather than something entirely separate.

This is also revealed in the resolutely middle-class nature of the Film Society and its members. As Vincent Porter notes, 'the Society's membership fee was expensive and it was impossible for the ordinary cinemagoer to buy a ticket for a single performance' (Porter 2010: 19). The three different subscription rates for the first season stood at three guineas, two guineas and one guinea and they generally shifted from season to season more or less in line with inflation. Given that the average wage in Britain was then about £200 per annum, this was not an insignificant sum and clearly targeted an upper-middle- and upper-class public. Interestingly the mainstream press of the day tended to describe the Society's members as bohemian and even, perhaps due to the Society's early enthusiasm for Soviet films, radical. After the showing of Pudovkin's *The End of St. Petersburg* in February 1929, *The Daily Sketch* reported:

> ... that at the end of performance, when the National Anthem was played, several distinct hisses were heard from the well of the theatre and many of the audience remained seated. [...] Many of those in the audience were sallow faced young men with long black hair. There were bearded youths and crop-haired girls. One young man wore an open-necked tennis shirt and another had a complete suit of blue velvet.
>
> (Robinson 1963: 285)

However, Iris Barry, in her response to Robinson's history, vigorously refutes this account of audience and event and is clearly furious at Robinson's decision to emphasise these press attacks and 'the sartorial peculiarities of the audience' in his study:

> There is no consideration of the purely <u>private</u> [her emphasis] nature of the showings nor a hint of the elegant (perhaps over-elegant) character of these manifestations – never were so many limousines seen in Regent Street on a Sunday afternoon – where the general decorum imposed by the presence of ladies-in-waiting from the Palace and of so many celebrities was only occasionally threatened by deliberate if polite booing of a nature-study 'short' (not mentioned) or a shout of acclamation mainly from Oxford and Cambridge students at the front of the hall, at some strikingly novel and effective bit of technique [...] in some of the Russian features.
>
> (Barry 1963)

So in Barry's recollections, memories borne out it must be said by the exclusive subscription costs alone, the Film Society was not a hot-bed of blue-velvet-suited radicalism but a thoroughly respectable gathering of film-lovers in which the only signs of agitation would come from youthful enthusiasm for cinematic excellence. To a certain degree, it was this very exclusivity which enabled the survival of the Society. High membership fees meant films could be shown in excellent facilities with full orchestral accompaniment thus leaving audiences keen for more. Arguably more significant was the Society's underlining of its members' intelligent, restrained (read middle-class) attitude to films in its attempts, during its second season, to obtain a permanent sanction from the London County Council for the showing of uncensored films on a Sunday afternoon. As Sexton remarks, 'The Film Society thus used its intellectual and respectable status as a cultural weapon, drawing a qualitative difference between its members and the audience that attended commercial cinemas' (Sexton 2008: 26). Programme notes for Season Three's screening of *Nana* in 1926 included an untranslated quote from Renoir: clearly it was assumed that this audience would not only have an interest in the best French films, they would also be conversant in the language (Programme Nineteen: 1972). This construction of a discerning, intelligent audience is one that has remained as the dominant stereotype for audiences for foreign cinema ever since and one which has had a significant impact on distribution and exhibition strategies as we shall see.

The Society's membership was then indisputably middle class. As membership declined towards the end of the 1930s, Phyllis Morris wrote to Sydney Bernstein suggesting a move to Sunday evening showings, a decision based firmly on the social class and habits of their members, 'Personally I think [. . .] that the growth of the "weekend cottage" habit has harmed us quite as much as has the increase in specialist cinema or the poorer quality of our programmes'. The class bias of the Society was both its strength (it ensured funds and the approval of the LCC) and in some ways its weakness as it limited its audience and thus its impact and constructed a set of perceptions as to what kind of people would pay to see 'foreign' cinema (middle-class, educated) which have largely remained in place ever since. Writing in *The Observer* Caroline Lejeune gives voice to this paradox as she both praises the Society's programmes and criticises its exclusivity and limited canon of taste:

> I haven't, in the past, given very much space in this column to the performances of the Film Society. That is not from any lack of admiration for its work, but because it seemed to me that the films which anybody could see in the local picturehouse were of more interest to the general public than the specialised fare of one group of London enthusiasts on Sunday afternoons. [. . .] The great value of the Film Society is that it creates appreciation of pictures in people

who have not yet discovered anything to excite their interest in the commercial film. For anyone in this country who wants to learn everything about pictures, the Film Society is an essential training ground.

(Lejeune, 'The Film Society Picks a Winner')

To some extent this 'exclusivity' was alleviated by the advent of the Continental cinemas, which began to offer a rather more accessible alternative to the Film Society. Moreover, the growth of the provincial film society movement reduced the metropolitan bias of non-English-language film exhibition making these films accessible to a rather wider range of audiences. Glasgow was the first to follow London with the establishment of a society in 1929 and this was swiftly followed by Edinburgh in 1930 and Birmingham, Leicester and Southampton in 1931. It is worth noting that membership charged by these societies was significantly lower than London: twenty-one shillings per annum in Edinburgh and ten shillings in Southampton as opposed to the Film Society's top rate of three guineas (Harvey 1932). The movement continued to grow in other cities and via the Workers' Film Society movement and became a dominant force for the dissemination of cinema outside commercial circuits, aided of course by the establishment of the National Film Library in 1935.

So it would be wrong to limit our account of the Film Society to a group of wealthy London film-loving socialites. The success of the Society was a major force in the national development of a movement which brought films which may well not otherwise have been seen to quite a broad range of audiences. Nevertheless, the middle-class exclusivity described above is undeniable and of course any society carries with it an element of distinction or selection. As the Film Society and its off-shoots became a key venue for the screening of French and other continental films, so these films took on that same 'distinction', arguably to the detriment of their broader distribution. This is not to deny in any way the importance of the Film Society in bringing French film to Britain. The Society was instrumental in showing a range of French films including experimental and avant-garde work and more mainstream narrative features which had otherwise failed to find British distribution: indeed more than one-fifth of the Society's programmes comprised French cinema. As Vincent Porter argues, the distribution of French cinema was highly precarious and by the mid-1930s was controlled by three specialist distributors, each linked to one of the specialist London cinemas, which themselves had 'barely a dozen French titles between them' (Porter 2010: 24). They were Denning Films (Fairfax-Jones/Hampstead Everyman), Reunion Film (Hakim/Academy) and Tobis Film Distributors, part of Tobis Maatschapij NV which had close links to the Curzon (24). Given this precarity, the continuing efforts of the Film Society in sourcing films and distributing to other societies were invaluable. Writing in 1975,

Thorold Dickinson, who had become fully associated with the Film Society in 1930, declared:

> It added to the excitement of foreign travel when one was able to unearth, and negotiate for, films unknown in Britain. In Paris my wife and I found Cocteau's *The Blood of a Poet*. In Berlin in January 1933, surrounded by incipient Nazism, we sat in a bankrupt unheated projection-room with only one projector, and saw the first export print of Machaty's *Ecstasy*, just arrived from Prague. To both films we were able to give the only uncensored performances outside their countries of origin.
>
> (Dickinson 1975: 9)

A particularly striking example of the Society's provision of films which would surely not have reached British audiences at this juncture without its existence is provided by the films of Jean Vigo. As David Robinson notes:

> The inclusion of Vigo films in Film Society programmes was a considerable act of faith in the 30s. Vigo [. . .] terrified the film renters to the extent that they mutilated his films before distribution; appalled the French censors who forbade public showings of *Zéro de Conduite*; and was misunderstood even by the most intellectually inclined British critics.
>
> (Robinson 1963: 238)

Despite, or perhaps because of, Vigo's contentious reputation, *Zéro de Conduite* attracted large audiences to the Society's screening. Robinson notes that, as the 1930s drew on, it became impossible 'to resist the feeling that the Society was beginning to lose its hold upon the public attention. Its work was done. The press notices became fewer and shorter. The membership was evidently going down' (ibid.: 27). Yet Vigo's film, unavailable elsewhere at that point, reminded members of the Society's original role, a role becoming increasingly redundant as other outlets provided the specialist fare it had made its stock in trade. Council minutes at the close of Season Thirteen(1937–38) noted that:

> The interest of the Film Society during the past twelve years in raising the general level of public taste has led to the establishment of a number of cinemas showing pictures of the type which in the past could only be seen at the Society's performances. Although this is a gratifying result, it has the practical effect of reducing the number of films available for showing by the Society.
>
> (cited in Robinson 1963: 330)

Accordingly, the Society's programmes were reduced from a season of eight performances to six 'at a correspondingly reduced subscription' (330) while four programmes of revivals were presented in association with the London Film Institute Society at the Forum Cinema in Villiers Street.

4. *Zéro de Conduite* (Jean Vigo, 1933).
Image courtesy of the BFI stills department.

So as the Film Society began to wind up its activities, what was its legacy? Without doubt its role in the exhibition of films which would have otherwise failed to win a showing in Britain was invaluable. The hard-won right to show uncensored films along with the founders' very real interest in the diversity of cinema meant that films from Russia, Germany, Japan and of course France found their way to a limited but genuinely interested British audience:

> The Film Society was a great force in establishing internationalism in the cinema. The council kept up an energetic correspondence with film people all over the world. They travelled Europe and further fields viewing and choosing film. They brought to this country, for the first time, the work of Bunuel, Cavalcanti, Clair, Cocteau, Eisenstein, Kinugasa, Lang, Lubitsch, Ophuls, Painlevé, Vertov and Vigo; and films from Japan, Hungary, Poland and Portugal. The Society played an enormous role in establishing the climate in which the Film Festival idea was able to gain ground in the 1930s and after the war.

(ibid.: no page numbers)

Beyond its specific role in creating a cosmopolitan film culture in Britain, the Society also forged important international links, links which led to the ten-day congress of international independent cinema at the Château de la Sarraz in Switzerland in September 1929, an event which in turn led to the establishment of the International League of Independent Cinema, created to aid distribution between the member clubs and societies (Sexton 2008: 17). In other words, the Film Society's interventions in transnational filmic exchange extended well beyond those Sunday afternoon showings.

Of particular significance here however is the role the Society played in the creation of tastes for, expectations and exhibition of 'specialist' film in the United Kingdom. The films shown by the Society throughout the 1930s became the basis of a 'canon' of cinematic excellence which to some extent has continued to define film, and determine what kinds of films are shown and where, ever since. As David Robinson remarks in the outline to his planned manuscript, 'To a remarkable extent the received history of the film was established in this country – and even, to a degree in Europe – by the Society's programmes' (Robinson 1961). The founders of the Society took their role very seriously – cinema, they believed, was important – and the films they chose to show did indeed provide a window on non-mainstream and foreign production which played a vital role in the construction of a serious film culture in Britain. Iris Barry's aforementioned 'irritation' at Robinson's history speaks volumes about her own guardianship of the Society's legacy: her desire to control the way in which the story is told suggests a firm belief in the importance of its contribution.

But if the Film Society and its regional off-shoots created a space for non-mainstream cinema in Britain, they were also instrumental in limiting that space, arguably to the detriment of the wider distribution of 'specialist' film, including French. French cinema became the province of the specialised exhibitor and the French cinema in question was defined by the intelligent but nevertheless restrictive tastes of a small group of individuals. The cultural significance of the Society and its perceived intellectualism are amusingly illustrated by Stella Gibbons' burlesque of the Society's films and audience in her 1932 comic novel *Cold Comfort Farm*:

> That audience had run to beards and magenta shirts and original ways of arranging its neckwear; and not content with the ravages produced in its over-excitable nervous system by the remorseless workings of its critical intelligence, it had sat through a film of Japanese life called 'Yes', made by a Norwegian film company in 1915 with Japanese actors, which lasted an hour and three-quarters and contained twelve close-ups of water-lilies lying perfectly still on a scummy pond and four suicides, all done extremely slowly.
>
> (Gibbons 1932: 93)

The Specialised Cinemas

While the so-called Continental cinemas were instrumental in hastening the demise of the Film Society, they could also be seen to counteract the rather limiting canonisation it engendered as they offered the potential for a wider range of 'specialised' film. The first of the 'Continental' picture houses was Eric Hakim's Academy in Oxford Street which opened its doors as Britain's first permanent 'art cinema' in 1931. Films were programmed by Elsie Cohen who began by programming one film per week and publicised her programmes through weekly press shows and, in another reminder of the limited number of people involved in Continental exhibition at this time, through preview screenings at the Film Society. As Vincent Porter notes, her first season was a six-week series of French films, including *Le Roi des resquilleurs*, *Jean de la Lune* and *La Douceur d'aimer* (Porter 2010: 20). The season was a success and the Academy began to advertise itself as 'The home of real French talkies' going on to première over thirty French films during the 1930s (20). The cinema quickly took on the reputation as the home of quality continental cinema. Writing in *Close Up* in June 1933, E. Coxhead declared:

> Everyone knows the Academy Cinema. When we say Academy, it is as often as not (and how shocked our grandfathers would be to hear it) that one we mean. It is more than a cinema; it is a policy, a promise, a guarantee. Something one has in common with other people, a topic of conversation, a means of making friends. [. . .] In my opinion, the greatest work of the Academy is the establishment of quite new relations between exhibitor and audience. As its ideas spread, the theatre itself will become less important; it will end as just one of a wide circle of theatres working on the same plan. But the spirit of co-operation which it has fostered will increase; the ideal of a thinking audience, as opposed to an audience which is spared all thought by the exhibitor's own policy, may finally become the most powerful factor in the Trade.
>
> (Coxhead, 1933: 133–37)

Coxhead's remarks are revealing as they demonstrate a real desire for the democratisation of cinematic taste (letting the audience choose its films) and yet a simultaneous exclusivity ('something one has in common with other people') which in many ways mirrors the members-only ethos of the Film Society. Certainly Cohen aimed to reach a wider audience through the Academy. Several rows of stalls were kept at very low prices and while much publicity was concentrated through a mailing list, Cohen ensured this spread beyond London thus offering those outside the city the chance to learn about particular films. As Coxhead hints, Cohen also planned a chain of Academies in every major British town although her attempts at expansion were to prove unsuccessful. She began programming at the larger Cambridge Theatre in London's Cambridge Circus but the size of the building made this venture unsuccessful and she abandoned it after only six months. Hakim also asked Cohen to programme another of his theatres, Oxford Street's Cinema House, in 1934. This was also to prove short-lived as Hakim's debts forced him to sell the cinema to the commercial D.J. James circuit later that year.

Cohen's work at the Academy was without doubt pioneering and provided a cinematic experience, open to all, not before available to British (or rather London) audiences. Turning once again to *Close Up*, an editorial of 1932 states, 'Actually, we are becoming so accustomed to assisting at the best Cosmopolitan talkies at the Academy that we are apt to forget the initial marvel of having a specialised theatre in sleepy London' (Anon. 1932a: 134). The Academy's success in attracting audiences for continental film led to competition and the opening of a series of specialised movie theatres across London and indeed further afield. In 1933 James Fairfax-Jones, Secretary and Treasurer of the Southampton Film Society, opened the Everyman Cinema Theatre in Hampstead. The cinema was funded by a group of like-minded friends, suggesting that, rather like the Film Society before it, this was a very personal and somewhat amateurish project. As Fairfax Jones recalled, 'It cannot be said that any of us associated with the venture had any very special knowledge of the film industry. We were animated with a laudable desire to have a small cinema at which we could give programmes of good films as a matter of regular policy' (Fairfax Jones 1994/95: 23). The policy was to 'conduct the Everyman on Film Society lines, reviving and presenting the best films, long and short, available from international sources; but with this difference, that the Everyman programmes were to be available to the public at large, rather than to a limited audience of subscribers' (23).

The venture was not at first a success, despite decent audiences for Hitchcock and Clair seasons. However, the showing in early 1935 of Robert Siodmak's *La Crise est finie* attracted good audiences and from then on the cinema 'reached a level of constancy which dispelled most financial cares and encouraged the expansion of ideas' (ibid.: 2). Just as the Academy was very much the work of Elsie Cohen, so the Everyman was the pet project of Fairfax Jones who not only selected films but also staffed the front desk, running the cinema as a hobby right up until his death in 1973. Among the 'best' films shown for the first time to the 'public at large' (rather than the members-only Film Society) was Vigo's *Zéro de Conduite* which, banned in France, was given a world public première at the Everyman in 1937. Fairfax Jones noted:

> The repercussions of this programme in various quarters were most interesting. *Zéro de Conduite* was clearly conceived and produced in all sincerity, with point and purpose. It accordingly merited serious criticism. All the critics disliked it and expressed their dislike in various ways. Some of them merely

slanged it, others tried to puzzle it out, others gave it headlines and smart journalism. The most reasoned and intelligent review came from *The Times* and the most deplorable piece of criticism I think I have ever encountered came from *The Observer*. Miss Lejeune awarded the film a series of facetious noughts without adding one word of reason or explanation. Speaking at the opening performance Basil Wright used the phrase 'Zero de Lejeune, or Nought for *The Observer*' – a remark which was greeted with immediate and sympathetic applause [. . .] The upshot was that more people than we thought possible came to see the film and it ran for five weeks. Never before had we such curious audiences or such curious audience response. Most people disliked *Zéro de Conduite*, although almost everybody thought the experimental shorts a very good collection.

(Fairfax Jones 1994/95: 24–25)

This account reveals much about the Everyman's remit at the time and indeed its legacy. The cinema was instrumental in showing films so far unavailable anywhere and was prepared to take risks to show what its programmers perceived as the 'best' work. These screenings, part of a regular cinema programme, were, like those of the Academy, more accessible to the general public than the Film Society's Sunday afternoon sessions. However, they were still of course only able to reach a limited audience. As Fairfax Jones remarked of the Vigo screening, 'But we have to remember that in the main it is the size – or rather lack of size – of the Everyman, which has but 260 seats, which enables us to conduct such experiments with any success. An audience sufficient to pack the Everyman would present a spectacle of pathetic desolation if transferred to any one of the local Odeons' (ibid.: 25). Despite the cinema's focus on 'international' cinema, the films shown still represented a relatively limited corpus of work which reflected the tastes of the programmers: French films were a very prominent feature of the Everyman's programmes both during the 1930s and after the cinema's post-war re-opening. One notes the reoccurrence of particular names with eight René Clair seasons and the regular reappearance of directors such as Duvivier, Allegret, Carné and Renoir. In other words, we can see the continuing formation of that great canon of French film of the period already begun by the Film Society. It is also worth noting audience response to *Zéro de Conduite* – a rush to the cinema to see this highly controversial film but a general antipathy to the work itself. Here we can see an early example of French film sold as 'shocking' (and then not necessarily enjoyed!), a marketing tactic which, as we will see, has remained in place ever since.

The Everyman's Hampstead location meant that it was not in direct competition with Cohen's Academy. However, the opening of the Curzon in Mayfair in March 1934, under the aegis of Captain H.G. Morrison and the Marquis of Casa Maury, undermined the Academy's status as the leading central London venue for continental films. The establishment of

5. Mireille Balin, Jean Gabin and Lucas Gridoux in *Pépé le Moko* (Julien Duvivier, 1937).
Image courtesy of the BFI stills department.

Studio One in 1936 provided further competition with the result, as Vincent Porter notes, that each cinema had to pay higher advances for the best films and thus, in an attempt to recoup their investments, held the more popular films over for longer (Porter 2010: 22). In other words, the growth in the continental picture houses did not de facto lead to increased choice and diversity in terms of the films. Between October 1936 and May 1937 Studio One screened *La Kermesse Héroïque* for eight months; the Curzon showed *Pépé le Moko* for seven weeks between April and May 1937 while the Academy held over *La Grande Illusion* for three months during spring 1938 (Porter 2010: 22). Other cinemas did jump on the band wagon, with venues such as the Berkeley showing continental films programmed by Elsie Cohen in 1937 and the opening of Casa Maury's Paris Cinema in Lower Regent Street in 1939.

This period of quite febrile competition was of course brought to a halt by the outbreak of war which, as the following chapter will reveal, was to have a significant impact upon the British exhibition of French film. Yet it is also striking that to some degree the very attempt to make continental,

6. A Peter Strausfeld poster advertising a re-release of *La Kermesse Héroïque* (Jacques Feyder, 1935) at Academy Cinema Two.
Image courtesy of the BFI stills department.

including French, film more accessible via the Continental theatres was also to contribute to the demise of this 'golden' period. By forcing a bidding battle for a body of films which itself was ever decreasing due to the approach of war, the competition between these cinemas undermined their ability to continue showing the films which they had made their stock in trade. Recalling the Academy of the 1930s in an interview in 1971, Elsie Cohen makes this very clear: 'The great days of the Academy in a way really ended about 1937, 1938, simply because of the Hitler position and the whole world situation generally. Nobody knew what was going to happen' (Cohen 1971: 12). She goes on to describe her competition with Casa Maury and the Curzon saying, 'from that moment really, the Academy began to lose its position, because we were fighting Casa Maury. He used to go and stay at the Ritz in Paris and pay God knows what, and take producers out and wine them and dine them. And from having been able to buy at reasonable prices for the Academy, I was really in competition then with a man who was prepared to pay anything' (12).

The End of an Era?

The impact of the 'Continental' cinemas, particularly the pioneering work of the Academy and Elsie Cohen, should sit alongside the programmes of the Film Society as a vital force in making available non-mainstream cinema to British audiences in the 1930s and more particularly in shaping a specific canon of films and tastes which would go on to define the French films shown in this country in subsequent decades. Writing in *Sight and Sound* in 1986, John Russell Taylor remarks:

> Elsie Cohen came out of the original Film Society, that astonishingly influential concern which introduced almost everybody of note in the Hitchcock/Bernstein/Montagu generation of the British cinema to the foreign wonders of film-as-art, with a burning conviction about the mission of the art house and its commercial viability for something much wider than the limited club audience.
> (Taylor 1986: 185)

Cohen of course continued that work at the Academy and her efforts were mirrored at the Everyman, the Curzon and of course further afield in Glasgow's Cosmo, for example. The 1930s was indeed a rich decade in terms of the British exhibition of French film with availability in London which has not been matched since. The spread of the film society movement to some degree moved that richness beyond the confines of London, allowing aficionados the opportunity to see a range of French films which would almost certainly have not otherwise reached British shores.

And yet we must not forget the limitations of this golden era. We owe much to the work of these cinematic pioneers – Cohen, Montagu, Barry et al. – yet they were indisputably a limited group with shared tastes and interests and in many cases shared backgrounds. This small coterie was to have a profound impact on the shaping of a canon of French film and of British expectations of what French cinema should be which to a great degree have defined British distribution and exhibition of the cross-channel product ever since. John Russell Taylor sums up the Academy cinemas as 'the kings of the middle way, catering to the intelligent middle-brow, middle-class audience' (ibid.: 186) and this essentially defines the audience for French film of the 1930s and arguably continues to do so today. The Film Society may have had a passion for the avant-garde but any cinematic excess was safely constrained by the exclusive, middle-class nature of its gatherings. In similar vein the continental cinemas showed 'good' French film to a 'discerning' audience. To enjoy French film by the end of the 1930s was to appreciate quality and good taste. As war reduced the flow of these 'quality' films to the UK during the 1940s and British film culture underwent a number of significant changes how would these audiences be catered for?

Note

1. Here he echoes a prevalent interest in the crucial role of the director in both French and British critical discourse of the period and prefigures the discourses of 'auteurism' which would emerge in the late 1950s.

Bibliography

Anon. 1930a. 'Vive la France! Bristol Showman's Alert Methods', *Kinematograph Weekly*, 12 June.
Anon. 1930b. 'Alhambra Theatre: Under the Roofs of Paris', *The Times*, 12 December (BFI Special Collections, BFI Clippings, vol. 1, item 3).
Anon. 1932a. '"Our" Academy', *Close Up*, June, 134.
Anon. 1932b. *Sight and Sound* 1(1), Spring.
Barry, I. 1926 (reprint 1972). *Let's Go to the Movies*. New York: Arno Press.
Barry, I. 1963. Notes on Robinson, D. *The Career and Times of the Film Society* (Film Society BFI Special Collection, item 45).
Betts, E. 1929. 'Why 'Talkies' Are Unsound', *Close Up* 4(4), April, in J. Donald, A. Friedberg and L. Marcus (eds), *Close Up 1927–1933: Cinema and Modernism*. London: Cassell, pp. 89–90.
Cohen, E. 1932/33. 'The Continental Film in England: A Survey and a Forecast for the Filmgoer', *Sight and Sound* 1(4), Winter.
Cohen, E. 1971. 'Elsie Cohen Talks to Anthony Slide About the Academy Cinema, Political Censorship and the British Cinema Scene in the Thirties', *The Silent Picture* 11/12, 1 July: 9–13.
Council of the London Film Society. 1972. *The Film Society Programmes 1925–1939*. New York: Arno Press.
Coxhead, E. 1933. 'Towards a Co-operative Cinema: The Work of the Academy, Oxford Street', *Close Up*, June: 133–37.
Dickinson, T. 1975. 'Then There Was the Time When . . .', *Film*, October/November: 8–9.
Donald, J. 1998. 'Introduction: From Silence to Sound', in J. Donald, A. Friedberg and L. Marcus (eds), *Close Up 1927–1933: Cinema and Modernism*. London: Cassell, pp.79–82.
Fairfax Jones, J. 1994/95. 'The Film's the Thing: First Years of the Everyman', *Picture House* 20, Winter: 23–25 (originally published in *Sight and Sound*, Autumn 1937).
Friedberg, A. 1998. 'Reading *Close Up*, 1927–1933', in J. Donald, A. Friedberg and L. Marcus (eds), *Close Up 1927–1933: Cinema and Modernism*. London: Cassell, pp. 1–26.
Gibbons, Stella. 1932 (2006). *Cold Comfort Farm*. London: Penguin Classics.
Gomery, D. 1980. 'Economic Struggle and Hollywood Imperialism: Europe Converts to Sound', *Yale French Studies* 60: 80–93.
Hake, S. 1993. *Cinema's Third Machine: Writing on Film in Germany 1907–1933*. Lincoln: University of Nebraska Press.
Hakim, E. 1934. 'Specialised Cinema or Film Society?', *Sight and Sound* 3(9), Spring: 10–12.
Harvey, J.M. 1932, 'Film Society Minutes', 5 April.

Hinxman, M. 1975. 'We Didn't Talk About Film Appreciation, You Just Liked Going to the Cinema', *Film*, October/November: 39.
Lejeune, C.A. 1939. 'René Clair on France's Cinema Industry', *The Observer*, 22 January (BFI Special Collection, BFI Clippings, vol.9, item 6).
Lejeune, C.A. No date. 'The Film Society Picks a Winner', *The Observer* (BFI Special Collections, Elsie Cohen Collection, item 11).
Macpherson, K. 1927. 'As Is', *Close Up* 1(1), July, in J. Donald, A. Friedberg and L. Marcus (eds), *Close Up 1927–1933: Cinema and Modernism*. London: Cassell, pp. 36–40.
Miller, H. 1925. 'An Independent Film Theatre', *The Evening Standard* (Film Society BFI Special Collection, item 11: Press Clippings Relating to the Film Society 1925–95).
Moore, B. 1934. '"Put Britain on the Screen" says René Clair', *Picturegoer*, 15 December: 21.
Nyman, K.A. 1934. 'Profit or Prestige? How the Public Gets its Films. A Problem for Exhibitors', *Sight and Sound* 3(10), Summer: 51.
Porter, V. 2010. 'The Exhibition, Distribution and Reception of French Films in Great Britain During the 1930s', in L. Mazdon and C. Wheatley (eds.), *Je t'aime, moi non plus: Franco-British Cinematic Relations*. Oxford: Berghahn Books, pp. 19–36.
Robinson, D. 1961. Outline for *The Career and Times of the Film Society* (Film Society BFI Special Collection, item 45).
Robinson, D. 1963. *The Career and Times of the Film Society* (Film Society BFI Special Collection, item 45, unpublished manuscript).
Rotha, P. 1930 (revised 1967). *The Film Till Now*. London: Spring Books.
Samson, J. 1986. 'The Film Society, 1925–1939', in C. Barr (ed.), *All Our Yesterdays. Ninety Years of British Cinema*. London: BFI, pp. 306–13.
Sedgwick, J. and Pokorny, M. 2005. 'The Film Business in the United States and Britain During the 1930s', *Economic History Review* 18(1): 79–112.
Sexton, J. 2008. *Alternative Film Culture in Inter-War Britain*. Exeter: University of Exeter Press.
Taylor, J.R. 1986. 'Academic Distinctions', *Sight and Sound* 55(3), 1 July: 184–86.
Thomas, Y. 1939. 'The Foreign Film Returns', *Sight and Sound* 8(29), Spring: 28–29.
Vincendeau, G. 1998. 'Hollywood Babel', *Screen* 29(2): 24–39.

Filmography

A nous la liberté (1931, René Clair)
Carnet de bal, Un (1937, Julien Duvivier)
Chapeau de Paille d'Italie, Un / An Italian Straw Hat (1928, René Clair)
Chute de la Maison Usher, La / The Fall of the House of Usher (1928, Jean Epstein)
Collier de la Reine, Le / The Queen's Necklace (1929, Tony Lekain and Gaston Ravel)
Coquille et le clergyman, La / The Seashell and the Clergyman (1928, Germaine Dulac)
Crise est finie, La (1934, Robert Siodmak)

David Golder (1931, Julien Duvivier)
Deux Timides, Les / Two Timid Souls (1928, René Clair)
Douceur d'aimer, La (1930, René Hervil)
Ekstase / Ecstasy (1933, Gustav Machaty)
En Rade (1928, Alberto Cavalcanti)
Finis Terrae (1929, Jean Epstein)
Grande Illusion, La (1937, Jean Renoir)
Jean de la lune (1931, Jean Choux)
Jour se lève / Daybreak, Le (1939, Marcel Carné)
Kameradschaft (1931, Georg Wilhelm Pabst)
Kermesse Héroïque, La / Carnival in Flanders (1935, Jacques Feyder)
Konets Sankt-Peterburga / The End of St. Petersburg (1927, Vsevolod Pudovkin)
M (1931, Fritz Lang)
Madame Sans Gêne (1924, Léonce Perret)
Maedchen in Uniform (1931, Leontine Sagan and Carl Froelich)
Marius (1931, Alexander Korda)
Million, Le (1931, René Clair)
My iz Kronshtadta / We From Kronstadt (1936, Efim Dzigan)
Nana (1926, Jean Renoir)
Opéra de quat'sous, L' / The Threepenny Opera (1931, Georg Wilhelm Pabst)
Paris Méditerranée / Into the Blue (1931, Joe May)
Pépé le Moko (1937, Julien Duvivier)
Quatorze juillet, Le / The Fourteenth of July (1933, René Clair)
Rien que les heures / Nothing But Time (1930, Alberto Cavalcanti)
Roi des resquilleurs, Le (1930, Pierre Colombier)
Roman d'un tricheur, Le / The Cheat (1936, Sacha Guitry)
Sang d'un poète, Le / Blood of a Poet (1930, Jean Cocteau)
Sous les toits de Paris / Under the Roofs of Paris (1930, René Clair)
Thérèse Raquin (1928, Jacques Feyder)
Westfront 1918 (1930, Georg Wilhelm Pabst)
Zéro de Conduite (1933, Jean Vigo)

2

Cinema Goes to War (1939–1950)

If the 1930s had proved a golden age for the British exhibition of French film, the outbreak of World War Two in September 1939 seemed to present a dire threat to this cinematic blossoming. The emergence of specialist cinemas, the growth in the Film Society movement and the increasing visibility of the 'Continentals', largely thanks to the efforts of a dedicated body of enthusiasts, all seemed precarious as the imperatives of war became paramount in Britain, and as France, source of so many of those 'Continentals', fell to the Nazis. And yet, early fears about the future of cinema, and French cinema in particular, were to prove somewhat exaggerated. The war years, rather than sounding cinema's death knell, saw it become an ever more prominent cultural presence and leisure activity. Despite the undeniable limitations imposed by German occupiers and Vichy authorities alike, French film production did not cease and via revivals of pre-war favourites the Gallic cinema retained a visible presence in the United Kingdom. The 1940s was then to prove a decade of paradoxes for the British dissemination of French cinema: a lack of new films due to the war would be countered by frequent and often popular revivals; these revivals would entrench the 'canonisation' of French cinema already begun through the exhibition practices and critical discourses of the 1930s; and yet as Hollywood films briefly fell away, particularly in the latter part of the decade, attempts were made to offer the French product as a popular and accessible alternative.

French Cinema during World War Two

As discussed in the previous chapter, by the end of the 1930s French film had become the dominant 'Continental' presence in Britain. Films from Germany had been a relative rarity since the coming to power of

7. Poster advertising a 1940s release of Jean Renoir's *Partie de Campagne* (1936). Image courtesy of the BFI stills department.

the Nazis in 1933, while Russian films had dwindled as Stalin took hold of Soviet Russia. Writing in *Sight and Sound* at the end of 1938, Arthur Vesselo remarked: 'The Continental cocktail this quarter is 80 per cent French, with a dash of Russian and Austrian to taste' (Vesselo 1938: 162). In another of his 'Continental round-ups', published in Spring 1939, he noted:

> The French films continue their triumphal march through the Continental cinemas, and even show tendencies to spread beyond those slightly confined boundaries. At one time in early June there were nine French feature-films playing simultaneously in West-End houses, as against an equal nine American and only four English. Such a situation must be quite unprecedented.
> (Vesselo 1939a: 78)

Vesselo is careful to remind readers that 'not *all* French productions are works of genius' – an interesting note of caution to which we shall return later – and yet it is clear that at this juncture French films, shown in subtitled or dubbed versions, were providing a very important alternative or even, via their occasional break-out to the non-specialist picture houses, addition to American and British fare.

The invasion of France by the Nazis in May 1940 which culminated in the formal surrender of Paris on 17 June 1940 would then pose a very real threat to British film connoisseurs, particularly those members of the Film Society and regular attendees of the Academy who relied on France for their fix of 'specialist' cinema. During the period of the so-called *drôle de guerre*, between the declaration of war in September 1939 and the invasion of France, Belgium, Luxembourg and the Netherlands in May 1940, the only fiction film produced in France was Duvivier's *Un Tel Père et fils* which was then not premièred until Autumn 1945. Film-making efforts were instead concentrated on propaganda films. Film's role in raising morale and combating Fascism was very clear to the French political and military authorities and by Spring 1940 France had produced, or was in the process of producing, around thirty films devoted to the defeat of Hitler and the defence of France. In addition, a series of short films showed efforts on the home front (*La France Continue*); the work of the navy (*La Marine Française*) and the air force (*Avions de France*); and even the results of Franco-British cooperation demonstrated through maps and animated drawings in *L'Effort Franco-Britannique* (Anon. 1940: 1). Following the fall of France, film-making more or less ceased until the end of 1940. However, in December 1940 the Vichy Government created the *Comité d'Organisation de L'Industrie Cinématographique* (COIC), an attempt to rationalise and strengthen the film industry which would form the basis of the later *Centre National de la Cinématographie* (CNC). As an element of the Vichy regime, the COIC introduced a number of repressive and anti-Semitic measures: Jews were forbidden to work in the film industry; trade unions were suppressed; and an obligatory professional identity card was imposed. Censorship was also stepped up as all scripts had to be approved by the COIC and then passed by the Vichy censor. The Germans established Continental films, a production studio based in Paris, and the vast majority of films were made in the occupied zone. This was to some extent the result of an early ban on French films crossing the demarcation line. Although this ban was lifted in 1941, meaning that any film passed by the German censors could be freely distributed throughout France, its initial impact created difficulties for film-making in the South and limited production significantly. Unsurprisingly American and British films were banned from French cinemas and many of those involved in the film industry, including leading figures such as Renoir, Clair and Duvivier, went into exile. Money was scarce and production budgets severely curtailed as an article published in *Sight and Sound* in 1942 makes abundantly clear:

> Unoccupied France now only possesses three sets of sound recording apparatus and four or five film cameras. The result is that hundreds of film actors and technicians are out of work. Another sad story concerns a recent film in which

was a scene where the star Jules Berry had to open a bottle of champagne. For some reason or another the scene had to be re-shot but as there was no other bottle available the same one had to be recorked and used over again. In the end the scene was cut as the champagne steadfastly refused to bubble!

(Anon. 1942: 11)

While the true impact of the war on French film production is still a somewhat contentious issue, it is now generally agreed that it was, perhaps surprisingly, a period of relative stability for those who chose and were permitted to continue making movies. Although output was reduced, the absence of Hollywood meant that French films dominated the box office, thus increasing domestic profits. Measures introduced by both Vichy and the Germans went some way to streamlining what had to all intents and purposes been little more than a cottage industry in the 1930s. While cinema-going remained much lower in France than in Britain,[1] attendance was frequent as cinemas provided affordable warmth and welcome distraction: audiences grew from 220 million in 1938 to over 300 million in 1943. Censorship of course posed a challenge to 'the ingenuity and inventiveness which had characterised the French cinema in the ten years before the war. Its greatest source of inspiration, everyday life and its human problems, was denied to it' (Hackett 1946: 2). Hackett claims that film-makers chose to 'ignore reality, a reality that was too painful and too close for artistic treatment', turning instead to historical literature, detective stories and fantasy and folklore for inspiration (2). One may of course dispute that film-makers of the period 'ignored' reality. Many of the films of the time would now be read in terms of their indirect but nevertheless important allusions to the realities of war and occupation. Nevertheless, it is fair to say that there was a shift from the focus on everyday contemporary experience which lay at the heart of so many of the important work of the 1930s to films which explored historical, mythical or allegorical themes.

Despite the undeniable difficulties faced by the French film industry during the war years, it did not collapse and once peace was restored in 1944 and those films made under the twin constraints of collaboration and occupation became more widely available, it was generally agreed that it had done rather more than survive. As Keith Bean reflected in 1944:

> It was grand news to learn, reliably, of French film production under the German occupation. Perhaps some of these two hundred films will be for the salvage bin – collaborative or merely not worth showing in competition with films produced in freedom and in less restrictive physical conditions of production. But we now know that the essential genius of French cinema has cherished its light under the bushel of Nazi domination. The first films shown here are an inspiring affirmation that the feeling of French film-makers for reality, for down-to-earth fidelity to life has survived.
>
> (Bean 1944: 65)

Cinema in Britain during World War Two

While France's film industry grappled with the impact of war and occupation, British cinema was faced with its own challenges. With the outbreak of war on 3 September 1939, all British cinemas were closed. On 11 September those outside urban areas were allowed to re-open and when the predicted bombings of Britain's cities did not immediately materialise, the Government permitted the re-opening of all cinemas until ten o'clock P.M. Only the cinemas of the West End were subject to additional restrictions as they were forced to close at six P.M., but by early November even these theatres were given permission to open until eleven. Film-going was not then to be prevented by the war although bomb damage and an embargo on cinema building certainly didn't make things easy for exhibitors. Moreover, a number of cinemas, notably some of the specialist picture houses dedicated to the showing of Continental film, were forced to close their doors. The Academy suffered bomb damage in 1941 and was closed, while Elsie Cohen's plans for a chain of Academies in Leeds and a number of other British cities were abandoned. George Hoellering, son of an Austrian theatrical impresario and Cohen's assistant at both the Academy and the Berkeley since 1937, was interned in 1940. Casa Maury's Curzon had closed for redecoration on 2 September 1939 but the declaration of war on 3 September resulted in its remaining closed until it was taken over by the Directorate of Army Cinematography for army screenings. His second cinema, the Paris Cinema, which had opened in 1938, also closed in late 1939 and was then requisitioned by the Office of Works and never operated as a public cinema again. The Everyman in Hampstead managed to survive the first few months of the war, showing a number of French films including *Hotel du Nord*, *Le Roman d'un Tricheur*, *Entrée des artistes*, *Les Otages*, *La Mort du Cygne* and Feyder's *Knight Without Armour*. However, it too was to bow to the inevitable and closed its doors in 1940. According to Peter Howden, it was then hired out and 'put on some quite commercial programmes for a couple of years because the European film market was not available' (Howden 1994/95: 40). The Cinema House on Oxford Street, which Elsie Cohen had begun programming in 1934, closed in 1940 but then re-opened in 1941, advertising itself as 'London's only Continental Cinema', a great marketing coup for that movie theatre but proof positive of the dire situation in which the 'specialist' cinemas found themselves.

If exhibition was precarious, British film-making was equally uncertain. Elstree studios were quickly requisitioned for war use while Pinewood and Denham were given over to food storage. Shortage of vital materials and the loss of key personnel to the war effort compounded these difficulties while increased taxation via an Excess Profits Tax and an Entertainments Tax, raised three times during the war, created serious financial constraints for all aspects of the industry (Richards 1986: 3). By October 1942 British domestic film production had reached an all-time low with only forty-six films made that year, a tiny proportion of the 600 films needed to enable British cinemas to operate successfully (1). But if Britain's film-makers were worried about the impact of the war, their American counterparts were similarly concerned. The loss of much of the European market meant that Hollywood was faced with the disappearance of a vital source of income. Writing in 1939 Ezra Goodman noted, 'Expenses and production budgets have been heavily cut, and the prevailing opinion is that as long as current conditions exist, the average top budgets will run to only half a million dollars, compared to the previous figure of approximately one million dollars for super-specials' (Goodman 1939: 106). This decline in both the quality and the quantity of Hollywood cinema (aided of course by the renewal of the Quota Act in 1938 which put a stop to the infamous 'quota quickies') was to provide a boost to the fortunes of domestic production. Although, as Jeffrey Richards notes, the production sector was forced to contract during the war years, what remained was considered very healthy and British films enjoyed an unprecedented popularity with critics and audiences alike (Richards 1986: 2).

This was partly due to the actual quality of the films with producers, Rank in particular, setting out to ape Hollywood by increasing budgets and making 'prestige' pictures which, it was hoped, would dominate the box office at home and abroad (Drazin 1998: 3). Popularity and critical esteem was also due to British patriotism – a desire to see the British way of life, British endeavours on screen rather than 'phoney' American fiction – and foreign admiration for Britain's courage in the face of adversity which made its cinema one that should be seen. Finally the decline in the American product provided both a space for the increased exhibition of British film and a mirror in which the quality of the domestic cinema shone all the more brightly. Writing in the *Sunday Express* in 1946, critic Stephen Watts suggested that this state of affairs was one that would outlast the war. 'British preferred' he states, going on to declare: 'I have heard more complaints about the general quality of films in the last year than ever before. British films at their best are preferred to run-of-the-mill Hollywood products. More and more people are resenting the amount of money we pay out each year for American films' (Watts 1946).

So what could so easily have proved a disastrous period for British cinema instead turned out to be a boom time, a period often described, in an echo of French cinema of the previous decade, as a 'golden age'. Variety was perhaps absent as smaller cinemas closed their doors and three large circuits, ABC, Gaumont and Odeon (the latter two both owned by Rank) dominated exhibition. Yet audiences were huge, rising from 987 million admissions in 1938 to a peak of 1,635 million in 1946,[2] attracted by morale-boosting and entertaining British productions and by the Technicolor charms still offered by Hollywood. Cinema-going became a dominant leisure activity as other forms of entertainment disappeared during the war. Contemporary trade magazines focused on box office above all else, and producers routinely sought a distributor before beginning production thus films were 'tailored to perceived box-office demands [...] the odds were stacked against anything different or original' (Drazin 1998: 8).

French Cinema in Britain in the War Years

So where did this leave French cinema in Britain? While the outbreak of war did not, as we have seen, bring a halt to French film-making, it did to all intents and purposes temporarily end the export of French film to the United Kingdom. That 'flood' of new French films which had fed the film societies and continental picture houses was reduced to a trickle by 1940, only to dry up entirely as France fell to the German invaders. This was to have a profound impact on all of Britain's 'specialist' exhibitors and arguably worst hit was the Film Society itself. Writing in 1975 to mark the fiftieth anniversary of the Film Society movement, Thorold Dickinson described the various challenges already facing the Film Society towards the end of the 1930s: the spread of the movement meant that many of those from the provinces who had come to London to attend the Society's screenings now joined an organisation closer to home; membership was also reduced due to competition from the specialised cinemas. He concludes:

> We no longer had a monopoly of foreign language cinema and the business men could outbid us, while the sources of good cinema were growing scantier, due to the rise of Nazism and Fascism, whose films were really awful, and to the interference of the Soviet Government in film production which was tending to conventionalise their output. [...] We all knew that war was inevitable and no one wanted to plan what to do when it did come. But our reputation was not that of the normal film society. From the beginning we had found, selected and introduced films in which the film trade could see no profit. We gave the only performances to which the critics came as to a first night. Our files, destroyed later by enemy action, made happy and proud reading. We did not want to lower our sights. So 'the day war broke out', in a dozen phone calls we closed the organisation down. And that was that.
>
> (Dickinson 1975: 9)

The demise of the Film Society was, as we have seen, swiftly followed by the closure of many of London's Continental cinemas. The absence of new Continental cinema was a very real concern for the specialist exhibitors as there was no longer a 'convenient stream of films passing to the [film] societies by way of the specialised cinemas in London' (Forsythe Hardy 1941: 29).

As John Ellis has revealed, the early 1940s saw an interesting shift towards a concept of British 'quality' film: cinema distinct from the producers' big-budget 'prestige' pictures which would have the artistic qualities more typically associated with French, German and Russian film in the 1930s (Ellis 1978: 16). Ellis argues that this was to prove a short-lived endeavour, undermined by the industry's economic crisis of 1948 and by the end of the war:

> By 1947 the strategy of encouraging more quality production, of exhibiting it widely through the circuits and backing it up with insistent newspaper and magazine criticism does not seem to have the desired effect. The good reception that was given to quality war-time pictures seems more and more to have depended on the fact of war rather than the fact of quality. The post-war quality film runs into problems with the mass audience who have problems understanding and appreciating them in the way they are offered.
>
> (Ellis 1978: 44)

Ellis contends that by the end of the 1940s the 'quality' film had retreated back to the specialised cinemas and was once again sought in the work of foreign film-makers (Italian Neo-realism in particular) and later via a re-evaluation of Hollywood genre films through the fledgling discourse of auteurism (46). What is worth noting is that this development of a discourse of British 'quality' from the early 1940s until the end of the decade should have coincided with the near absence of new French and other continental films from British screens. While the 1930s saw the establishment of a concept of 'art' cinema largely through the films of continental Europe, a process which to a great extent will re-emerge in later decades, the 1940s and the impact of the war seems to offer a brief hiatus in which British cinema and the 'prestige' pictures of US studios such as MGM are offered as a quality alternative. This critical focus on quality went hand in hand with the huge growth in cinema audiences already described and it may seem probable that the two would be in direct opposition: the mass audience's desire for entertainment versus a much more selective belief in cinema's potential for art. And yet, writing in 1947, Dilys Powell, influential film critic on *The Sunday Times*, remarked, 'The British public, always a cinema-going public, has become doubly so during the war years. And with the increase in numbers, a certain sharpening of public taste is to be observed. Themes which would once have been thought too serious or too controversial for the ordinary spectator are now accepted as a matter of course' (Powell 1947: 39).

So the British cinematic landscape of the early 1940s would seem to offer somewhat ambivalent prospects for the exhibition of French film:

cinema-going was a hugely popular leisure activity but many of the venues which had showed French movies had closed their doors; there was a growing critical interest in 'quality' cinema and a 'sharpening of public taste' and yet the very films which may have appealed to that taste were no longer arriving from France; films had of course become a hugely important means of propaganda yet audiences also craved escapism, films that were not about the on-going war (Richards 1986: 11). Writing in a questionnaire handed out to members of the Tyneside Film Society in Summer 1938, just weeks before the declaration of war, one respondent declared, 'Surrounded every week-day with the dinginess, dullness, and ugliness of industrial Newcastle and its sordid labouring class streets I crave for film showing us something *beautiful*' (Dyer 1938: 79). Interestingly, and not altogether surprisingly given its huge success on the society circuit, members selected Feyder's *La Kermesse Héroïque* as their favourite film of the season. Whether this would have been the selection of the above quoted respondent is debatable as s/he went on to complain, 'I have not been well satisfied with the films shown to us; several have interested me, yet they are lacking in the *beauty* which I want' (79). Nevertheless, what these remarks do suggest is a desire for cinema which was removed from the exigencies of war, from the daily lived experience of the average British cinema-goer, for a beautiful, quality cinema – in many ways the very type of cinema so often provided by the products of France in earlier years.

The Film Societies in the 1940s

Despite all the obstacles thrown in its path, French film was not to disappear from the United Kingdom during the 1940s. Crucial to its pre-war presence was of course the growing and increasingly popular presence of the film societies. If we turn our attention once more to the Tyneside Film Society in 1938 we can find clear evidence of this popularity as Ernest Dyer, the Society's chairman, weighs up the pros and cons of increased membership, 'On Tyneside last winter, with a membership of 1,200, we were able to show nine programmes [. . .] for a subscription of only 12*s*. a member, and yet to finish up – in spite of a grant of £20 to initiate a Children's Cinema Council, and a similar allocation to a dinner – with a balance on the season's working of over £200' (Dyer 1938: 78). Large membership also increased the society's standing with exhibitors and he notes, 'we are often able to secure the public exhibition of films that would not otherwise have been booked and to ensure the box-office success of films that have "flopped" in other towns' (78). Dyer acknowledges that a downside of these large numbers is the risk that choice of films may not be quite as 'courageous' as when the society had only forty members to consider. However, he counters this by claiming the society has indeed been more courageous 'because now we don't much care if we do lose a few hundred members, whereas before it would have been calamitous to lose a score' (78). He proudly declares, 'we are no longer looked upon as a body of amateur highbrows, but as a consumers' organisation' (78). This latter claim was perhaps somewhat over ambitious. As the film society movement and membership of many organisations grew, they were indeed taken more seriously by the film industry; nevertheless they remained to a great extent the domain of the film aficionado with a definite leaning towards the highbrow.

The original London Film Society was to close its doors shortly after the outbreak of war in 1939, and a number of other societies quickly followed suit. However, it was not all doom and gloom. Some groups, including a number of the Scottish societies, continued throughout the war and the period even saw the development of some new societies aided in part by a change in the law relating to the Sunday opening of cinemas. Indeed Peter Price attributes the opening of the Cambridge Film Society in 1941 directly to this development: as 'the need to Entertain the troops overtook the need to observe the Day of the Lord' so 'the films of Jean Vigo and Len Lye finally got a local showing as an incidental by-product' (Price 1975: 11). While the dearth of new films from the continent was to create problems for film society programmers, it could also be argued that it helped to increase membership of the societies which continued to function. Whereas the keen film fan may once have made the trip to London to catch the latest French import at the Academy, he or she would now join the local society and watch the best films of the previous decades. Of course those trips into London would have also become more difficult as rationing and the other restrictions of war time took hold. But trips out of London also impacted upon film society membership and growth, notably in the formation of the Colwyn Bay Film Society to accommodate government workers evacuated from London. The film societies were also aided by the National Film Library. Established in 1935, it was subject to a major reorganisation in 1941 and a new catalogue was produced. Films from the library's 'preservation' collection, which included the recently donated films of the London Film Society, were made available for public circulation and the library's collections became staples on the film society circuit, a vital resource in the war years in particular. Writing in 1943, H. Forsythe Hardy remarked:

> It is fortunate that, at this difficult period, the National Film Library should have shown itself ready and eager to help the film societies. [. . .] The collection of the London Film Society having been placed in its care, it has decided to make available dupe loan prints of those films which film societies would like to show. A select list has been made and this contains many films which hold a special and significant place in the history of the film.
>
> (Forsythe Hardy 1942: 63)

While the war years did not see the demise of the film society movement, it really began to take off in the immediate post-war period. The development of 16 mm projectors for war-time use meant that film societies could operate with smaller audiences in much smaller venues. This saw the demise of a number of the larger societies projecting on 35 mm in large cinemas, particularly as even more relaxed Sunday opening laws meant these cinemas could now be used for purely commercial screenings. However the smaller 16 mm societies proliferated. In 1945 the Federation of Film Societies was formed in England and the BFI began a booking agency to provide films for both this society and its Scottish equivalent. Membership of the English Federation grew from forty-six societies in 1945 to 190 by 1948. Olwen Vaughn (of whom more later) had programmed films at the Academy during the war under the guise of the London Film Institute and film enthusiasts relied upon it for a dose of French and other Continental cinema (Drazin 1998: 240). In 1945 she set up the New London Film Society along with Rodney Ackland showing films at the Scala Theatre in Charlotte Street, including a festival of French film in Autumn 1946. The Society showed silent classics alongside newly arrived work from the continent and ran successfully for ten seasons until its role was taken over by a newly invigorated British Film Institute (Drazin 1998: 243).

The war-time survival and post-war expansion of the film society movement were of course crucial to the continuing presence of the French cinema in Britain during the 1940s. While the specialist cinemas did not disappear entirely from the British cinematic landscape – the opening of Glasgow's Cosmo in 1939, the first purpose-built Continental and repertory cinema outside London, was of particular significance – it was to a great extent the remaining film societies which kept the flame of 'art' cinema and by extension French cinema burning through the dark days of the war. Societies in Manchester, Belfast, Liverpool, Aberdeen, Dundee, Bradford, Cambridge, Edinburgh, Colwyn Bay, Chester, Norwich, Tredegar, Glasgow, Ayrshire and of course London continued to show the 'best' of French film of the 1930s. Approximately thirty-nine French films were circulated around these societies between 1939 and 1945 and a small group was to prove particularly popular: *Un Carnet de bal* (Duvivier, 1937) was to receive screenings at nine societies; *Le Jour se lève* (Carné, 1939) received seven: *La Kermesse Héroïque* (Feyder, 1935) and *Roman d'un tricheur* (Guitry, 1936) each received six; while Pagnol's *La Femme du Boulanger* (1938) was shown at five societies during the period.

Above and beyond the actual exhibition of French film, which was inevitably limited by the constraints of war, it was their role in supporting and disseminating film as art which made the continuing presence of the film societies so important, arguably to British film culture more broadly, and specifically to the maintenance of an albeit limited place for non-English-language cinema in the United Kingdom. Discussing the future of the film societies in 1945, Norman Wilson remarked:

> For nearly twenty years the film societies have been concerned with establishing, in the first place, the claims of the film as a medium of expression with almost limitless possibilities, and, latterly, in educating a wider public to understand and appreciate the unique qualities and emerging virtues of this great medium. The pursuit of these objects, largely attained by bringing together in selective programmes the best productions of the Continent, which few people would otherwise have seen, was undoubtedly a major contribution to the development of an intelligent cinema and to the advancement of the art of film in this country. [...] There are still millions of filmgoers whose tastes are deplorably low; there are still too many producers who pander to these tastes, or further degrade them. [...] The film societies, therefore, still have a two-fold main task to perform: one, to increase the general standard of public taste in films, and so increase the general standard of production; and, two, to create a smaller specialised audience for the experiments of advanced film workers.
>
> (Wilson 1945: 37)

Wilson concludes his article by suggesting a number of ways in which the film society movement may be carried forward; however, he reminds his readers that the showing of the latest French or Russian 'masterpiece' is the 'original and primary aim of the film societies and must never be neglected' (38). His comments thus make abundantly clear the societies' vital role in maintaining and extending the presence of the 'Continentals', an increasingly challenging task as enticing new product ceased during the war, and in educating the British cinema-goer in the myriad possibilities of the art of film. In this sense the film society movement, already central to the construction of a serious film culture in the 1930s, can be linked to Ellis' description of an extended concept of 'quality' film in Britain in the 1940s. The aim to produce a 'quality' or serious British product was closely entangled with the societies' role in educating its audience in the 'art' of film. Moreover, critical discourse often held up the serious 'Continentals' as a model for the quality British film. Writing in 1938, George Pearson calls for a renewal in British cinematic art, claiming that it will be possible 'if like France we can believe there is more joy in the cinema, technique apart, over one revealing glimpse through fiction, of life as we truly know it, than for a hundred puppet romances in gilded covers, without sincerity' (Pearson 1938: 151). It was of course the film societies which played a major role in making the Continental 'model' available.

As discussed in the previous chapter, the presence of French film in Britain was to a great extent shaped by a small band of cinephiles: Elsie Cohen, Ivor Montagu, Thorold Dickinson et al. This was no less the case in the 1940s and worth noting here is the aforementioned Olwen Vaughn.

Charles Drazin has argued that 'The best place to go and find the spirit that shaped the British cinema of the 1940s would not have been the sound stages of Denham or Pinewood or Ealing but a town house not far from Piccadilly. A small signboard, decorated with a fleur de lys, hung outside no.4 St James's Place and announced "Le Petit Club Français"' (Drazin 1998: 235). Le Petit Club was set up by Olwen Vaughn, an ardent Francophile, in the summer of 1940 and was intended as a place where the Free French in London might find something of the country they had left behind. However, why this is of particular interest here is that Vaughn was both a Francophile and a cinephile and the visiting French were joined by film-makers and film-lovers of all kinds, making the club into a key space for the promotion of cinematic culture, in particular French cinematic culture, in London. Of course Vaughn was not alone in providing a meeting place for the Free French. As Robert and Isabelle Tombs have revealed, in the early part of 1940 the British government was active in promoting the Free French image and various activities were organised and promoted in this service (Tombs and Tombs 2006: 574). Nevertheless, the Petit Club was alone in fostering Franco-British relations and cinematic culture in tandem and is of particular significance because of Vaughn's central role in the film society movement. She had formed the International Federation of Film Archives (FIAF) in 1938 with Iris Barry, Henri Langlois of the Cinémathèque française and Frank Hensel of the Reichsfilm archive; became secretary of the newly established British Film Institute in 1933; had been closely involved with the original Film Society and had also organised screenings for the Forum Cinema at Charing Cross. As we have seen, during the war she ran the London Film Institute Society which became such an invaluable resource to serious film enthusiasts and was to form a close partnership with Denis Forman's revitalised BFI. Vaughn was then a figure of great importance in the construction of a cinephile culture in pre-war Britain and throughout the war years. What is of particular interest here is that her love for the fostering of a British cinephilic culture via the film society should have gone hand in hand with her love and support for French culture even during the darkest days of the war. Just as the French films released on a repertory circuit at the film societies during the war years can be seen to have underwritten the value of French film and its potential to influence British film culture, so Vaughn's activities via le Petit Club Français and the London Film Institute Society encouraged an appreciation of French culture at a time when, to British audiences at least, it could so easily have appeared to be entirely moribund.

Repertory, Revivals and Canonisation

If after the fall of France the flow of new French films to the United Kingdom came to a halt, French cinema did not disappear from British screens but the remaining Continental picturehouses and film societies became reliant upon re-releases of earlier films, including some of the silent works of the 1920s. As Forsythe Hardy noted, 'Programmes can [no longer] be composed almost automatically, as they sometimes were, by booking a French feature and a couple of shorts' (Forsythe Hardy 1942: 63). This was obviously a source of some concern for the specialist exhibitors. Writing in Spring 1943, the programmer of the Bradford Civic Playhouse outlined the difficulties with which cinemas such as his were obliged to contend:

> For a Society which has specialised in continental films for years [ours] are unusual programmes, and bring up the cause of our greatest anxiety. How long can we continue with this policy, [of showing reissues, British Council shorts, Yugoslav films etc] and how compete with the commercial theatre with a changed policy? Our Society shows films to the public nearly every alternate week, and is the only cinema in a very large area still showing continental films. To our audience revivals are not only for the second, but often for the third or fourth time, and exhaustion point is very quickly reached. We find that while the audiences during the week keep up their numbers well, and more and more people are learning to appreciate the best continental films, the Sunday audiences of the connoisseurs are dwindling. Over the past six or seven years we have given them so much that there is nothing they haven't seen!
> (Anon. 1943a: 87–88)

While one can sympathise with the programmer's predicament, his claim that audiences 'are learning to appreciate the best continental films' is telling. For it would seem that the necessary creation of a repertory system for French film during the war years played a vital role in fostering an appreciation of that cinema and establishing a canon of great works. This was a process which had begun in the 1930s, but the very shortage of new material in the war years, the enforced revival of earlier films which subjected them to repeated scrutiny and the reliance on the collections of the NFL contributed actively to the selection and entrenchment of a 'canon' of great works. If we look at the French films showing on the regional film society circuit during the war years and during post-war revivals, we are struck by the recurring presence of films such as *La Grande Illusion*, *Quai des brumes*, *La Marseillaise*, *La Bête humaine*, *Hotel du Nord*, *Les Bas-fonds*, *Le Jour se lève* and *Sous les toits de Paris*, not all greeted with uniform critical praise at the time of their initial UK release, but now seen as some of the great works of a golden period in French film history. Indeed this 'canon' of the 1930s has to a great extent become a critical orthodoxy in British accounts of the period. Although the quality of many of these films is undeniable, it does seem that the enforced creation of a repertory circuit of select French films during the war years may have played a crucial role in constructing these perceptions.

French film was a 'safe bet', a mark of quality, and in these straitened times the revival of the best of the pre-war French product made perfect sense to programmers at the film societies and the remaining specialist theatres. Writing in *The Observer* in June 1943, Caroline Lejeune describes responses to her recent request for help in choosing revivals for a repertory cinema in the north-west of London (The Envoy in Kilburn High Road). She is astonished by the level of response: 'I was prepared for several dozen letters. I received many hundreds. They came from places as far afield as Aberdeen and Newport, Torquay and Lancaster. Many were from Servicemen, suggesting the films they would like to see on their next leave in London. There seems to be little doubt that the idea of revivals is popular' (Lejeune 1943). The results, she claims, are unequivocal. Nearly one third voted for *Un Carnet de Bal* closely followed by *Citizen Kane*. Fifteen votes behind came another group of films which included the 'best' of Hollywood (*Mr Deeds*, the films of the Marx brothers and Astaire-Rogers) as well as a number of continental pictures, notably *La Kermesse Héroïque* and *Sous les toits de Paris*. Other French films selected by Lejeune's readers included *Le Million*, *Pépé le Moko* and *La Femme du Boulanger*. It is worth remarking that many of these films were simultaneously doing the rounds of the film societies, perhaps increasing their popularity hence the call for further revivals. Lejeune concludes, 'If any general conclusion can be drawn from this survey it is simply that the best films remain the best films, and the best people know them'. The 'best' people in terms of film culture were so often the film society members and specialist movie theatre customers whose tastes dictated which films would be revived thus ensuring that their status as the 'best' of cinema became almost unassailable. The place of French cinema in this selection of the 'best' is nicely illustrated by yet another poll, this time among the patrons of Glasgow's Cosmo cinema, who were asked in May 1940 to choose which films from the previous January to January period they would like revived. Eight films were selected and all but one are French: *Un Carnet de* Bal (611 votes); *La Kermesse Héroïque* (479); *La Femme du Boulanger* (438); *Amphitryon* (419); *Alerte en Méditerranée* (392); *La Grande Illusion* (385); *Otages* (368) and *La Mort du Cygne* (360) (Oakley 1940: 9). This process of 'distinction' was aided by the reduction in the number of French films shown in the United Kingdom in the war years. Whereas thirty-four French films had been released in Britain in 1938 and thirty-two in 1939, these numbers fell dramatically to sixteen new releases in 1940, three in 1941and 1943 and only one in 1942. This dramatic shortage was filled by the re-release of earlier films and yet it was a relatively small body of preferred works which were selected to fill the gap: a total of only around thirty-nine French films was shown at the film societies between 1939 and 1945 and via this frequent repetition many of these films gained both audience and a status which remains to this day.

'What's So Special About All These Foreign Films?'

Writing in *Picturegoer* a few years after the war in 1948, Eric Goldschmidt asks 'What's so special about all these foreign films?' (Goldschmidt 1948: 17). 'Many of us get alarmed when specialized or foreign films are mentioned' he claims. '"A highbrow diet" we say, presuming that extra-special people go to see *The Last Chance, Carnet de Bal* or *Shoe Shine*. But considering that each of these films has had an audience of about 3,000,000 in this country, there must be an astonishing number of highbrows, or else the films weren't really "specialised" at all' (17). Of course the films selected by Goldschmidt here achieved a level of success not managed by many of the foreign films released in the United Kingdom. Nevertheless, his question is pertinent. What was the British critical perspective on French cinema in the 1940s? Clearly the films' position on the film society circuit identified them as 'special' but how was this echoed or indeed instigated by those who had the power to shape wider public taste?

Let us recall Arthur Vesselo's warning back in late 1938, quoted at the start of this chapter, that not *all* French films are works of genius. In a later piece, published in Spring 1939, Vesselo describes a catalogue he has compiled, under the auspices of the BFI, of all films made up to and including 1934 still available for hire in Britain. He reminds his readers that any assumptions about the Continental cinema listed should be taken with a very large pinch of salt given the tiny proportion of films which reaches British screens:

> Continental films have never achieved more than a limited foothold in Great Britain, and that is, of course, one, though not the only, reason why it is quite unsound to assume that any accurate relationship exists between the proportionate numbers of films available and those actually produced in the several countries. On the same basis, the miniature groups of Continental films listed may be taken in general to represent not the whole scale of production in each country (as the British and American groups do) but only the higher ranges.
> (Vesselo 1939b: 111)

He reinforces this affirmation of the 'selective' nature of the French film shown in the U.K. by stressing the distinction bestowed upon the films by their exhibition in the film societies and specialist movie theatres:

Since current English-speaking feature films are monopolised by the ordinary public cinemas, these classes of films are necessarily excluded from [film] society performances, with the result that a sharp and for the most part unreal distinction arises. Normal performances as such are labelled 'popular'; society performances as such, being much rarer (and in this respect the specialist cinemas fall into the same category), are considered 'cultural', and their content, even though in certain ways limited by purely external conditions, is felt to be on a higher plane that what is seen elsewhere.

(Vesselo 1939b: 110)

Vesselo's remarks are prescient and of course go to the very heart of this volume's argument: that French cinema in Britain has long been a selective body of work, unable to fully represent French cinema as experienced in France and whose identity and status is to a great extent determined by particular forms of distribution and exhibition. Vesselo neatly illustrates his thesis in his review of Renoir's *La Bête humaine*, then recently released in the United Kingdom (Vesselo 1939a: 79). He does not dislike the film, indeed states that it has 'a great deal that is of value' (79). And yet his praise is mitigated: the film has 'certain defects', 'weaknesses [. . .] in structure', 'an unevenness of balance in the presentation of the engine-driver's character'. Overall perhaps *La Bête humaine* 'attempts too much' (79). While differences in critical opinion are not of course unusual, it is worth comparing Vesselo's somewhat ambivalent account of the film to the process of canonisation which later deemed it one of the great French works of the 1930s and one of the great films by Renoir. It seems likely that its repeated screenings across the film society circuit during the war years would have played a key role in this process.

Vesselo's slight reservations vis à vis *La Bête humaine* notwithstanding, French cinema was held in high esteem by many critics in the 1940s. French films were praised above all for their fine acting, their realism, their dialogue (perhaps surprisingly given the on-going doubts about the relative merits of dubbing and subtitling), their aesthetic sensibilities and their overall 'quality'. Thus Roger Manvell, writing about Marcel Carné in *Sight and Sound* in 1946, states:

In 1939 *Le Jour se lève* was produced and when this was exhibited during the War in London, it was recognised as a masterpiece in the true tradition of the best French cinema, which combines rich human characterisation supported by unusually fine acting with the quality called realism. This realism implies faithfulness to the true situations and emotional reactions of human life together with the careful reconstruction of background and the atmosphere of locality.

(Manvell 1946a: 4)

Writing two years later in 1948, D.A. Yerrill defines what he perceives as 'true realism', advocating a number of French films as ideal exemplars (Yerrill 1948a: 23–24). Dilys Powell in turn declares in 1948:

The French, a people with a deep and tender feeling for the under-side of life, the shadowed pavement of the street, the human unfortunate, have made their best films on the theme of undisciplined life. Renoir, Carné, Duvivier, René Clair, have shown us the crook, the vagabond, rather than the *bourgeois* home; the picture has been translated into a kind of poetic realism which found beauty in the smoky confusion of the railway viaduct, the quayside, the murky back-street.

(in Cook 1991: 5)

Powell's positing of poetic realism, a gritty but aestheticised realism, as a distinguishing factor of the French cinema is one that remains in place to this day. Quality and fine acting are somewhat nostalgically praised in a 1943 review of Duvivier's 'immensely French and immensely civilised' *La Fin du Jour*: 'French film art as we best remember it, and the acting is nothing short of superb' (Anon. 1943b). Reviewing *La Femme du Boulanger* upon its first U.K. release in 1939, Graham Greene declares, 'It is a long film with a small subject, but the treatment is so authentic that it seems over far too soon, and the acting is superb' (Greene 1939). On the occasion of its revival in 1942, William Whitebait claims the film 'bears seeing a second and a third time; Raimu's performance, the story given a stir by every breeze of gossip, the florid conversations, summertime, a village, the classical topics of joking and the feeling for human appetite make this film as evergreen as anything that has come into the cinema' (Whitebait 1942).

Ample evidence of the generally high esteem in which French cinema was held by British critics in the 1940s, despite or perhaps due to the war time embargo, is provided by reactions to the planned remaking of *Le Jour se lève* in 1946. As it was learned that Hollywood producers planned to remake the film and destroy all remaining copies, many critics urged their readers to go and see it at its 'last' run at Studio One. Richard Winnington describes this as 'the most saddening experience of all my years of cinema' (Winnington 1946); Patrick Kirwan in the *Evening Standard* declares, 'this will be your last chance to see the film. Hollywood has bought the rights, which means that the original will disappear and some bowdlerised and sugar-coated version will take its place' (Kirwan 1946a); meanwhile an unnamed critic in *Time and Tide* states, 'It's a case of look they last on all things lovely. What impresses me is that Hollywood which knows so much about the adequacy of second best should fear the best so much. You wouldn't think they'd find beauty lethal' (Anon. 1946a). While this hostility to the remaking of earlier cinema is far from unusual, it is striking to what extent the British critics rallied round Carné's films, underlining its status and value and urging film-goers to see it before it disappeared, they feared, for ever. *Le Jour se lève* and French cinema more broadly then continued to represent quality for British critics; it provided a reliable 'gold standard' against which other cinemas could be judged (and, in the case of much American and British film, found lacking) and which could be offered to the 'serious' film-goer as a relatively sure value. Not surprisingly, then, Keith Bean welcomes with open arms the return of new French films to British screens in 1944:

> It was the fact that French cinema made the magic shadow show something more than a tale told by an idiot that was the pre-eminent factor in giving French films a predictably satisfying quality. More than any other national output the French output seemed imbued with that spirit which – in gaiety or whimsy or satire or straight drama – made screen story-telling something more than sound and fury signifying nothing. The return of French films to our screens throws up again the contrast of much of the output from the studios of the English-speaking world, the contrast of the three dimensional beside the pasteboard. With memories of the rich contribution of the French before the war, one welcomes the prospect of this force renewed in the cinema.
> (Bean 1944: 65)

'They Don't Want to Miss Anything Good. And They Don't Want to Be Told What is Good for Them'

Critical acclaim for French cinema was not of course necessarily echoed by public preference. The confinement of French cinema to the film societies and remaining specialist cinemas during the war years meant that, as in the 1930s, it remained for the most part an 'acquired taste'. Writing in 1948, Sidney Bernstein notes the disparity between critical opinion and public taste:

> Some of my best friends happen to be critics. But to turn to the film reviews in newspapers and periodicals for a sampling of public taste can be most misleading. Since finally the public makes up its own mind, the most condemning notice can sometimes herald a successful film, just as a West End *succès d'estime* can flop when it meets the acid comment of average filmgoers who, in home, office or factory, give last night's movie a thorough picking over. Upon their findings depends the word-of-mouth publicity which can kill or acclaim.
> (Bernstein 1948)

Bernstein asks, 'What do the British public want?' and replies, 'They don't want to miss anything good. And they don't want to be told what is good for them'. He argues that to a great extent their taste is based on what they see and what they see is decided not by the critics but by the distributors who need to supply the demands of around 3,500 British cinemas showing up to 200 feature films a year (Bernstein 1948). Much as the critics may praise the latest Continental, its screening on a small circuit of specialised venues will thus prevent the broad 'word of mouth' publicity which Bernstein claims leads to significant box-office success. This brings us back to the fundamental question of the vital role of distribution and exhibition in British perceptions of French cinema: the specific ways in which the films are made available inevitably shapes audiences and expectations. Critical discourse also plays its part but to some extent may 'preach to the converted'. As D.A. Yerrill notes, also in 1948:

> It is true the critics *are* read by that section of the public which 'shops' for its films and which is more essential to the life of the film as an art form than that which buys a cinema seat much as it buys a tin of Ministry of Food salmon (for want of anything better). The former section of the film-going public is that which would be heard demanding films in a good tradition if someone were to tell them what such a tradition is, and where such films are to be found on the rare occasions of their appearance.
>
> (Yerrill 1948b: 98)

Interestingly Yerrill praises France where 'they really go to town with criticism and every kind of film news' with the result that 'the French public are really film conscious and acutely aware of their own country's efforts'. He sounds a note of caution which speaks volumes about British attitudes to French intellectual life, suggesting that the French attitude can be 'a bit of a bore' but claims that it would be 'useful to take a small step in that direction' (99). Yerrill concludes by stating that 'it is more profitable to give the public what it wants than what is good. It is up to the critics to prove that the producers' arithmetic and diplomacy are both bad and that what is good in fact coincides what is liked and what is wanted' (99).

That Yerrill should make this claim at this juncture is striking as the very endeavour he describes – proving that 'quality' films (read Continentals) could in fact be 'popular' films – became a significant feature of the British cinematic landscape in the years following the war as we shall discuss in the next chapter. To a great degree this was dictated by the very pressing need for more films. British production was still suffering the effects of war-time limitations while audiences and the demand for new films remained high. The decision to introduce a 70 per cent tax on American film profits in June 1947 saw Hollywood blocking the export of films to Britain. Rank, the UK's dominant producer, embarked upon an attempt to fill the huge gap left by this embargo with the hasty production of up to sixty films a year. This was not sufficient to plug the shortfall and in Spring 1948 the government repealed the tax, leading to a flood of Hollywood films to the immense detriment of Rank's hastily produced and often poor quality screen fillers (Drazin 1998: 5). Another solution to the shortfall and, upon the return of Hollywood, a means of increasing choice was offered by the Continentals. Rank had realised the potential of foreign cinema as early as 1946 as Patrick Kirwan notes in *The Evening*

Standard: 'Mr. Rank, from whom all cinematic blessings flow, promised a series of the best French films for the British screen' (Kirwan 1946a). Rank was a dominant force in British film culture of the 1940s. Beginning in 1936, J. Arthur Rank had built a vertically-integrated film company, buying distributors, cinema chains and production companies. The Rank Organisation financed half the films made in the UK between 1941 and 1947, controlled over 600 cinemas and was the major film distributor. Via purchase of a 25 per cent stake in Universal Pictures, Rank was able to secure American distribution for their own productions and a ready supply of Hollywood films for their cinemas. However, the need for more films, the quota obligation to show non-American product, and the Cripps' Plan which obliged the main circuits to give screen space to independent producers meant that the distribution and/or exhibition of some continental films on the Rank circuit seemed an attractive, not to say necessary, prospect.

Rank was not alone in this endeavour; Roger Manvell notes in *Sight and Sound* in Spring 1946 that MGM had 'rather tumbled over themselves to sell [Austrian director Leopold Lindtberg's *The Last Chance*] as a masterpiece' thanks to their 'admirable plan to give non-American films a chance on the non-specialised market' (Manvell 1946b: 27). However, Rank's dominance of the British cinematic landscape at this juncture makes their role in the distribution and exhibition of continental films of particular significance. Interestingly Rank's Foreign Film Department was run after the war by Julia Wolf who, as we saw in the previous chapter, was responsible for the subtitling of so many of the Continental films shown in the UK in the 1930s, notably all films shown at the Curzon after its opening in 1934. We can but assume that Wolf's very evident love and admiration for the cinema of the continent would have had some influence on the Rank company's decision to get involved in the British dissemination of this work.

The first Continental film to be distributed by Eagle Lion, Rank's distribution arm (later renamed General Film Distributors), was the Delannoy-Cocteau picture, *Love Eternal* (*L'Éternel Retour*, 1943). The film was shown in June 1946 at the re-opening of the Curzon thus setting in place a pattern that was to be repeated until the end of the decade: French films would be shown at the Curzon, either through the Curzon's own distribution arm (GCT, later Curzon Film Distributors) or another, including Eagle Lion. If the film proved a success at the Curzon, it was considered by Rank for distribution on the commercial circuit both in London and the provinces. In this sense the Curzon became a testing ground for the commercial potential of 'specialised' film, a role it continues to play to this day. The cinema had been acquired by H.H. Wingate's General Cinema Theatres in 1940. As both a distributor and an exhibitor, Wingate was clearly dedicated to the British dissemination of foreign-language films. Indeed, as his son and current Chairman Roger Wingate notes, this was very much a family affair with Wingate's wife brushing up her school-girl French and undertaking Berlitz courses in Italian in order to subtitle French and Italian imports![3] This dual identity as both the exhibitor of 'specialised' cinema and the space in which its potential for broader appeal could be tested is revealing. To a great extent this embodies the transformation from 'art-house' enclaves to still relatively exclusive but rather more accessible, arguably more middle-brow venues, which would be undertaken by many of the Continental theatres from the late 1940s onwards. If the Academy with its echoes of the experiments of the Film Society could be seen to represent the exhibition of Continental film in Britain in the 1930s, so the Curzon with its move to a more commercially savvy middle ground symbolises that of the late 1940s and 1950s.

Love Eternal was swiftly followed by Christian-Jaque's *Symphonie Fantastique*, again shown at the Curzon and then distributed commercially by Rank. Neither film was considered a wise choice by critics of the day. Many found the 'Wagnerian' elements of the Cocteau-Delannoy film highly questionable given its context of production. Moreover, neither film was seen to represent the best of France. Patrick Kirwan declared, 'As critic, sitting below the salt and receiving only the crumbs from the cinematic feast, it is not my task to criticise policy, but if [*Love Eternal*] is intended to popularise French films with the general public I think it is a pity one more representative was not chosen as a curtain-raiser' (Kirwan 1946b). Caroline Lejeune describes Rank's decision to select this film to 'woo the British public to an appreciation of French stars, French technique, and French notions in the cinema' as 'idiotic' for '*Love Eternal* [. . .] is a remarkable film; a fascinating and at moments a very beautiful film; but the one thing it is not is a typically French film' (Lejeune 1946). Rather less charitably, an anonymous critic in *The Spectator* states, 'As heavy, Teutonic and improbable as a bowl of sliced sausage-meat, it is charged with the eventual task of introducing to hundreds of provincial audiences that world of insight, wisdom and humour which is the French cinema' (Anon. 1946b).

This condemnation of the film's 'Teutonic' characteristics speaks volumes about anti-German sentiment of the period. However, each of these remarks also makes plain a very strong critical sense of what French cinema should be like and what the public ought to see. This is in many ways a great compliment to French film; the critics are disappointed that those elements which have made French cinema great (realism, humour, artistry) are not represented here. However, it also says much about a critical tendency to label, to construct clear and potentially limiting definitions of what should constitute French cinema in the U.K., and in some ways to claim ownership: if French film was going to be sent out to the

8. Poster advertising a post-war release of *Pépé le Moko* (Julien Duvivier, 1937) and *Paris 1900* (Nicole Vedres, 1947).
Image courtesy of the BFI stills department.

'masses', the critics, it seems, were keen to have their say on what kind of French film should go their way. It also of course raises the question as to why *Love Eternal* and subsequently *La Symphonie fantastique*, a biopic based on the life of Berlioz which was to meet with similar critical ambivalence, should have been selected by Rank for broad distribution. To some extent choice was based on what was available: a relatively limited group of films made in France during the years of war and occupation. Both of these films had achieved significant critical and box-office success in France so in that sense seemed a sensible choice. It should also be noted that the films which British critics saw as defining French cinema, the earthy, realist works of the 1930s, were not a prominent feature of French war-time production for the reasons discussed above. Both *Love Eternal* and *La Symphonie fantastique* with their recourse to myth and history were rather more typical of a body of work in which, as Roger Manvell notes with a telling taste of the auteurist discourses which lay ahead, it was not always easy to find a common feature beyond 'the outstanding importance of the controlling artist' (Manvell 1946/47: 153). Moreover, it may well be that these were films which appealed to Rank's personal tastes. It is worth noting that Maurice Cloche's *Monsieur Vincent* (1947) was also considered by Rank for broader distribution. This was partly due to the film's commercial appeal. It ran for fifty-two weeks at the Curzon in 1947–48 and interestingly was re-released in a dubbed version at the Jacey cinema in Marble Arch in 1965 (Anon. 1965). However, it may also be that the film, a life of St Vincent de Paul paid for by subscription from Catholic organisations in France, appealed directly to Rank's deeply held religious convictions.

It is certainly the case that this critical response to the films underlines the dual position in which French cinema found itself in Britain by the mid-1940s. On the one hand there was a clear move towards popularisation as evidenced by Rank's plan for non-specialist distribution described above. An article in *Sight and Sound* in Autumn 1948, while acknowledging that 'captioned' films are an 'acquired taste', describes the efforts of an independent cinema in Bedford to prove that it is possible to show such films without loss of money (Dellow 1948: 129). The cinema manager, a Mr John Chetham, points out the difficulty of programming foreign films: simply 'slipping' a Continental into a 'normal' programme would inevitably lead to a flop.

> It seemed that normal cinema audiences were not willing to have such pictures thrust down their throats, while the people who liked them, not generally being regular cinema goers, often knew nothing about the films until it was too late [. . .] The difficulty is to select a programme that will not result in both sides being dissatisfied – the continental lovers because they do not like the commercial picture, and the rest because they do not like continental film.
> (Dellow 1948: 129)

Of course this is a dilemma which has continued to vex British distributors and exhibitors to this day. Attempts to widen the appeal of more commercially oriented French films via particular forms of distribution and exhibition strategy, including dubbing, have often proved unsuccessful, failing to appeal to the mainstream movie-goer and disappointing the French aficionado: consider for example the dubbed versions of huge French hit *Les Visiteurs* in 1994 and *Taxi* in 1999. Nevertheless Mr Chetham perseveres in his efforts, showing Continental films on Sundays and targeting advertising at schools, debating societies and music groups. In other words, he very explicitly sets out to create an audience for 'specialised' cinema, fully aware that it was not his 'normal' audience but something rather different and that the creation of this audience would gradually develop interest among 'regular patrons', beating the 'conservative British objection to something new, an objection that is particularly strong in the case of films where the language spoken is not English' (130). Those who came to see the films 'seemed to appreciate the quality, and most of them came again and again' and Chetham notes that the more serious films proved the most popular, suggesting that this was still a relatively 'serious' or 'cultured' audience. This suspicion is borne out by Chetham's remarks on the need to select appropriate supporting programmes ('travelogues and popular science films were definitely unpalatable to the average continental viewer') and the importance of creating an 'encouraging' atmosphere through the selection of music to be played before the programme and during intervals: 'We obtained new records of light music, operatic overtures such as "Marriage of Figaro" and pieces like "Eine Kleine Nachtmusik". Pieces like "It Must be Jelly 'Cos Jam Don't Shake Like That" were discreetly slipped to the bottom of the pile' (130).

These experiments in extending the audience for 'foreign' films at this small, provincial theatre provide a neat illustration of the place of French cinema by the late 1940s. On the one hand it remained the staple of the 'specialist' film-goer as revealed by Mr Chetham's choice of music, second features, advertising and programming. This continuing specialisation was reinforced by the on-going presence of French cinema on the film society circuit and in the re-opened Continental picture houses. These theatres were clearly marked as 'different' from the commercial circuits, both through their choice of films (witness the revival of French 'classics' of the 1930s at the Everyman between 1946 and 1949) and their methods of promotion (consider Peter Strausfeld's distinctive linoblocks for the Academy from 1944).

And yet there was also a recognition that French cinema could appeal beyond these somewhat rarefied venues either through broader commercial distribution or, as Allen Eyles points out, as additional or second features in independent theatres (Eyles 2005: 34). Both critics and industry

9. A Peter Strausfeld poster for a screening of René Barberis' *Ramuntcho* (1937) at The Academy.
Image courtesy of the BFI stills department.

insiders seemed aware that while many of the works of French cinema were indeed 'great', not all French films were of high quality: *Vautrin* (Pierre Billon, 1944) is described by *The New Statesman* as proof 'that France can maltreat actors and authors as blithely as anyone' (Anon.1946c). There was an understanding that French film could possess a commercial appeal and that distribution outside the specialist networks and using new forms of promotion and exhibition (notably dubbed prints) may well be the means of exploiting that potential. Recall Eric Goldschmidt's question of 1948, 'What's so special about all these foreign films?'. As he interviews people waiting in line in London's Oxford Street to see foreign films, he comes to the conclusion that there is nothing 'special' about this audience, it was not 'riddled with addicts or epicures, fops, faddists or fellow travellers. It was just ordinary' (Goldschmidt 1948: 17). What is specialised, argues Goldschmidt, is not the audience nor indeed the films, but the very means in which they are made available to the British public:

> Probably the most pernicious factor blocking the wider showing of specialised films is the very word 'special'. So long as the legend persists – misleading and useless though it is – that foreign films should be roped off and filed away for

the benefit of a handful of lost souls, the inhabitants of Portsmouth, Putney and Perth won't get a chance of taking sides in this argument. As for the cinema managers – perhaps one can get them to take a look at those Oxford Street queues on a Saturday night. Then they'll see the clearest evidence that there's nothing special about foreign films.

(Goldschmidt 1948: 17)

How ironically prescient Goldschmidt's words now seem as non-English-language imports to the U.K. were identified by the now-defunct U.K. Film Council under the umbrella term 'specialist film'. Nevertheless, at the end of the 1940s his pleas for a broadening of attitude towards and options for foreign cinema did not fall entirely on deaf ears as developments in the 1950s described in the next chapter will reveal.

Notes

1. Charles Drazin claims that at the end of the war the average French person was going to the cinema eight times a year while the average Briton was going twenty-eight times (Drazin 1998: 8).
2. http://www.screenonline.org.uk/film/facts/fact1.html (accessed 26 May 2010).
3. http://www.actproductions.co.uk/iabout_company.asp (accessed 19 May 2010).

Bibliography

Anon. 1940. 'Newsreel: Comments of the Quarter by *Sight and Sound* Contributors', *Sight and Sound* 9 (33), Spring: 1–2.
Anon. 1942. 'In France Today', *Sight and Sound* 11(42), Summer: 11.
Anon. 1943a. 'Yorkshire Enterprise', *Sight and Sound* 11(44), Spring: 87–88.
Anon. 1943b. 'La Fin du Jour', *Manchester Guardian*, 17 April.
Anon. 1946a. *Time and Tide*, 18 May.
Anon. 1946b. 'The Cinema', *Spectator*, 22 January.
Anon. 1946c. *New Statesman*, 20 December.
Anon. 1965. *The Times*, 25 November.
Bean, K. 1944. 'Keith Bean's Reflections', *Sight and Sound* 13(51), October: 65–66.
Bernstein, S.L. 1948. 'Film and British Taste', *News Chronicle*, 5 August.
Cook, C. (ed.). 1991. *The Dilys Powell Film Reader*. Manchester: Carcanet.
Dellow, R. 1948. 'Provincial Specialist Theatres', *Sight and Sound* 17(67), Autumn: 129–30.
Dickinson, T. 1975. 'Then There Was the Time When . . .', *Film*, October/November: 8–9.
Drazin, C. 1998. *The Finest Years: British Cinema of the 1940s*. London: Andre Deutsch.

Dyer, E. 1938. 'What Do They Like?', *Sight and Sound* 7(26), Summer: 78–79.
Ellis, J. 1978. 'Art, Culture and Quality: Terms for a Cinema in the Forties and Seventies', *Screen* 19, Autumn: 9–49.
Eyles. A. 2005. *Odeon Cinemas 2: From Arthur J Rank to the Multiplex*. London: Cinema Theatre Association /BFI.
Forsythe Hardy, H. 1941. 'An Open Letter to the Film Societies', *Sight and Sound* 10(38), Summer: 29–30.
Forsythe Hardy, H. 1942. 'Testing Time: A Challenge to the Film Societies', *Sight and Sound* 11(43), Winter: 62–64.
Goldschmidt, E. 1948. 'What's So Special About All These Foreign Films?'*Picturegoer*, 18 December: 17.
Goodman, E. 1939. 'Hollywood is Worried', *Sight and Sound* 8(31), Autumn: 106.
Greene, G. 1939. 'La Femme du Boulanger', *Spectator*, 9 June.
Hackett, H. (1946). 'The French Cinema During the Occupation', *Sight and Sound* 15(57), Spring: 1–3.
Howden, P. 1994/95. 'Fun to Run a Cinema', *Picture House* 20, Winter: 34–42.
Kirwan, P. 1946a. 'French Films: Where are They All Going?' *Evening Standard*, 10 May.
Kirwan, P. 1946b. 'I Like My French Film French', *Evening Standard*, 2 February.
Lejeune, C.A. 1943. 'The Films', *Observer*, 27 June.
Lejeune, C.A. 1946. 'The Films', *Observer*, 2 February.
Manvell, R, 1946a. 'Marcel Carné', *Sight and Sound* 15(57), Spring: 4–5.
Manvell, R. 1946b. 'Films of the Quarter', *Sight and Sound* 15(57), Spring: 24–27.
Manvell, R. 1946/47. 'Continental Films of the Quarter', *Sight and Sound* 15(60), Winter: 153–54.
Oakley, C.A. 1940. 'Mr. Cosmo Takes a Bow', *Sight and Sound* 9(33), Spring: 9.
Pearson, G. 1938. 'Lambeth Walk to Leicester Square', *Sight and Sound* 7(28), Autumn: 150–51.
Powell, D. 1947. *Film Since 1939*. London: British Council.
Price, P. 1975. 'Early Days in Cambridge', *Film*, October/November: 11.
Richards, J. (ed.). 1986. *Britain Can Take It*. Oxford: Blackwell.
Tombs, Robert and Tombs, Isabelle. 2006. *That Sweet Enemy: The French and the British from the Sun King to the Present*. London: William Heinemann.
Vesselo, A. 1938. 'Vermouth, Vodka and Beer', *Sight and Sound* 7(28), Winter: 162–63.
Vesselo, A. 1939a. 'Misprints and Limitations', *Sight and Sound* 8(29), Spring: 77–79.
Vesselo, A. 1939b. 'Searchlight on Veterans', *Sight and Sound* 8(29), Spring: 109–11.
Watts, S. 1946. 'Films', *Sunday Express*, 8 December.
Whitebait, W. 1942. 'The Movies', *New Statesman*, 17 January.
Wilson, N. 1945. 'Film Societies– The Next Phase', *Sight and Sound* 14(54), July: 37–38.
Winnington, R. 1946, 'A Slight Case of Murder'.
Yerrill, D.A. 1948a. 'The Technique of Realism', *Sight and Sound* 17(65), Spring: 23–24.
Yerrill, D.A. 1948b. 'On Film Critics', *Sight and Sound* 17(66), Summer: 98–99.

Filmography

Alerte en Méditerranée / Alert in the Mediterranean (1938, Léo Joannon)
Aus den Wolken Kommt das Glück / Amphitryon (1935, Reinhold Schünzel)
Bas-fonds, Les (1936, Jean Renoir)
Bête humaine, La (1938, Jean Renoir)
Un Carnet de bal (1937, Julien Duvivier)
Citizen Kane (1941, Orson Welles)
Entrée des artistes (1938, Marc Allégret)
Éternel Retour, L' / Love Eternal (1943, Jean Delannoy)
Femme du Boulanger, La (1938, Marcel Pagnol)
Fin du Jour, La (1939, Julien Duvivier)
Grande Illusion, La (1937, Jean Renoir)
Hotel du Nord (1938, Marcel Carné)
Jour se lève, Le / Daybreak (1939, Marcel Carné)
Kermesse Héroïque, La / Carnival in Flanders (1935, Jacques Feyder)
Knight Without Armour (1937, Jacques Feyder)
Letzte Chance, Die / The Last Chance (1945, Leopold Lindtberg)
Marseillaise, La (1938, Jean Renoir)
Million, Le (1931, René Clair)
Monsieur Vincent (1947, Maurice Cloche)
Mort du Cygne, La (1937, Jean Benoît-Lévy)
Mr Deeds Goes to Town (1936, Frank Capra)
Otages, Les (1939, Raymond Bernard)
Quai des brumes (1938, Marcel Carné)
Pépé le Moko (1937, Julien Duvivier)
Ramuntcho (1937, René Barberis)
Roman d'un Tricheur, Le / The Cheat (1936, Sacha Guitry)
Sciuscià / Shoe Shine (1946, Vittorio de Sica)
Sous les toits de Paris / Under the Roofs of Paris (1930, René Clair)
Symphonie fantastique, La (1942, Christian-Jaque)
Taxi (1998, Gérard Pirès)
Tel Père et fils, Un (1943, Julien Duvivier)
Vautrin (1944, Pierre Billon)
Visiteurs, Les (1993, Jean-Marie Poiré)

3

'SAUCY AND NAUGHTY AND WITTY AND CHIC'*
Can French Films Fill the Gap? (1950–1959)

The 1950s was to prove a challenging period for the film industry. If the rigours of the war years had seen people flocking to the cinema in search of entertainment, warmth and a modicum of safety, the 1950s ushered in a range of enticing alternatives. Other forms of leisure, some of them unavailable during the war, replaced film-going for many and it became increasingly common to see the conversion of a movie theatre to dance or concert hall. The improved comfort of the domestic space meant that staying at home became an ever more attractive option, even more so in those homes equipped with a television set. Indeed the marked rise in television ownership after the BBC's highly successful live transmission of the Queen's Coronation in 1952 was to prove a very real threat to cinema-going and the beginning of a rivalry which in greater or lesser degrees has bedevilled the film industry ever since. British cinema audiences fell into a steady decline as the decade progressed while movie theatres diminished from a post-war total of 4,700 to 3,050 in 1960 to only 1,971 by 1965.[1]

If times were hard for the British film industry, things were no easier in Hollywood. The much documented anti-trust decree of 1948 which led to the break-up of the major Hollywood studios was to have a profound impact on the industry, notably causing a significant reduction in production which was in turn to cause significant problems for British exhibitors. Hollywood had also felt the impact of television as early as the late 1940s and this new competitor joined forces with the upheavals provoked by the end of vertical integration to plunge the American film industry into turbulent and economically challenging times. Audiences declined dramatically dropping from a weekly total of 90 million in 1947 to only 51 million by 1952 (Maltby 1995: 156). Attempts were made to lure audiences back into the movie theatres with Technicolor, Cinerama, 3D and other technical delights. Cinema Scope in particular was widely adopted by the Hollywood industry during the 1950s and was perceived as a lasting solution to box-office decline, unlike the more gimmicky 3D and Cinerama (Balio 1990: 27). The British industry was rather more reticent about these innovations. As Su Holmes remarks, much has been made of the reluctance of the Rank Organisation and smaller exhibitors to make the costly changes necessary to screen Cinema Scope with stereophonic sound (Holmes 2004: 137). Nevertheless, by the end of 1955 more than half of British cinemas were equipped to show widescreen films (Murphy 1992: 103). However, none of these novelties, however expensive or extensively publicised, was to offer a lasting solution and audience numbers continued to fall dramatically.

While exhibition was being separated from production and distribution in the United States, it is worth noting that British film exhibition at the end of the 1940s and into the 1950s was a very tightly controlled affair. A committee appointed by the Board of Trade to examine the 'Distribution and Exhibition of Cinematograph Films' and chaired by Sir Arnold Plant reported in 1950 that 'under the present organisation of the industry, the average cost of production cannot be recovered from the cinemas in Great Britain, and overseas returns are negligible for the vast majority of [British] films' (Crow 1950: 9). The Plant Committee noted that there were, in 1948, about 4,800 commercial cinemas operating in Britain. In all they had a seating capacity of 4,200,000 and each seat was filled approximately seven times per week. The cinemas could be split into three groups according to their size: fewer than 500 seats; between 500 and 1,500 seats; more than 1,500 seats. Exhibition was dominated by the larger cinemas, notably the 'super cinemas' which represented around 10 to 15 per cent of total screens but sold 30 per cent of all tickets (Crow 1950: 9). The larger cinemas' dominance of exhibition was furthered by their concentration in the hands of the three main cinema circuits: Rank's Odeon and Gaumont-British picture houses and the Associated British Picture Corporation's ABC circuit. These three circuits owned only 947 cinemas at the close of the 1940s and yet they represented one third of total cinema seating capacity. Indeed they owned around 70 per cent of the larger cinemas. This meant that 'a booking with one of them is essential if a British Producer is to have any hope of recovering his costs of production' (9). The Plant Committee made a number of recommendations to increase competitive trading into the system of distribution and exhibition yet it is clear that the landscape of the late 1940s/1950s favoured the major circuits and the big-budget crowd-pleasing films. A key suggestion was a move away from the practice of showing cheaper old films on Sundays in favour of normal weekday programmes. This was intended to extend the screen time for mainstream features and was a potentially lucrative move for exhibitors. However, those cheaper old films which were being asked to make way for the weekday programmes were often the Continental films not sufficiently crowd pleasing to merit showing at other times. In its ambition to improve the career of home-grown production, the Plant Committee thus threatened to limit even further the British presence of the 'Continentals'.

A Specialised Film Culture in the 1950s

These were then difficult times for the British film industry, not helped of course by similar turbulence in Hollywood. An editorial in *Sight and Sound* in August 1950 opined:

> British and American trade papers have recently reflected the increasing alarm of the industry at falling box-office returns. This state of affairs is, of course, perennial and seasonal, although television has now joined the weather as a scapegoat: [...] In the past, blame for a box-office slump has usually been attached to some extraneous cause – war, weather, or competition from other media – but now the slogan and the war cries seem to show some appreciation that what is needed is, simply, better pictures.
> (Anon. 1950b: 227)

What is interesting is that the editorial does not suggest that the expensive technical wizardry of Hollywood's bigger-budget productions may represent these 'better pictures'. Rather it offers the 'strange, the foreign, the experimental' as a possible solution to audience dissatisfaction (227):

> both in Britain and the U.S.A. a new kind of audience is growing, joining film societies, encouraging the development of specialist cinemas and 'art theatres'. If this public increasingly deserts the commercial cinema, the latter has only itself to blame; meanwhile, it is generally agreed that the ordinary public, with money shorter and rival entertainments becoming more attractive, is more selective and even, perhaps, more adventurous.
> (Anon. 1950b: 227)

The article suggests that with production diminished in both Britain and, to a lesser degree, the U.S., it may be time for exhibitors to broaden their definition of what constitutes a 'good' (or commercially attractive) picture, coinciding more closely with critical viewpoints and including 'such continental successes as *Bicycle Thieves* and *Jour de Fête*' (227).

This acknowledgement of changing audience tastes and the accompanying call to give more prominence to the 'specialised' film is interesting. Without a doubt there was a need for more films to fill U.K. screens at this juncture and, as we shall go on to discuss, the 'Continentals' were indeed mobilised in varying degrees to fill this gap. There was also an audience for these films: the 'specialised' audience of the film societies and art houses first constituted, as we have seen, in the 1930s. Another article in *Sight and Sound*, in February 1950, notes the 'successful growth of the Film Society Movement' (Anon. 1950a: 45), which had continued to develop across the United Kingdom since the end of the war. Norman Wilson remarks that:

> one of the most interesting recent developments in Britain has been the rapid growth in the number of film societies, which has increased from 46 to over 200 since the end of the war [. . .] Nearly every large town now supports and enjoys its own organisation which presents each winter a series of selected programmes, drawn from international sources. In the larger centres these are generally shown in commercial cinemas, usually on Sundays, with audiences ranging from about 250, to over 3,000. But the movement is by no means confined to the cities and towns. With the great advances in 16mm projection since the end of the war, it is now economically possible to provide performances of under a hundred, and this has enabled groups to be established in quite small communities and in the most outlandish areas.
>
> (Wilson 1951: 61–62)

The specialised cinemas were also a continuing and increasingly visible element of the British cinematic landscape. Writing in *Picturegoer* in February 1953, David Marlowe describes a cinema in Stoke Newington, London, which has 'gone all Continental – right up to a no-smoking rule' (Marlowe 1953: 18):

> The cinema – recently redecorated, refurnished and renamed – is the Vogue Continental. The films are postwar products of French, Italian and other Continental studios: successful pictures that have proved themselves. The picturegoers are people who'll book in advance and sacrifice smoking for the sake of the show. You might call it a test case cinema. For if the Vogue becomes the vogue with picturegoers it may encourage a number of provincial managements to go the Continental way.
>
> (ibid.: 18)

Marlowe's account of the Vogue is revealing. He notes the success of many of the films from across the Channel which with their 'powerful, poignant realism' or 'courageous treatment of subjects that are still styled strong meat here' are 'appealing to a widening audience' who no longer take for granted 'that Hollywood and our own studios are the home of everything screen worthy' (ibid.: 18). Yet while celebrating this acknowledgement of the quality of the Continental product, Marlowe is careful to stress the limitations which continue to constrain its presence in Britain:

> Why don't more 'locals' show 'Continentals'? It's a question that's often been posed by writers to Picturegoer's 'Focus on Films'. It's an idea that Picturegoer has supported with sympathy – although we've pointed out some pitfalls, too. Let's be realistic about it. To please art-of-the-film-conscious West End audi-

ences with Continental fare is one proposition. To get the same week-by-week support from the entertainment seeking population of a London suburb is another.

(ibid.: 18)

Somewhat ironically from a contemporary perspective, Marlowe criticises the cinema's decision to introduce a smoking ban (a Continental innovation) fearing this will put off prospective film-goers: 'British picturegoers are only too anxious to see what Continental studios have to show. But will they be willing to go *à la continentale* all the way? Forsake the familiar satisfaction of a smoke in the stalls? Why should they?' (18).

Marlowe's brief account of the opening of the Vogue Continental neatly encapsulates the place of 'foreign' film in Britain in the early 1950s. A 'specialised' film culture did indeed continue to thrive as evidenced by the burgeoning film society movement, the BFI's inauguration of a permanent repertory programme drawn from the archives of the National Film Library, the opening of the National Film Theatre on London's South Bank on 23 October 1952 and the emergence of new Continental

10. Vittorio de Sica, John Ford and René Clair celebrate the opening of the NFT in October 1952.
Image courtesy of the BFI stills department.

picture houses. However, certainly in the very early years of the decade, this film culture was to remain resolutely 'specialised, the domain of the 'art-of-the-film-conscious' and to a great extent London's middle class. While the film society movement did indeed expand and some screenings were, as Norman Wilson remarks, very successful, many of the smaller societies struggled to grow their membership. The anonymous film society secretary writing in *Sight and Sound* in February 1950 notes, 'It seems to be a difficult task, in our town of sixty thousand inhabitants, to increase our membership beyond 200. Although the loyalty and interest of the faithful fifty is there, it is an uphill and often disheartening struggle to put a 16mm. society on to a firm financial footing' (Anon. 1950a: 45).

There existed a continuing perception of Continental film as 'special' or 'different' to the products of Britain and Hollywood, a perception fostered in many ways by the on-going canonisation of earlier films, described in Chapter Two, in publications such as *Sight and Sound*. Critics continued to stress the quality and the realism of French films, particularly those of the 1930s. Thus while singling them out for special praise, they simultaneously set them apart from the mainstream filmic offer. Leonard England notes the tendency to divide film between 'the sort of film that the public likes' and 'the sort of film that the critics think is good' (England 1951: 43). Although he queries the extent of this divergence, he does acknowledge that in some areas, notably foreign cinema, public taste rarely mirrors critical acclaim: 'The limited general education of the cinema going mass public also automatically puts all foreign films out of the running [for box-office success] . The problem goes far deeper than language, and will not be solved by dubbing; the whole idiom of a French or an Italian film is strange to the audience' (44). Writing a few years later in 1956, Walter Lassally commends the specialised cinemas and film societies for their part in bringing 'intelligent and artistic' films to the notice of the British public. However, he is pessimistic about the true extent of these developments, claiming that it can be safely assumed that less than 1 per cent of Britain's film-goers attend the 'specialised' shows (Lassally 1956: 12). He largely attributes this reluctant audience to typical British attitudes towards art and culture: 'Nowhere else in the world does this latter word have such a disagreeable connotation as in Britain. Whereas on the continent the artist is traditionally respected, the average Englishman will cheerfully condemn him with the term "highbrow" and will defend to the death his right to remain ignorant in these matters' (12).

While Lassally's words may seem a little harsh, his picture of British tendencies towards anti-intellectualism is certainly not entirely unfair and, as we saw in Chapter One, was to play its part in the establishment of a place for French film in the United Kingdom. However, by this stage resistance to the Continental product was also very closely bound up with quite well established mechanics of distribution and exhibition and the expectations they engendered: audiences for foreign films tended to be small because they were usually shown in specialised venues understood to be 'different', not 'for' the average cinema-goer. And it should be noted that those who did not share in the loathing of the highbrow described by Lassally often had a vested interest in keeping the Continentals 'special', thus ensuring a level of cultural distinction which set them apart from the mass cinema audience. In a letter to *Picturegoer* in March 1953, a Miss M. Grafton of Goodmayes, Essex, writes, 'I am all for restricting Continental films to specialized cinemas. I do not feel that such typically foreign efforts as *La Ronde* and *Les Belles de Nuit* are seen at their best when screened at the ordinary local cinemas, and I get the impression that a good French film in the same programme as, say, a Hollywood Western is rather like drinking fine Bordeaux with an Irish stew!' (Goodmayes 1953). While the washing down of a plate of stew with a glass of fine French wine may now seem an entirely uncontroversial affair, it is clear that in the early 1950s there still existed a strong sense of the distinctive nature of Continental cinema. Audiences and opportunities for its consumption were indeed increasing but it was, to a great extent, still contained within a specialised circuit of exhibition. In the words of Major W. de Lane Lea, founder of leading dubbing company De Lane Lea Processes Ltd., 'The sub-titled [read Continental] film is excellent for foreign residents here, for bi-lingual individuals, for language students, for intellectuals; and of course its snob value is tremendously important' (De Lane Lea 1953: 10).

Sex and the 'X'

A development which was to have a significant impact on the place of Continental cinema in Britain during the 1950s was the advent of the X certificate in the U.K. in 1951. The BBFC implemented the certificate to cover all films considered unsuitable for under sixteens, and it was originally intended to replace the existing H certificate and enable the exhibition of 'adult' orientated features which might previously have fallen foul of the censors. Interestingly many of the first X certificate films were foreign – for example Max Ophüls' film of 1950 *La Ronde* which created great controversy when released in the U.K. in 1951. As Tom Dewe Matthews (1994: 126) remarks, 'Under the new category British audiences were introduced to a golden age of World Cinema through the films of Fellini, Bergman, Kurosawa, Mizoguchi, Rossellini, Renoir and many others'. In order to position films within the new category rather than ban them outright, many were initially cut dramatically. However, as the decade progressed and cinema's status as an 'art' form worthy of the protection and respect accorded to other arts became increasingly accepted, so this censorship decreased. Writing in *The Sunday Times* in April 1952, film critic Dilys Powell announced her firm support of the new X certificate and the status it accorded cinematic production:

> It is significant that people should complain when every film programme in London is not designed for audiences under sixteen years old. We don't (except at Christmas) order the stage for the benefit of children; but until the censorship adopted its present enlightened policy we did so order the screen. And then the high-and-mighties attack the cinema for being childish! It can be little else as long as we refuse to admit to it the adult subject and the adult comment. Now the Censor has made a first step towards allowing it in this country to become adult. The X certificate is, paradoxically, a relaxation of censorship, not a new restriction. I for one am thankful for it.
>
> (in Cook 1991: 400)

Interestingly, Powell praises the certificate as it both brings Britain into line with the 'Continent' and enables British audiences to see more foreign films. That it should indeed have been instrumental in opening the market to previously banned films was clearly a positive move. However, the impact of the X certificate on 'Continental' productions was arguably not entirely positive. As an editorial in *Sight and Sound* in October–December 1951 points out, a number of exhibitors were guilty of the 'squalid exploitation' of the certificate, using it in their publicity to suggest sensational thrills. The article reveals that the Cameo-Polytechnic cinema in London had discontinued its policy of showing Continental films because its governors disliked X films and as such 'much of the profitable continental product is not available' (Anon. 1951: 51). In other words, a slippage occurs between the X as applied to sensational cinema (of which a fair number are French and other foreign sex films of one kind or another) and the X as 'a valuable minority legislation in an industry that seldom caters for minorities'. This is significant in terms of pervasive perceptions of French cinema as 'risqué'. According to an article in *Sight and Sound* in January–March 1954, seventy-two films received the X certificate in the first three years of its existence. Of these, thirty-eight were foreign-language films and twenty-six were French. The writer praises the 'high calibre' films permitted screenings thanks to the new certificate, but laments the tendency to screen 'sensationalist' films promoted as 'the Xiest show in town' and suggests 'that [the fact that] the letter "X" was chosen for the new category was in itself surely an unnecessary gift to the exploiters' (Anon. 1954c: 123–24)!

So, in short, the French cinema became to a great degree associated with the X certificate and by extension with both its support of more serious cinema and the far more sensationalist fare it also denoted. Writing in *Sight and Sound* in Summer 1956, Walter Lassally, after lamenting the British disregard for culture as we have seen, expressed his regret that only 1 per cent of British film-goers regularly attended the growing number of specialised films shown by the film societies and repertory cinemas. He stated:

> In this context, the 'X' certificate, created to enable adult audiences to see adult films, has been particularly abused. Dozens of continental films of dubious quality have had long runs in London's specialised cinemas often backed up by lurid advertising campaigns shrewdly based on X and sex, while really adult films such as *Cristo Proibito*, *I Bambini ci Guardano* and *Ugetsu Monogatari* have not as yet received a single public showing in this country. Even some Film Society programmes have shown an unworthy tendency to pander in this way to their box office at the expense of more significant productions.
>
> (Lassally 1956: 12)

While the X helped to label Continental cinema as both 'racy' and 'challenging', it was essentially in its racy guise that it attracted significant numbers of movie-goers. It did enable the exhibition of films which may otherwise have fallen foul of the BBFC. Censorship in France tended to be more focused on political censorship than Britain where 'although the Board (BBFC) rightly claims that violence is what it abhors, sex is really the heart of the matter' (Wilcox 1956: 207–8). In this sense the X did indeed enable a more enlightened approach to cinematic exhibition which was of great benefit to many Continental productions. Margaret Hinxman notes the X-rated exhibition of *Manon*, *Occupe-toi d'Amélie* and *Le Diable au corps*, all of which had failed to conform to the ordinary 'A' standards: 'des Grieux can now fondle his dead Manon and Amélie can flit from bedroom to bedroom with the comforting assurance of the British censor's qualified approval' (Hinxman 1951: 57).

However, and perhaps more importantly, the X certificate was seized upon by distributors and exhibitors as a means of selling their films to curious and thrill-seeking British film-goers.[2] This did not go unnoticed by the BBFC who, as John Wilcox points out, 'more than once issued a warning of disapproval to distributors who proudly display the "X" on posters calculated to titillate' (Wilcox 1956: 208). It should also be noted that in 1952 the Rank-owned circuits banned X films from their cinemas which, given the relatively significant numbers of X-rated Continentals, actually increased curtailment of foreign exhibition to some extent. Yet despite the Board's disapproval and Rank's ban, the use of the X rapidly became a prominent feature in the marketing of many Continental films and stars. Take Gala Film's distribution of Henri Decoin's *Chnouf* starring Jean Gabin and Magali Noel in 1956. The X rating was prominently displayed on publicity materials and was subsequently taken up by critics who stressed the X certificate and the brutality and adult themes which had provoked it: 'super-tough, super-cynical thriller' (*Manchester Guardian*),

'Explosive rough-stuff' (*Kinematograph Weekly*), 'Excellent strong-meat entertainment for those of strong stomach' (*Today's Cinema*).³ Miracle Films arguably benefitted further from the X certificate when they released Vadim's then titled *And Woman . . . Was Created* (*And God Created Woman*) in 1956. The film opened at the Cameo Royal Charing Cross in March 1957 and much was made in the press of the fact that the film had been initially banned and then released with cuts in France. Publicity trumpeted its daring charms and the X certificate which had enabled its release. However, as Anthony Carthew notes, such marketing was somewhat disingenuous as despite the X rating, as in France, the film had been cut considerably before release (Carthew 1957). A nice example of this discrepancy between titillating marketing and the actual cuts the X still enforced is provided by a critic in the *Evening Standard* who notes, 'It is only fair to warn prospective audiences that the naked embraces displayed on the stills outside the cinema have been blue-pencilled from the film. The censors took exception to the bare facts' (Anon. 1957b).

The advent of the X was without doubt an important development in the distribution of non-English-language cinema in the United Kingdom as it enabled exhibition of films which would have otherwise been banned by the censors and limited to specialist showing in film societies. In this sense it played its part in fostering a serious film culture and in making 'serious' but daring films available to wider audiences. Yet via its commercial exploitation –'the X-iest shows in town' – the certificate fostered and entrenched perceptions of Continental cinema as risqué, provocative and perhaps somewhat seamy. As we shall see in later chapters, this was a perception which was to prove problematic for French cinema in particular in later years.

'Adult, Intelligent, Sophisticated – and in Good Taste': Continentals to the Rescue

The confinement of the Continental cinema to a relatively rarefied circuit of specialist theatres and film society screenings which had typified exhibition patterns in the 1930s and the 1940s was to be challenged as the decade progressed. The changes in Hollywood described previously meant that there was a real product shortage in the United Kingdom and to a great extent it was due to this that the 1950s offered such potential for the exhibition of French films in Britain. While the major circuits were just about able to fill their screens, second and third run cinemas increasingly turned to Continental films to fill their schedules and about half of these films came from France (Harper and Porter 2003: 246). As the decade progressed, the number of Continental films shown on British cinema screens began to rise. As Charles H.V. Brown wrote in

Kinematograph Weekly on 16 December 1954, in 1946 only thirty-eight foreign features were shown in British cinemas; by 1953 this number had risen to seventy-seven. In 1946 only twenty cinemas regularly showed foreign films. By 1954, 100 cinemas were regularly showing Continental films while another 150 showed them on an occasional basis, a small proportion of the whole but almost a sevenfold increase all the same. Of these 'Continental' films a significant number were French. In 1952 *Picture Post* claimed that 491 cinemas in Britain were exhibiting French films occasionally, four times as many as in 1950 (cited in Holmes 2005: 241). As Joachim Lembach remarks in his study *The German Cinema in Great Britain after 1945* (2003), the 1950s represents the first (and some may claim the last) foreign film boom in British cinemas (15).

A fruitful source of information regarding the presence of Continental films in the British market during the 1950s is the *Continental Film Review* and the very emergence of this publication in November 1952 says much about attempts to broaden the films' appeal. Although by the time it folded in 1982 the magazine did little more than focus somewhat pruriently on semi-clothed starlets, in its early incarnation it set out to bring European film to a much wider public. The magazine was aimed very specifically at a readership that enjoyed all the pleasures of the Continent – food, travel, cinema and, of course, 'fine Bordeaux' – and not simply a highbrow 'art' cinema audience. The opening editorial stated:

> We like Continental films, we like opera in Italy and jazz in Paris, we like night clubs in Hamburg or the view of the Rhine from the Drachenfels, we like to buy records that remind us of the pleasant times, we do not eschew sentiment and, if there are such things, we might be sceptical romantics. This magazine is for those who enjoy good Continental films, have been to the Continent, are going to the Continent, would like to go to the Continent and for those whose imaginations have been so stirred that they will forever be hankering to return to that bistro in Paris, that coast run into Trieste, that railway to Pompeii, that restaurant in Vienna [. . .] In other words, 'philes' of all Continental countries will be able to indulge their tastes from month to month, not from holiday to holiday.
>
> (Anon. 1952: 3)

We can see a real shift in perception here as the film-goer envisaged by the *Continental Film Review* is not the blue-velvet-suited intellectual of the Film Society of the 1930s described in Chapter One. Rather s/he is a cosmopolitan, fun-loving individual open to the pleasures of the Continent and the emotional pull of music and film. While the magazine certainly aimed for broad appeal with much focus on stars (Martine Carol, Brigitte Bardot and Fernandel for example feature heavily), articles on travel and tourism and a 'Continental Star Calendar' displaying a selection of scantily clad young actresses, it also took its role as a promoter of Continental cinema quite seriously. Information on all Continental releases in the United Kingdom was provided, the films were reviewed and feature articles focused enthusiastically on key films and figures. An editorial in July 1953 shows a keen awareness of the difficulties facing foreign film in Britain, noting that the attractions of the 'sensational and novel' (3D and stereoscopic screens) and the rush to imitate the X-rated sexual antics of *La Ronde* (of which more later) risked limiting the Continental presence. However, the magazine strikes an optimistic note, affirming the consolidation of Continental film distribution which, it believed, would ensure a wide selection of the best products (Anon. 1953a: 3).

In many ways the *Continental Film Review* was right to be optimistic. Non-English-language releases were indeed becoming a more prominent feature of the cinematic landscape and were slowly beginning to move beyond the confines of the specialist circuits. In 1952 two French films (*Mr Wonderbird*, an Anglo-French animation, and Clair's *Night Beauties*) made history by being the first non-English-language films to be selected for the Royal Command Performance. Then in 1954 Kenneth Rive of Gala Film Distributors and Sir Albert Clavering of Cameo-Poly Distributors announced their collaboration. Already responsible for Continental screenings at the West End's Cameo-Poly, Continentale and Berkeley and Hendon's New Classic, they announced their intention to extend their activities to five further West End cinemas and to screens in major cities beginning with Manchester and Bristol (Anon. 1954b: 3). The joining of forces between these two major Continental distributors was clearly significant. It enabled a broader and more powerful distribution network for the Continentals both within central London and further afield. Moreover, the very fact that such a consolidation was deemed sensible at this juncture underlines a contemporary belief in the increased commercial potential of the non-English-language product. Publicity for one of the group's cinemas, the Cameo-Poly, suggests such expectations may not have been misplaced. 'Only three films in thirty eight weeks' trumpets the advertisement: 'In the past thirty eight weeks one third of a million people have seen *French Can Can*, *The Fiends* and *The Light Across the Street* at the Cameo-Poly which has only 600 seats [. . .] the Cameo-Poly is confident of maintaining its pre-eminence in offering a choice of entertainment that is Adult, Intelligent, Sophisticated – and in good taste' (Anon.: 1956a: 8).

An editorial in the *Review* in May 1955 celebrated the fact that the month had seen more Continental film bookings than ever before and also noted the success of two newly opened Continental Picture Houses in Aberdeen and Glasgow. Certainly it seemed that the magazine was correct in its assumption that there was an audience for non-English-language film and the very presence of the magazine itself is testament to that constituency. Moreover the *Continental Film Review*'s enthusiastic advocacy of all things continental, its praise for the pleasures of foreign films and their stars, were surely instrumental in extending that constituency and aiding in the gradual move of the foreign films from the specialised circuits to rather wider audiences and more varied venues.

Selling French Film on the British Market

Developments in the British market, notably the need for extra films to fill the gap left by the decline in Hollywood production, were matched by a concerted effort on the part of the French film industry to increase the international distribution of the domestic product. Although the years of war and occupation had proved extremely challenging for French film production, there was a concerted effort to revivify the industry and to build on some of the more positive developments of the 1940s. Developments in co-production agreements brought extra financial resources into the beleaguered French industry and a growing focus on big-budget crowd pleasers set out to grow audience numbers. As the *Continental Film Review* notes in August 1956, 'By the middle of July twenty-eight films were being made in the French studios – the highest figure for a long time. Up to this date, fifty-nine films had gone into production as against forty-eight last year for the same period. Spectacular colour productions are on the increase, what might be called quickies are on the decrease' (Anon. 1956b: 4). A particularly significant development given our focus here was the establishment in January 1949 of Unifrance. Unifrance was created with the express purpose of promoting French cinema in overseas markets and it rapidly set up bureaux and organised activities in a number of countries deemed to have the potential to increase the presence of French film. As Robert Cravenne, Unifrance's first director, explained in *Kine Weekly* in 1953, while the quality and prestige of French cinema was undisputed, a need had now been recognised for a more focused international distribution:

> On the international plane, producers understood as early as 1949 the necessity for common action and, with government support, founded an association for the distribution of French films in the world. This is how 'Unifrance Film' a propaganda organisation was born. At present increasing emphasis is being put on its economic and near-commercial role, by facilitating exchanges, easing difficulties and generally representing each individual producer abroad. The main role of 'Unifrance Films' has been to popularise our pictures, our film stars, our film production.
>
> (Cravenne 1953: 6)

A French Film Festival sponsored by Unifrance, supported by the French Embassy and attended by the Queen, was held in London in February 1953 and the event trumpeted the 'mainly adult but seldom highbrow' nature of recent French cinema. In the words of Ingram Fraser, then

Managing Director of British distributors Films de France: 'Among Continental productions, those from France enjoy special box-office advantages. France is the Englishman's most favoured tourist haunt and ten people speak French for every one who speaks another language. The very differences between French and English life can be turned to advantage' (Fraser 1953). It is worth noting that Fraser's comments were published in a special issue of *Kine Weekly* devoted to this first 'officially sponsored' festival of French films as this in itself underlines both the extent of Unifrance's promotional efforts and the British trade's recognition of the commercial potential of the French product. The event was deemed a 'huge success' and the magazine cites long runners such as *La Ronde* (shown for eighteen months at the Curzon alongside 'more normal film entertainment') as evidence that French films were regaining the popularity they had enjoyed in pre-sound days (Anon. 1953b: 3).

The difficulties facing French cinema did not go unnoticed. Jacques Flaud, then director of the *CNC*, remarks upon the limited presence of French films in Britain, 'France is Great Britain's nearest neighbour, and yet Great Britain is the only country of all France's neighbours into which it is difficult for French films to penetrate' (Flaud 1953: 5). He urges closer cooperation between the two nations, indeed positions cinema as a crucial means of reinforcing international understanding in the post-war context, and concludes by stating: 'I have no fear of contradiction by my English friends when I say that British films encounter no difficulty or antagonism in their attempts to penetrate the French market. I hope that after this London film week French producers may be able to detect an equally encouraging state of affairs on your side of the Channel' (ibid.). Nevertheless, *Kine Weekly* sees the festival as a turning point in French cinema's fortunes. The problems and shortages facing the British industry described previously, along with Unifrance's valiant efforts at promotion, seemed to offer potential for a far more visible and commercially profitable place in the British market. In the words of Philip Kutner, General Sales Manager of International Film Distributors:

> The international film [...] can provide with its freshness of outlook, its very 'difference' of treatment and milieu, a contrast which not only excites and interests in itself, but by contrast will also highlight the regular film fare. [...] In the past couple of years French pictures have enjoyed unparalleled success in London and have repeated this success throughout the country. Many exhibitors were quick to grasp the box-office significance of showing films of international origins, and have been well repaid. Other exhibitors, reluctant at first, but when finally induced to book them, have had their doubts dispelled by box-office results. [...] the international film today is no longer the preference solely of the minority and art-theatre patron, but attracts, interests, appeals to and satisfies the ordinary family-type audience.
>
> (Kutner 1953: 9)

Of course Kutner was hardly an impartial observer: as Sales Manager for an international distribution company he had a keen interest in increasing the market for the 'Continentals'. However, his account of a developing British interest in all things foreign and the potential for market growth is echoed by other writers of the time and is reinforced by the establishment and success of the French Film Festival itself and, as we shall see, by the box-office careers of a number of non-English-language films throughout the decade. Ingram Fraser remarks that more foreign pictures were imported to Britain in 1952 than in any previous year and more showing time was devoted to them in both London and the provinces. 'The reason behind this trend is the obvious one that the right kind of Continental film is better box-office than the average routine picture' (Fraser 1953: 9).

It would seem that the early 1950s did indeed herald a second golden age for French cinema in the U.K. with wider distribution, broader audiences and increasing attention paid to its films, directors and stars. As an article in *Films and Filming* announced in 1955, 'French studios are aiming for world markets with international stars and stories that are full of human interest' (Anon. 1955: 6). Given the paper's own interest in Charles Boyer, Martine Carol, Simone Signoret, Gérard Philippe et al., these efforts were clearly met with a certain degree of success. In 1957 the *Continental Film Review* discussed Unifrance's 'all out effort' to capture world markets with films accompanied by stars 'going everywhere' and a distribution deal signed by producers Raoul Levy and Ray Ventura with Columbia for distribution of six films, including Roger Vadim's *Les Bijoutiers de la Clair de Lune* featuring star of the moment Brigitte Bardot (Anon. 1957a: 10). The writer concludes by stating 'this is undoubtedly a great commercial period for French films'. However, the writer regrets the reliance on 'styles and formulae created at least twenty years ago' and somewhat presciently calls for a 'fresh experimental period; for an avant-garde; for new ideas and stories, not remakes' (10). It is somewhat ironic that this call for an avant-garde should come just as the rejection of the *cinema de qualité* was beginning to take off in France, leading to the *nouvelle vague*, a cinematic movement which, as we shall see in subsequent chapters, in many ways put paid to the much vaunted commercial potential for French films in the Britain during the 1950s.

Filling the Gap: Continental Circuit Release

In an article published in *Kinematograph Weekly* in July 1956 Ingram Fraser asks, 'Can Continentals Fill the Gap?' His response is equivocal:

> For a Continental film to be acceptable to the great British public, it has to have several distinct qualities: basic simplicity of story, with the emphasis on

action rather than on dialogue; an atmosphere, expressed in the characters and the setting, that is not to be found in a British or American production; and on the whole better acting and higher production values than a comparable Hollywood or British film, in order to overcome the initial handicap of being foreign.

(Fraser 1956: 25)

That handicap was of course largely created by the need for dubbing or subtitling, the presence of what an article in *Picturegoer* on 3 March 1954 termed 'unknown, unpronounceable stars' and, crucially, the exhibitors' reluctance to take a risk. A number of films meet his criteria, including *Le Salaire de la peur* (Henri-Georges Clouzot, France/Italy, 1953), *Les Diaboliques* (Henri-Georges Clouzot, France, 1955), *Du Rififi chez les hommes* (Jules Dassin, France/Italy, 1955), the work of Tati and a farce starring Brigitte Bardot entitled *Cette Sacrée Gamine* (Michel Boisrond, France, 1956). However, he concludes that much of the remainder consists of 'strong sex dramas', X-rated films which could find an audience but which were not suitable for general booking. This sense that much of the Continental production present in the U.K. was risqué sex drama is echoed by Reg Whitley in *The Daily Mirror* on 2 December 1955. He condemns Clouzot's *Les Diaboliques*, describing it as 'a suspenseful but

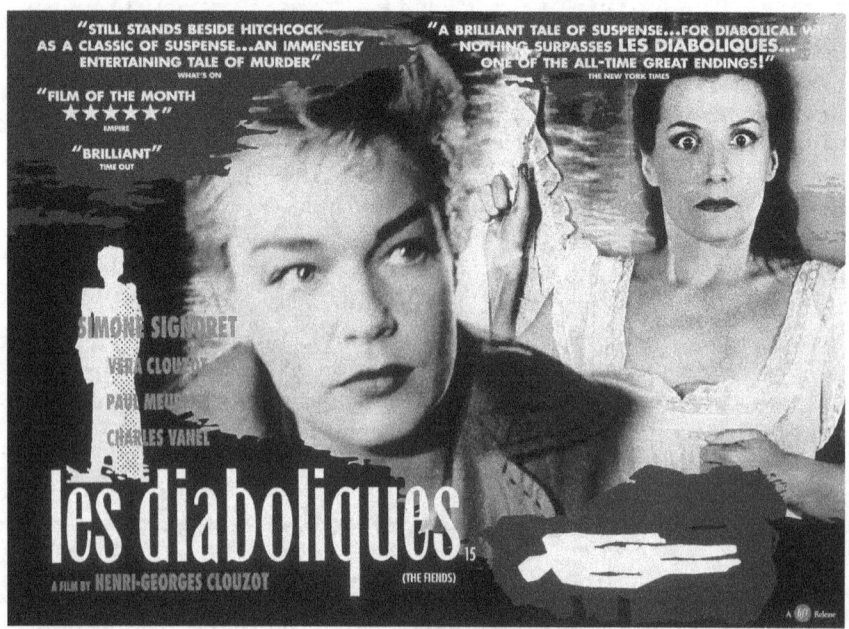

11. A poster advertising a much later re-release of 1950s success *Les Diaboliques* (H.G. Clouzot, 1955).
Image courtesy of the BFI stills department.

sordid slice of French life' and urges 'it is high time something was done to stop the dumping here of so many Hollywood and Continental pictures which are bound to get X' (Whitley 1955). While he does acknowledge the American provenance of some of these 'gruesome' movies, it is significant that it should be a French film that he holds up to particular scrutiny. In another article, published in *Tribune* almost a year later, R.D. Smith makes no bones about his dislike of Clouzot's film and the connections between its subject matter and national identity, labelling it 'vulgar, nasty and French' (Smith 1956). In other words, the British cinematic landscape of the 1950s displayed a certain ambiguity in terms of the potential space accorded to French cinema: in many ways a good time for a French film to make its mark on British film culture due to the product shortage previously discussed yet still subject to the rather reductive discourses which limit the dissemination of the 'foreign' product.

Nevertheless Clouzot's *Wages of Fear* was the first French film in the U.K. to break through to circuit release and to a great extent it is this which marks the 1950s as a second (and perhaps last) Golden Age for French film in Britain. The prominent status of *Wages of Fear* within British cinema was reinforced when the British Academy of Film judged it film of the year in 1954. It is not perhaps surprising that this film should be the 'break-through' movie for this was indeed a film which seemed to combine admirably the 'local' specificities and the 'international' (read Hollywood) appeal highlighted by Sarah Street as essential for successful export (Street 2002). Clouzot's film was a co-production and as such very much part of the French industry's concerted effort to create an exportable product described above. It featured a multi-national cast (Yves Montand, Charles Vanel, Folco Lulli and Peter Van Eyck). Its dialogue was limited, so translation became less problematic, and what dialogue there was incorporated Italian, English, German and Spanish as well as the dominant French. This was indeed a film which had the potential to appeal to audiences more accustomed to the films of Hollywood. As Derek Granger wrote in *The Financial Times*, 'Filmgoers should be aware, then, that they will be submitting themselves to a fairly gruelling ordeal and that they will also be seeing a film containing elements of toughness and violence which we have come more to associate with the American thriller (the kind of thing which Mr. John Huston might do in his fierce "Sierra Madre" mood) than with the close-quartered intimacy of the best French films' (Granger 1954). Interestingly Granger stresses the ways in which Clouzot's film differs from dominant British perceptions of French cinema and mirrors more closely some Hollywood production, yet still makes a point of underlining the film's French provenance and reinforcing specific forms of perception and hence reception. As Granger continues he refers to the film's 'disquieting undercurrent of feeling [. . .] that bleak and pessimistic quality which has dominated the intellectual temper of post-war France'. As such the film is simultaneously held up as 'different' to the majority of French production – a violent, suspenseful action film – and yet in some ways still part of that identity – bleak, philosophical and intellectual.

The film's distributors and exhibitors appeared to make a concerted effort to avoid the treatment normally accorded to continental cinema. There was the major booking on the part of the Odeon chain and a publicity campaign which did indeed set out to foreground the film's decidedly non-typically French action/adventure elements. Publicity for both *Le Salaire* and Clouzot's later film *Les Diaboliques/The Fiends* compared Clouzot to Hitchcock and claimed that he was even more 'hard-hitting'.[4] The original British poster for *Le Salaire* places the lorry at the centre of the image with the word 'explosives' prominent on its front. Alongside this is a close-up image of Montand while across the top of the poster are the words 'dynamic', 'tremendous' and 'shattering'. At the bottom is a quote from the *Daily Express* describing the film as 'the tensest picture I have ever seen'.

In contrast, the original French poster eschews gripping adjectives and features only the names of the two French stars (Montand and Vanel) and the film's title. Interestingly the image shows a close-up of Jo (Vanel) resting on Mario (Montand). In other words where the British poster stresses action, adventure and excitement the French version foregrounds

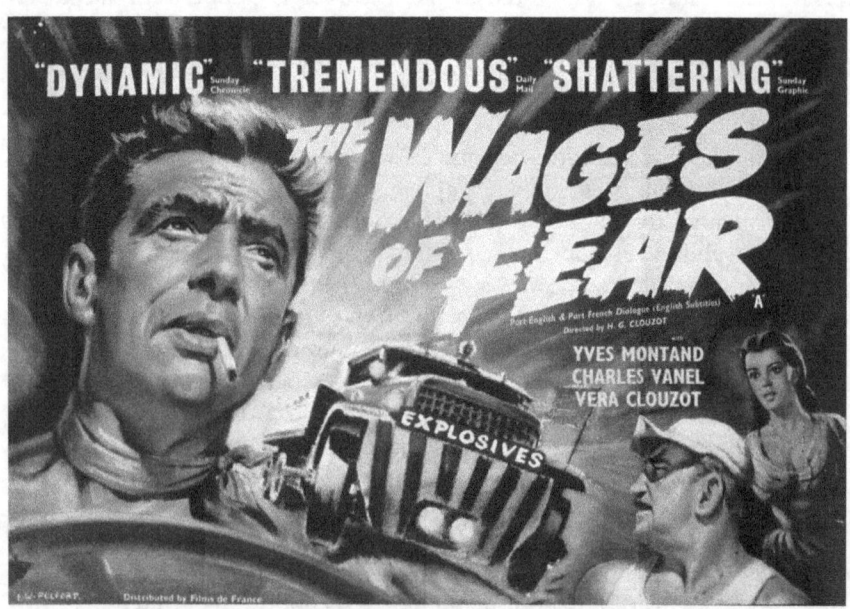

12. British publicity poster for *The Wages of Fear* (H.G. Clouzot, 1953).
Image courtesy of the BFI stills department.

the relationship between the two men. Nevertheless, contemporary British reviews made a point of stressing the film's national origins (largely due to Clouzot's identity it was generally described as a French film), thus re-locating it within dominant perceptions of French cinema and inviting modes of reception arguably different to those solicited in France where its national identity was surely not at stake. This is perhaps best summed up in a short but rather defeatist piece in *The Evening Standard*. The writer states:

> In a strange week we must now record that once again the French have proved themselves the supreme masters of film making without being the supreme conquerors of the box office. *Le Salaire de la peur* is a tremendous film ... Compared to this film most of the popular offerings at the cinema look like peep-show entertainment. It is a masterpiece. But who wants to see a masterpiece?
>
> (Anon. 1954d)

The Daily Sketch is less pessimistic, praising the film, criticising its then limited distribution and urging its readers to see the film if it 'should come their way' and 'to start griping' if it did not (Anon. 1954e). Of course, this pessimism was to prove somewhat unfounded as the film did indeed make its way onto the major Odeon circuit. However, these remarks speak volumes about the place for foreign cinema at the time and assumptions on the part of distributors, exhibitors and critics about the limitations of audience taste which remained firmly in place despite the apparent attempts at change we noted earlier. The film is French and hence a 'masterpiece'. The film is French and as such destined to commercial failure.

That Clouzot's film should, to some extent, have avoided the constraining agendas and strategies in which the vast majority of French film in the U.K. had previously been situated is of course noteworthy – it was after all a significant commercial success. And yet even this 'cross-over' film did not entirely escape the dominant critical and commercial discourses which produced particular constructions of French cinema for British audiences, thus potentially reshaping reception and ultimately the film itself. Although other films (*The Fiends*, *Rififi*) similarly went on to achieve wide circuit release, the practice, with very rare exceptions, did not outlast the decade suggesting the powerful nature of these longstanding perceptions and expectations.

So we should perhaps resist the temptation to see the 1950s as a true 'golden age' for the dissemination of French cinema in the U.K. Despite an undeniably increased presence, the distribution and exhibition of foreign-language production remained limited and curtailed in a number of ways. American and British cinema remained the dominant feature of the cinematic landscape and only a handful of non-English-language films found their way onto major circuit release. As the monthly round-up of

Continental film releases in the *Continental Film Review* revealed, a relatively broad geographical spread of exhibition venues was to some extent undermined by a limited corpus of films (only a handful of films were considered suitable for general bookings). Moreover, as we have seen, and as Lembach confirms, the development in the wider public's taste for foreign films coincided with a dramatic decline in cinema attendance in the period as television replaced going to the pictures as a favourite leisure pursuit (Lembach 2003: 14). The impact of this decline on mainstream cinema was significant and yet the 'art-house' film with its distinctive identity and 'specialist' audience remained relatively unscathed.

And so we come back to those overweening definitions outlined in the Introduction. Despite the mainstream release of a number of foreign-language films and an increase in the number of French films distributed in the U.K., the majority continued to be constrained by quite limiting definitions of what French cinema should be. Writing in *Sight and Sound* in 1954 Leslie Halliwell discusses the running of a specialised cinema, the Rex in Cambridge:

> We are persevering in the hope of making sub-titled films popular with the 'masses' but it is not easy. That is why much continental film advertising has become so garish. Most distributors are as eager as the critics that their films should be properly received by intelligent audiences but they are business men as well as connoisseurs ... and so *Dieu a Besoin des Hommes* becomes *Isles of Sinners*, and *Altri Tempi* suffers a sea-change into *Infidelity*.
>
> (Halliwell 1954: 201)

Sex or specialised, it seems, remained the choice for much continental cinema in the 1950s. And if the X-rated thrillers and 'sex' films seemed to offer some exhibitors potential for a new if not always entirely successful commercialisation, they also engendered critical disappointment which threatened the art-house status which guaranteed French film some presence in the U.K. In other words, attempts to broaden French cinema's appeal, to move it beyond the confines of specialised exhibition, created a rather thorny double bind: how to retain French cinema's reputation for quality and thus its existing audiences while simultaneously reaching out to a new public in search of more popular fare? Films such as Clouzot's *Wages of Fear*, which were able to obscure to some degree their 'Frenchness' and mobilise stylistic and narrative traits more commonly associated with Hollywood, were able to negotiate this situation and achieve, as we have seen, critical and commercial success. In this sense Clouzot's film can be seen to prefigure that much more recent 'breakout' French hit, *The Artist*. This 'Hollywoodisation' of French cinema is something which we see resurfacing in later years, notably in the 1990s via the films of Luc Besson, in an attempt to broaden French cinema's appeal on the global market. And yet it is a strategy which both now and in the 1950s carried risks and uncertainties for French film. Attempts to reach out to new audiences were not guaranteed success and there was a very real danger of losing existing audiences who disliked a commercialism they did not expect from the French product. *The Manchester Guardian* sums up 1957's French Film Festival as 'an unimpressive anthology, a sorry reminder of better days of French film-making' (Anon.1957c): it would seem that by the end of the decade, striking a balance between commercial success and the maintenance of its critical reputation was a challenge that French cinema in Britain was yet to achieve. As the following chapter will reveal, the arrival of the French New Wave on British shores in the 1960s was to make this balancing act even more precarious.

Notes

* Publicity for *An Artist with Ladies* starring Fernandel, *Continental Film Review*, December 1953.
1. http://www.screenonline.org.uk/film/cinemas/sect4.html(accessed 28 October 2010).
2. See Wheatley (2010) for a detailed discussion of marketing using the X certificate.
3. All quotes taken from Press Pack for *Chnouf* produced by Gala Distributors.
4. Gala Publicity Bulletin for *Les Diaboliques*.

Bibliography

Anon. 1950a. 'Film Societies: The Other Side', *Sight and Sound* 18(72), February: 45.
Anon. 1950b. 'The Front Page', *Sight and Sound* 19(6), August: 227–28.
Anon.1951. 'The Front Page: X-Appeal', *Sight and Sound* 21(2), October–December: 51.
Anon. 1952. 'Let Us Introduce Ourselves', *Continental Film Review* 1(1), November: 3.
Anon. 1953a. 'In the Foyer', *Continental Film Review* 1(9), July: 3.
Anon. 1953b. 'A Royal Occasion', *Kinematograph Weekly*, 19 February: 3.
Anon. 1954a. 'Continentals to the Rescue', *Picturegoer*, 27 March: 8.
Anon. 1954b. 'In the Foyer', *Continental Film Review*, April: 3.
Anon. 1954c. 'Report on the X'. *Sight and Sound* 23(3), January–March: 123–24.
Anon. 1954d. 'The French Again', *Evening Standard*, 11 February.
Anon. 1954e. 'The Wages of Stupidity', *Daily Sketch*, 24 February.
Anon. 1955. 'Boyer is Back in Paris', *Films and Filming*, October: 6.
Anon. 1956a. Advertisement for the Cameo-Poly, *Continental Film Review*, July: 8.
Anon. 1956b. 'Record French Production', *Continental Film Review*, August: 4–6.
Anon. 1957a. 'News From France', *Continental Film Review*, June: 10.
Anon. 1957b. 'Et Dieu Crea la Femme', *Evening Standard*, 14 March.

Anon. 1957c. 'Perhaps the Film of the Decade', *Manchester Guardian*, 30 March.
Balio, T (ed.). 1990. *Hollywood in the Age of Television*. Boston: Unwin-Hyman.
Brown, C.H.V. 1954. 'Continental Films Can Make Profit for the Small Exhibitor', *Kinematograph Weekly*, 16 December: 185.
Carthew, A. 1957. 'Censors' Scissors Take the Sex Away from Brigitte', *Daily Herald*, 12 March.
Cook, Christopher (ed.).1991. *The Dilys Powell Film Reader*. Manchester: Carcanet.
Cravenne, R. 1953. 'Revival Aimed at World Markets', *Kinematograph Weekly*, 19 February: 6.
Crow, D. 1950. 'Days of Reckoning', *Sight and Sound* 18(72), February: 9–12.
De Lane Lea, W. 1953. 'The Art of Dubbing: Hear All See All', *Kinematograph Weekly*, 19 February: 10.
Dewe Matthews, T. 1994. *Censored: The Story of Film Censorship in Britain*. London: Chatto and Windus.
England, L, 1951. 'The Critics and the Box-Office', *Sight and Sound* 20(1), May: 43–44.
Flaud, J. 1953. 'This Golden Opportunity', *Kinematograph Weekly*, 19 February: 5.
Fraser, I. 1953. 'Appetite Grows with Eating', *Kinematograph Weekly*, 19 February: 9–15.
Fraser, I. 1956. 'Can Continentals Fill the Gap?', *Kinematograph Weekly*, 5 July: 25.
Granger, D. 1954. *Financial Times*, 15 February.
Goodmayes, M. 1953, letter to 'Focus on Films', *Picturegoer*, 14 March.
Halliwell, L. 1954. 'Strictly for Eggheads', *Sight and Sound* 23(4), April–June: 201–2.
Harper, S. and Porter, V. 2003. *British Cinema of the 1950s: The Decline of Deference*. Oxford: OUP.
Hinxman, M. 1951. 'The British Board of Film Censors', *Films in Britain 1951*, London: BFI, pp.57–58.
Holmes, S. 2004. 'Looking at the Wider Picture on the Small Screen: Reconsidering British Television and Widescreen Cinema in the 1950s', *Quarterly Review of Film and Video* 21(2): 131–47.
Holmes, S. 2005. *British TV and Film Culture in the 1950s: Coming to a TV Near You*. Bristol: Intellect.
Kutner, P. 1953. 'Now It's French Without Tears', *Kinematograph Weekly*, 19 February: 9.
Lassally, W. 1956. 'The Cynical Audience', *Sight and Sound* 26(1), Summer: 12–15.
Lembach, J. 2003. *The German Cinema in Great Britain after 1945*. Lewiston, NY: Edwin Mellor Press.
Maltby, R. 1995. *Hollywood Cinema*. Oxford: Blackwell.
Marlowe, D. 1953. 'Ici On Parle Français', *Picturegoer*, 28 February: 18.
Murphy, R. 1992. *Sixties British Cinema*. London: Routledge.
Smith, R.D. 1956. 'Vulgar, Nasty – and French', *Tribune*, 16 November.
Street, S. 2002. *Transatlantic Crossings: British Feature Films in the USA*. London: Continuum.
Wheatley, C. 2010. 'The Language of Love? How the French Sold *Lady Chatterley's Lover* (Back) to British Audiences', in L. Mazdon and

C. Wheatley (eds.), *Je t'aime, moi non plus: Franco-British Cinematic Relations*. Oxford: Berghahn, pp.81–100.
Whitley, R. 1955. 'This is Xasperating', *Daily Mirror*, 2 December.
Wilcox, J.1956. 'The Small Knife: Studies in Censorship', *Sight and Sound* 25(4), Spring: 206–20.
Wilson, N. 1951. 'A Window on Europe', *Films in Britain 1951*, London: BFI, pp. 61–2.

Filmography

Altri Tempi / Infidelity (1952, Alessandro Blasetti)
Artiste, L' / The Artist (2011, Michel Hazanavicius)
Bambini ci Guardano, I / The Children Are Watching Us (1944, Vittorio de Sica)
Belles de nuit, Les / Beauties of the Night (1952, René Clair)
Bergère et le ramoneur, La / Mr Wonderbird (1952, Paul Grimault)
Bijoutiers de la Clair de Lune, Les / Heaven Fell That Night (1958, Roger Vadim)
Cette Sacrée Gamine / Mam'zelle Pigalle (1956, Michel Boisrond)
Cristo Proibito, Il / The Forbidden Christ (1951, Curzio Malaparte)
Diable au corps, Le / Devil in the Flesh (1947, Claude Autant-Lara)
Diaboliques, Les / The Fiends (1955, Henri-Georges Clouzot)
Dieu a besoin des hommes / Isles of Sinners (1950, Jean Delannoy)
Et Dieu créa la femme / And Woman . . . Was Created (1956, Roger Vadim)
French Can Can (1954, Jean Renoir)
Jour de fête (1949, Jacques Tati)
Ladri di biciclette / Bicycle Thieves (Vittorio de Sica, 1948)
Lumière d'en face, La / The Light Across the Street (1955, Georges Lacombe)
Manon (1949, Henri-Georges Clouzot)
Occupe toi d'Amélie (1949, Claude Autant-Lara)
Razzia sur la chnouf / Chnouf (1955, Henri Decoin)
Rififi chez les hommes, Du / Rififi (1955, Jules Dassin)
Ronde, La (1950, Max Ophüls)
Salaire de la peur, Le / The Wages of Fear (1953, Henri-Georges Clouzot)
UgetsuMonogatari / Tales of Ugetsu (1953, Kenji Mizoguchi)

4

THE FRENCH NEW WAVE ON BRITISH SHORES (1959–1970)

How to balance commercial success and critical standing? If this was the question that British distributors and exhibitors of French cinema were struggling with at the end of the 1950s, the subsequent decade seemed to offer a solution of sorts, albeit one that was short-lived. For 1960 was the year that saw the arrival of a new kind of French film on British shores, one that has left a lasting impression on perceptions of Gallic cinema amongst U.K. critics, academics and film-goers. This was, of course, the era of the French New Wave.

Although coined by French journalist Françoise Giroud, editor of the weekly paper *L'Express*, to describe the new socially active youth class, in the British context the term *nouvelle vague* has come to refer to a group of young critics-turned-film-makers whose debut films were all produced at the turn of the decade, and who ushered in a new paradigm of French film-making. Amongst the names most commonly associated with it are those of François Truffaut, Jean-Luc Godard, Claude Chabrol and Alain Resnais. The significance of these men, their films, and the banner under which they are so frequently grouped within contemporary British discourses of French cinema cannot be overstated. Consider, for example, this quote from Joe Queenan, written some fifty years after the *nouvelle vague*'s inception:

> The New Wave was just that – a wave – that rolled in and then rolled out over the course of 10 years. Not all the New Wave films were good, and not all have stood the test of time, but the ratio of good to bad and great to good was high enough to make it an unprecedented moment in the history of cinema. No one in the year 2009 will make a better film than *Les Quatre Cents Coups*, *Hiroshima, Mon Amour*, or *Jules et Jim*. No one will make a more daring film than *Pierrot le Fou*, *Alphaville* or *Weekend*. No one will make a more adventurous film than *Paris Nous Appartient* or a more influential film than *A Bout de Souffle*. No one will make a more anachronistic, stranger film than *Les Parapluies de Cherbourg*.

And no one will make a nuttier film than *La Chinoise* or *La Gai Savoir*. This was not a wave, it was a Tsunami.

(Queenan 2009)

Naturally there were other types of French film showing in British cinemas during the 1960s: as Geoffrey Nowell-Smith has pointed out, the two biggest foreign-language hits of 1959 and 1960 respectively were Jacques Tati's almost-silent slapstick *Mon Oncle*, and Claude Autant-Lara's bedroom farce *Le Jument Verte / The Green Mare's Nest*, both of which received a first-run at Gala's Cameo-Poly theatre before going on to receive a circuit release (Nowell-Smith 2010: 121). But as Queenan's eulogy suggests, the *nouvelle vague* is the key phenomenon that structures British perceptions of French cinema of the 1960s; indeed one might well say that it is the key phenomenon that structures British perceptions of French cinema *tout court*.

And yet the retrospective image of the French New Wave does not necessarily match the image it had when it first arrived in the U.K.: British perceptions of this moment have changed significantly in the period since the New Wave first hit British shores. True enough, when François Truffaut's *Les 400 Coups* was given its première at the London Film Festival in 1959, British film-makers and cinephiles raved about this exciting new cinema, lamenting the comparative banality of so much British production. But the response of distributors, exhibitors, audiences and critics to the glut of films that were to follow was not altogether enthusiastic. The *nouvelle vague* in its 'purest' form, for want of a better word, only lasted several years (if that); and its critical and commercial success was followed by recrimination and disappointment as the films coming from France in the later half of the decade failed to live up to expectations. Moreover, in comparison with the relative exposure of French film during the 1950s, the films associated with the *nouvelle vague* banner were seen, for the most part, by a relatively restricted section of society – variants on the same audiences who had patronised French cinema at the film societies and independent art houses of the 1930s and 1940s. There is a neat irony in the fact that the *nouvelle vague*, for all the initial splash it made, may well have quelled the tide of more commercial French films into the circuits seen during the 1950s, as we shall go on to examine.

The First Splash

Although the term had not yet become common currency at the time they were screened, the first *nouvelle vague* films available to British audiences were Truffaut's short *Les Mistons* (1957) and Chabrol's first feature, *Le Beau Serge* (1958). Both films were shown by David Robinson at the

National Film Theatre (NFT) in London in early September 1958 under the Free Cinema banner. Billed as a 'French Renewal', the programme notes to the two films succinctly capture British attitudes to French cinema, at least within certain circles, at the end of the 1950s:

> It is an open secret that the past few years have seen a catastrophic decline in the French cinema. A few lonely names survive; but generally the great tradition of the past has been submerged in a flood of catchpenny productions – films noirs cheaply imitative of American toughies, synthetic co-productions, a depressing succession of sensational, pseudo-erotic romances.
> This year have come the first indications of a turn of the tide: and FREE CINEMA is happy to present, for the first time in London, the work of a new generation of French film-makers who will, we believe, prove to be of decisive importance. Of particular significance is the fact that these directors are mostly not of the industry: they represent the irruption into actual film-making of a group of critics who, by their outspoken writing in the magazine *Cahiers du Cinéma* have established themselves as passionate lovers of the cinema, and sworn enemies of the conventional and uncreative. Their films are made with an absolute rejection of 'safe' commercial considerations. They are important, and should be seen.
>
> (Anderson 1958)

Note the distinct hostility towards the mainstream cinema in Anderson's rallying cry. It is significant that the films of the *nouvelle vague* were first welcomed into British cinema by a certain school of film-goer – cineliterate, esoteric in their tastes, attendees of the art houses and specialised cinemas – who firmly opposed the 'Hollywoodisation' of French film described in the previous chapter and who championed art above industry. This initial ringfencing of the *nouvelle vague* films as unconventional and anti-commercial sits uneasily with its later success on British screens. It may also, ironically, have contributed to a shift in critical attitudes to the films of Truffaut, Chabrol et al. It is worth bearing in mind as we proceed through the chapter that from the very outset, these films were 'important' precisely because they were not 'industrial'.

These first films do not seem to have caused a particular stir. The only review of *Le Beau Serge* published in 1958 appeared in *The Tribune*, written by Derek Hill (1958), in which he comments that there were, as far as he knew, no plans for a commercial release for the film; and it would in fact be another three years before *Le Beau Serge* would be picked up by the Gala distributors. At the London Film Festival that autumn, the French films chosen by the festival director Richard Roud were Jacques Baratier's *Goha* (1958), which according to Nowell-Smith 'died without trace' (Nowell-Smith 2010: 119), and Louis Malle's *Les Amants* (1958), whose subsequent release and reception in Britain (the film opened at the Cameo-Poly one year later) was overshadowed by controversy surrounding the cutting of a scene of a cunnilingus and the banning of its poster, carrying a picture of Rodin's sculpture *The Kiss*, from London's Underground ('We banned it because we find that some posters lend themselves to defacement which can embarrass other passengers', a spokesman for the Transport Commission reportedly told *The News Chronicle*) (1959a).[1] The film, which did well at the box office, was ambivalently received by the critics and most coverage focussed on its (im)moral values ('it curls a Gallic lip at the moral of *Brief Encounter*', states *The News Chronicle* [1959b], while Roy Basil in *The Star* sneers, 'how these French love l'amour'[Basil 1959]). However, in amongst the censorship debates and national stereotyping could be found several references to the work of the so-called 'French New Wave'. For David Robinson, champion of the new French cinema, *Les Amants* was 'another ripple' (Robinson 1959a); Campbell Dixon describes the twenty-seven-year-old Malle as 'teetering on the crest' of the *nouvelle vague* (Dixon 1959); while Dilys Powell, in *The Sunday Times*, is a little less ambivalent when she states that this is a film 'of exceptional interest, belonging to the New Wave' (Powell 1959).

Interestingly, Powell adds that this is the third time that she has seen the film, following the LFF screening and a viewing in Paris seven months earlier. When the film appeared in London's West End one year later, it was in a rather different context. For by this time, word of the nouvelle vague had begun to spread. The screenings of *Le Beau Serge* and *Les Mistons* had been followed up in the Winter 1958/59 issue of *Sight and Sound*. As Nowell-Smith points out, this issue was practically dedicated to the New Wave. It contained a tribute to André Bazin, who had died in November, by Louis Marcorelles, and an interview by Bazin with Jean Renoir and Roberto Rossellini. Separately, but in the same issue, Marcorelles reported from Paris on the making of Jacques Rivette's *Paris Nous Appartient*, on the fact that Chabrol had made *Le Beau Serge*, that Truffaut was shooting *Les 400 Coups*, and that Resnais was in Japan shooting *Hiroshima Mon Amour* (Nowell-Smith 2010: 1,190).

Le Beau Serge and *Les Cousins* were released in Paris more or less simultaneously, in February and March 1959 respectively, a fact mentioned by several foreign film correspondents but which received scant attention otherwise in the British press. Then in May 1959 *Les 400 Coups*, *Hiroshima Mon Amour* and *Orfeu Negro* debuted at the Cannes Film Festival, leading *The Daily Worker*'s Special Correspondent to declare that, 'The French cinema today seems to be a leading force not only in this festival but in Western Europe generally. Neo-realism, dead now in Italy, has been reborn in France' (*Daily Worker* 1959). It would be almost another year before these films would appear in commercial U.K. cinemas, but already they were being heralded by the British trade press as the first splash of what would be termed the *nouvelle vague* – *Sight and Sound* and *Films and Filming* had both used the term several times before *Les 400 Coups* opened

13. A Curzon poster for Marcel Camus' *Orfeu Negro*, which arrived on British shores already garlanded with prizes.
Image courtesy of the BFI stills department.

the Cork Film Festival on 23 September 1959 (where it was shown under the title *Up to Some Mischief*).

Accompanied by an appearance from the non-English-speaking Jean-Pierre Léaud, the film's première at the Savoy was described by *The Irish Press* (1959) as 'gay', and Léaud as 'the essence of Gallic aplomb'; 'the French programme got a delighted reception from a captivated audience', *The Dublin Evening Press* meanwhile reported (1959). It was however during the film's gala screening at the LFF in October 1959 (along with *Orfeu Negro* and Georges Franju's *La Tête Contre Les Murs*) that the special status of French cinema in Britain was confirmed. Attended by Jacques Flaud, the director general of the CNC, Jean Chauvel, the French Ambassador to London, and Truffaut himself, the evening of 25 October saw an honorary award made to the French cinema industry, as 'the country which has given its young directors the most possibilities to create great cinema, and which has been rewarded by a body of films of an exceptional maturity' (*Libération* 1959). The award was presented, ironically enough, by *Brief Encounter* star Celia Johnson, who declared that: 'the great classics of the French cinema remain in our memories; this new generation of directors seem capable of repeating their success. They have undeniable talents, and their films have taken festivals across the globe by storm' (*Les Echos* 1959). The French press trumpeted this success, citing M. Jean Néry's announcement (Unifrance's official representative in Great Britain) that:

> The success that new French films are seeing with British distributors and audiences is highly significant. The interest surrounding the films of Truffaut, Franju and Camus films in London is indicative of a slow, but definite, evolution in British tastes. The New Wave films have definitely made ripples here.
> (*Nice-Matin* 1959, authors' translation)

By the time of *Les 400 Coups*' British première, Chabrol's *Les Cousins* had already played for two weeks in September at the Curzon. The film was well received in the British press, who praised the 'young Frenchman' Chabrol for his part in 'a movement away from what might be called the Americanisation of the French Cinema, when slickness was all and films were concerned with types rather than human beings, back to the cinema of the young Clair, Carné and Renoir, when all that really mattered was the interplay of personalities and ideas' (Hollingworth 1959). For the most part though these writers did not use the term 'New Wave'; the exception being Hollis Alpert (1959), in *The Saturday Review* (who gives Chabrol's name alongside Truffaut, Camus, Malle and Edouard Molinaro as the constituents of a 'group of new and often young filmmakers who in the past eighteen months have made several striking films'). However, four months later, when *Les 400 Coups* opened commercially at the Curzon in March 1960, the British press apparently felt duty bound to provide their readers with some explanation of the film's provenance and what exactly this New Wave might consist of. *The Guardian* informed its readers that the 'La Nouvelle Vague' was 'indeterminate', but 'on the whole, an agitation among the young', 'essentially dedicated to realism', and 'rebellious' (1960). Across the range of publications, *Les 400 Coups* received unilateral praise,[2] and Truffaut was heralded as the most promising of the young ginger group, the great white hope of a national industry whose golden age had previously been perceived by some to be long past. As Campbell Dixon, echoing Hollingworth's earlier praise of Chabrol's film, puts it: 'If he continues to develop, this young man may play a great part in restoring the prestige the French screen has lost since the triumphs of Clair and Carné, Clouzot and Clément' (Dixon 1960). Even *Playboy* magazine saw fit to review the film, describing it as 'the best foreign film of 1959' (*Playboy* 1960).

The acclaim was compounded by the fact, heavily underlined in the film's publicity material, that it had already won the New York Critics' prize, the best foreign film Oscar and the best director award at Cannes in

14. A UK poster for François Truffaut's *Les 400 Coups*, distributed by Kenneth Rive's Gala.
Image courtesy of the BFI stills department.

1959. Across the Curzon's poster, featuring the infamous final freeze-frame of Jean-Pierre Léaud, these awards were emblazoned in a font almost as large as the title itself. (A later Gala release of the film abbreviated this to the simple phrase 'award winning' above the title; Truffaut's name, once almost unknown, now taking prominent status.) The prominence of Cannes in particular points to the increasing prestige of the French award in film marketing; as *The Daily Record* notes, by this point, a prize from this particular festival would give a film 'a head start with the intellectuals', making it 'a back marker with the commercial cinema circuits' (1960).

Distribution

While the festival hype played a significant role in the marketing of *Les 400 Coups*, this was not the case for Gala's release of *Hiroshima Mon Amour*: so as not to spoil its release, the distributors had deliberately withheld the film from the 1959 London Film Festival. Its British première therefore took place at its first commercial screening on 8 January 1960 and, to celebrate the event, Gala renamed one of their cinemas, previously the Roxy Westbourne Grove, as the International Film Theatre.

According to Geoffrey Nowell-Smith, this was something of a significant event because up to then Gala could not really count as a prestigious distributor/exhibitor (Nowell-Smith 2010: 120). Nowell-Smith claims that at the beginning of the decade, the company owned six cinemas in London showing mainly Continental films, but that 'Continental' in this context meant exploitation, since most of the films shown were soft-core films which the British censor had allowed in with an X certificate and which had more sex content than was allowed in British or American films (120). At this juncture, he states, the exhibition of 'serious' foreign films fell, for the most part, to the same three prestige cinemas that had dominated the scene for the past two decades: the Academy, the Curzon and the Paris Pullman in Chelsea. Nowell-Smith states that the only two other independent West End distributor/exhibitors were the Classic chain (eight cinemas in central London and the suburbs), which did not do new releases; and the two Cameos – the Cameo Royal in Charing Cross Road and the Cameo-Poly in Regent Street, on the site of the London Polytechnic where the first Lumière shows took place in Britain in 1896 – which were also on the art/sex boundary. However, he fails to take into account that, following the series of merger agreements that took place in 1953 and 1954 (detailed in the previous chapter), Kenneth Rive's Gala group had joined forces with Sir Albert Clavering's Cameo-Poly group under the inspired title of Gala-Cameo-Poly distributors in the second half of the 1950s, a 'tie-up' (Baker 1964: 49) which continued into the 1960s and put them in a very prominent position in terms of foreign film exhibition. A press release issued on 16 May 1954 states that the combined group owned a total of seven cinemas in London, four of which were first-run houses in the West End; in 1964 Rive gives the figure as eleven (Baker 1964: 49). Gala, moreover, had agreements with Columbia to handle all their foreign-language films in Britain (Baker 1964: 64), and with the Jacey chain of cinemas (notorious for its predilection for X-rated foreign fare) to show all their continental pictures at Jaceys in the provinces (*Today's Cinema* 1953, 1954).

Be that as it may, in 1960 most of the serious business in the field was still done by a small handful of firms, many of which operated a policy of vertical integration: the Academy had Studio One, their distribution arm; the Curzon had United Artists, while the Paris Pullman was closely allied with Contemporary Films (and, indeed, in 1967 Charles Cooper, Head of Contemporary, would, with ex-BFI head James Quinn and Ralph Stephenson, take over the cinema as an outlet for Contemporary's product – Summers 1975: 12–13). In addition there were distributors Connoisseur films, founded in 1952 by William Pallanca, formerly of Films de France and the Academy Cinema, with whom he maintained close links and who provided a showcase for the majority of Connoisseur's releases (NFT Programmes 1977).

So there may be some truth to Nowell-Smith's claim that Gala's première of *Hiroshima Mon Amour* at the grandly renamed International Film Theatre was not only the occasion of the arrival of the *nouvelle vague* on British commercial screens but an inaugural moment for the 1960s art-film culture as a whole. Yet he might not only be overstating both the significance of this moment and its impact, but also overlooking its source. For while Gala do indeed emerge as the most prolific distributors of French films in Britain during the 1960s (distributing a total of seventy-eight French films for commercial release, as opposed to Connoisseur's fifty-six and Contemporary's forty-two, the two next most prolific),[3] this may be attributable primarily to the agreements struck with Cameo-Poly and then, in April 1960, with Ingram Fraser's ailing Films de France. This agreement saw Gala undertake to handle the physical distribution of all of Films de France product henceforth, offering the company a much wider distribution pattern, and Gala a substantial list of top continental successes, including *The Game of Love* and *La Main Chaude* (*Kine Weekly* 1960).

As for the sex/art binary discussed in the previous chapter, a quick survey of Gala's marketing campaign for *Hiroshima* suggests they might not have moved as far away from their existing reputation as exhibitors of risqué French film as supposed. Featuring a prostrate Emmanuelle Riva, eyes closed, her body sheltered by the broad, bare back of her lover, whose shoulders she clasps tightly, the image is framed at the top by the film's title, in flaming lettering, and below by an equally incendiary 'X'. At the lower corners of the rectangular poster are two taglines: on the right, 'A woman's hand caresses, strokes and claws a masculine shoulder . . .'; on the left: 'To be able to live one must forget . . . HIROSHIMA, the atomic bomb, this love and that'. A subsequent promotional spread, issued to regional cinemas that rented the print from Gala's distribution arm, featured only the text: 'THE FILM THAT TOOK LONDON BY STORM!' laid over a collage of reviews from the national papers, the most prominent headlines amongst which read: 'Guilty love in the East and West', 'Brief Encounter Japanese Style' and 'Lovers in Hiroshima'. The press release, meanwhile, describes it as 'a story of an adult love'. The focus, it would appear, was placed on amour, rather than Hiroshima. In a nod, too, to more commercial audiences, while the film was for the most part shown with subtitles, British actress Moira Lister was hired to give the early, voice-over commentary to the film in English.[4]

Indeed, how far Gala ever really intended to change tack is debatable. In the same month as *Hiroshima* premièred at the International Film Theatre, Alexandre Astruc's X-rated Maupassant adaptation *Une Vie* opened at the Gala Royal, billed as 'A Study in Sexual Betrayal' and with its publicity offering a remarkably familiar image of a prone woman naked, her lover's wide shoulders sparing her modesty.[5] Gala would subsequently go on to have moderate success with two more X-rated French films – *Les Liaisons Dangereuses* and *Le Repos du Guerrier* – in 1962 and 1963 respectively: the former, whose literary reputation precedes it, had been the subject of a notorious three-year battle with the French censors; the latter, a Brigitte Bardot vehicle whose title translates as 'The Warrior's Rest', Rive saw fit to name *Love on A Pillow* until the censor insisted he revert to the literal sense if he wanted the film to be passed. Neither could be described as a *nouvelle vague* film; both, according to the British press at least, fell firmly on the sex side of the sex/art border; and at least one of them, *Le Repos du Guerrier*, was shown principally in a dubbed print on the National, Rank's 'third' circuit' (Baker 1964: 46). For his part, Rive was unrepentant. Responding to an article in *The Daily Cinema* critiquing his advertising methods, he stated that:

> I have never made a pretence about what I stand for . . . I hope I'm a showman and my object is to fill cinemas, to the benefit of my co-directors and shareholders and also those of the companies with whom I deal, and I find I never have complaints at this end of the operation.
> [. . .]
> Let us get things in their right perspective – I would be more than pleased to show only films on their artistic merit and my company can certainly never be condemned for not having tried this.
> [. . .]
> Strange as it may seem, I intend to carry on selling films in a manner that fills the cinemas, when I am wrong the public will let me know, if they want 'True Heart Susie' I will most happy to oblige, but until then I'll use every trick of the showman to bring them to that little window which is my only guide to whether I'm right or wrong.
>
> (Rive 1960)

Cult Film

The Gala-Cameo-Poly group did however score one huge hit with a *nouvelle vague* film (of sorts) whose appeal was based purely on its intellectual and artistic challenges. Distributed by its subsidiary, Compton-Cameo, Alain Resnais' second film to arrive in Britain, *L'Année Dernière à Marienbad*, was marketed in a remarkably different manner to *Hiroshima*. The posters that Compton-Cameo produced for this film featured highly stylised, avant-garde graphics; there were no stills or images of the players, and the actors' names were absent in favour of the film-makers'. The comments of the French press featured heavily in the film's marketing campaign – an unusual move at the time for distributors of foreign film, who preferred to rely on festival reviews from recognisable outlets amongst the British and North American press. As for festivals themselves, a list of prizes was issued to newspapers featuring no mention of Cannes or the Oscars, rather the Golden Lion (Venice), International Critics Prize (Mexico) and the yet more esoteric Prix Méliès (Association of French Cinema and Television Critics).

The pressnotes meanwhile deviated from the norm in crediting not only director Resnais with the film's authorship, but also the screenwriter, Alain Robbe-Grillet, a celebrated French novelist. Indeed, Robbe-Grillet's contribution played a pivotal part in the film's promotion and reception. In tandem with the film, the working film script (or ciné-roman) was released by John Calder Publishers, with the tagline 'Now that you have seen the film, you will want to read the film novel'. (The same company also released hasty translations of three novels by Robbe-Grillet, *The Voyeur*, *Jealousy*, and *The Erasers* [1962a, 1962b, 1962c] in order to capitalise on Robbe-Grillet's sudden renown amongst British intellectuals.) Across a range of publications, joint interviews with Resnais and Robbe-Grillet were published, either on the basis of original material or as rehashes of pieces that had originally appeared in the French press. Much mention was made in the press of the film's literary connections and overtones. As David Robinson puts it in his review of the film for *The Financial Times*:

> The authors of *L'Année Dernière à Marienbad* have scarcely ceased to write, explicitly and persuasively, about their film – in articles and interviews, in the published scenario (already available in English!) and in the peculiar little leaflet which was hastily and nervously prepared to forearm the audience at the Venice Festival, where the film won the Golden Lion. The English version at the Cameo-Poly adds yet another gloss in an oddly-conceived opening title, which begins: 'This film may surprise you . . .' and which is simultaneously read aloud by a pedagogical voice for the benefit of illiterate aficionados of the Nouvelle Vague.
>
> (Robinson 1962)

The Times describes the film as 'an alliance between nouveau roman and nouvelle vague' (1962); *The Daily Telegraph*, in an extended piece considering the relationship between the film on the page and on the screen, describes it as 'an essentially literary achievement' (Gibbs 1962a). *The Listener*'s March edition meanwhile devoted not one but two articles to the film: a discussion by critic Eric Rhode on Robbe-Grillet's career and aims (Rhode 1962), and an analysis of the film in relation to various literary traditions, from the French symbolist poets to Plato to Shakespeare (Millar 1962). For Gavin Millar, the author of this last piece, the film's interest 'does not lie solely in its director, although he is one of the most distinguished of the "New Wave" of French film-directors, but also – perhaps principally – in the fact that the scenario is by Alain Robbe-Grillet, a leading figure in the new French school of "anti-novelists"' (Millar 1962).

Millar continues to comment that: 'It has even been suggested that M. Resnais and M. Robbe-Grillet are not entirely agreed on the meaning of their joint effort, and that it has indeed no single meaning at all' (Millar 1962). Here is where Robbe-Grillet's authorial status really came into its own, in terms of popular reception at least – that is, in terms of the significant fuel it added to the raging debate about what *Marienbad* really 'meant'. In fact, even before its release in February *Marienbad* had prompted seemingly endless columns of critical speculation and debate. In a two-page centrespread published in the *Observer Review* in January 1962, entitled 'Masterpiece or Insoluble Riddle', John Weightman describes the film as 'the event of the season' in Paris:

> It is still showing to full houses at three cinemas and has just been the subject of a two-page discussion in *Le Monde*. The *Canard Enchaîné* has used the theme for an end-of-the-year skit on 1961 in Gaullist France. The film has also rated in addition to innumerable shorter articles, a 6,000 word study in Sartre's review, *Le Temps Moderne* [. . .] Some say people claim that it is the most intelligent film ever made; others say it is the most tedious. [. . .] At least ten different interpretations of the film have been put forward.
>
> (Weightman 1962)

The Guardian's film critic meanwhile writes that 'It has not really taken [*Marienbad*] long to reach a commercial cinema in London, but it seems a long time because, in the five months since this puzzle picture first saw the light of day at the last Venice Film Festival, words enough to fill volumes have been spent on it' (*Guardian* 1962).

The use of the phrase 'puzzle picture' is particularly telling. For in many ways, *Marienbad*, along with Jacques Rivette's *Paris Nous Appartient*, released by Contemporary Films at the Paris-Pullman in July of the same year, and Nico Papatakis' *Les Abysses*, released by Gala in 1963, inaugurates a pair of tropes that have long since been associated with French film in Britain. 'Puzzle films' or 'problem pictures' on the one hand, 'vogue films' and 'cult pictures' on the other, those open-ended narrative films which demand watching and rewatching, interpretation and reinterpretation, have appeared and reappeared throughout the history of French cinema in the U.K. – indeed one could trace a direct line from *Marienbad* to Austrian director Michael Haneke's French-language *Caché*, which like its predecessor broke out of the art houses and into the circuit cinemas on the basis of the acres of column inches devoted to elucidating its mysteries. It is in fact a discussion of *Paris Nous Appartient* in the British magazine *Sight and Sound* that sees one of the first uses of the term 'cult film' (Arkadin 1962: 189). Although it never gained a circuit release, the film, popular with students, artists and intellectuals – the very figures that it depicts – became one of the sleeper hits of 1962, playing for over eighteen months at U.K. cinemas across the country, despite its opaque narrative, and was re-released in 1966. A quick flick through the papers of the time reveals a huge amount of press coverage dedicated to analysing, describing, explaining, eulogising, declaiming and debunking these films. And the myriad theories spilled off the page and onto the screen, as the BBC devoted several episodes of its programme, *The Critics*, to exploring the enigmatic film (including Derek Prouse on *Marienbad* in November 1961; Gabriel Pearson on *Paris Nous Appartient*, August 1962; and Edgar Anstey on *Muriel*).

Such films moreover have a tendency to split audiences and critics into those who see them as artistic masterpieces, and those others who claim they are the pinnacles of pretentiousness. The division is neatly captured by Isabel Quigley in the *Spectator*, writing at the time of *Marienbad*'s release:

> Response to *L'Année dernière à Marienbad* seems to me mostly a matter of temperament, not aesthetics. You are the sort of person this thing appeals to or you aren't. You accept the idea of making a work of art that has no definable meaning, or rather is self-confessedly ambiguous and might mean anything at all, the joint authors of which don't agree on what, at a particular moment, they are saying, or you don't.
>
> Me, I see that I'm not and I don't. I have brooded over what seems to me this painstaking and pretty piece only to find it a tease and a nonsense; in fact, something of a monstrous legpull (which for all I know it may be).
>
> (Quigley 1962)

It is noteworthy that Quigley proves the exception to a general trend for the broadsheets and cultural magazines (*The Listener*, *The Spectator*, *The New Statesman*, for example) to treat the film seriously, and for the red-tops to scoff at it as the cinematic version of the Emperor's New Clothes. Quentin Crewe, in *The Daily Mail*, dismisses it as 'the most highly specialised form of boredom' (Crewe 1962); Ernest Betts, in *The People*, asks whether it isn't 'the biggest spoof ever put over by the French cinema?' (Betts 1962); and Paul Dehn of *The Daily Herald*, perhaps lingering under the influence of *La Jument Verte*, ingeniously describes it as a 'pretentious' and 'banal' update on the French bedroom farce, 'which has been thriving on this sort of 'Haven't I met you somewhere before' flummery for nearly a century' (Dehn 1962).

A Very Long Wait

Below is an extract from Dilys Powell's Marienbad Diary, published in the *Sunday Times* on 25 February 1962, reproduced in its entirety since it powerfully evokes the sense of anticipation surrounding the arrival of *Marienbad* on British shores.

> **1961: September.** Read reports from Venice Festival of enigmatic new film, directed by Alain Resnais from script by Alain Robbe-Grillet, which makes '*Hiroshima, Mon Amour*', look old-world if not winsome. Criteria of film-making overthrown, everyone in an uproar, and it wins the Grand Prix.
> **October.** Embark on a preparatory course of Robbe-Grillet. Sit up nightly over '*La Jalousie*'. Transfixed. Why didn't somebody tell me?
> **November.** Watch television programme introduced by Derek Prouse and including flashes from enigmatic new film, directed by etc. When is the damn thing coming to London?
> **December.** Sudden appearance *passim* of articles about enigmatic new film etc. Determined to preserve element of surprise so don't read articles, but am half demented with expectation. Shall I nip over to Paris where film is running?
> **Christmas.** Harold Hobson, back from one of his Paris forays, presents me with Robbe Grillet's published script of enigmatic new etc. After battle with curiosity stick to decision not to read before seeing film.
> **1962: January 1.** Everybody still writing articles enigmatic etc. Pallid with frustration.
> **January 25.** Admitted to private preview. Hallelujah, it's superb.
>
> (Powell 1962)

As Geoffrey Nowell-Smith has pointed out, the films associated with the *nouvelle vague* tended to come to Britain with a six- to eighteen-month delay (Nowell-Smith 2010: 118). The impact of the delay wasn't always negative: often a long-building sense of anticipation surrounded many of these films, a sense nicely captured by Dilys Powell's account of waiting for *Marienbad*. In the case of that film, the advance hype worked to its advantage: *Marienbad* was one of the biggest *nouvelle vague* hits in the U.K. and brought substantial box-office returns for Compton-Cameo. For other films, however, the delay between their French releases and their British ones could have a far less happy effect.

Writing in 1964, Arkadin speculates over the various causes of such delays: sometimes, he states, the reasons were purely financial, with producer and potential British distributor unable to agree on a possible advance guarantee; sometimes it would simply be a question of taste; there may potentially be severe censorship issues to be confronted; or sometimes the film may have been the property of a major Hollywood company which had a financial stake in it and no longer knew what to do with it – as was the case with Chabrol's *Landru* and the portfolio film *L'Amour à Vingt ans*, both of which were bought up by Twentieth Century Fox to tide them over a dearth of product (Arkadin 1964: 90). When Arkadin asked the three largest British distributors of continental product, William Pallanca of Connoisseur, Charles Cooper of Contemporary Films and Kenneth Rive of Gala about these time delays, their responses suggested they were generally harmful to the film's prospects. Of his usual practice of waiting two or three years for a film's price to drop if he deemed it unreasonably high, Cooper stated that 'by that time you often don't want to buy the film anyway, it's not in the news any more, people want newer films', pointing to Le Petit Soldat (made in 1960; released in 1963),[6] as an example of a contemporary product that had suffered in this way (Arkadin 1964: 90).[7]

Another of Godard's films, *A Bout de Souffle*, the film that for many marked only the beginning of the *nouvelle vague*'s arrival on British shores, offers another surprising example of the deleterious effects of the long wait for its arrival. By the time it opened at the Academy in early July 1961, *Sight and Sound* had already published an article by Jacques Siclier in which he declared the *nouvelle vague* over and done with, a comment reiterated in David Robinson's review of the film, in which he states that 'the nouvelle vague has been and gone, even though it has left 'a permanent impression' (Robinson 1961). Isabel Quigley gives perhaps the most well-rounded portrait of the ambivalence surrounding *A Bout de Souffle* writing in *The Guardian* on 8 July:

> For once a cinema's advertisement does not exaggerate. The Academy advertises Jean-Luc Godard's *A Bout de Souffle* as 'the most eagerly awaited new film of the nouvelle vague', and although 'new' is hardly accurate (the film is two years old and one of those that gave the New Wave its original impetus and excitement), certainly the film that *Sight and Sound* called 'the group's intellectual manifesto' is one that anyone with an interest in what the cinema is up to has been waiting to see. Few films have been so widely discussed before their public showing; and, as it turns out, few can ever have seemed such obvious prototypes or have embodied so many attitudes and techniques that have since been imitated, exaggerated, caricatured and (therefore) weakened, even made absurd.
>
> (Quigley 1961a)

Writing elsewhere, Quigley states that: 'A bewildering amount of the French New Wave is known to homebound filmgoers only by hearsay. About the movement so much has been written, rumoured, argued, gossiped and shouted from the rooftops (as if it were a single wave of talent, instead of individual directors of very different capacity) that one feels overfamiliar, wary' (Quigley 1961b).[8]

A Bout de Souffle was thus critically hamstrung by a double problem: on the one hand, it could not fail to disappoint given the rapturous praise it had been receiving in the British press for nearly two years; on the other, while the more celebrated film was awaiting release, a plethora of second films and second-rate imitations had filled the cinemas, rendering what had once appeared so fresh and original to Paris audiences and festival attendees somewhat over-familiar and even clichéd. Between 1959 and

1960 some sixty-seven directors had found their opportunities to make their first feature films (Robinson 1961), many of which had already made their way over to Britain. Other New Wave directors such as Truffaut and Chabrol had already shown second, third and even fourth features in the U.K. (*Tirez sur la Pianiste / Les Bonnes Femmes*) before Godard's first film arrived. Added to this was the fact that several older directors, such as Marcel Camus, were producing works that were now being bracketed, rightly or wrongly, within the *nouvelle vague* category. Marcel Carné's *Les Tricheurs*, given a sexed-up English title by Gala (*Youthful Sinners*) and released at the Cinephone in January 1961, three years after it won the *Grand Prix du Cinéma* and two years after Truffaut's debut first surfaced in the U.K., was just such a film – although it, too, was judged by the standards of the *nouvelle vague* and found wanting. 'It is more polished, more assured, and more portentous than the films of the Jeune Cinéma Francais', writes the programmer of the Queen's University Belfast Film Society, 'but they are speaking with the authority of youth' (Queen's University of Belfast Film Society 1961). Isabel Quigley comments that 'anyone who goes to the cinema these days will know exactly what's coming' and *The Times* sees it as 'old-fashioned melodrama with a top-dressing of fashionable reference' (Quigley 1961c). Dilys Powell was meanwhile prompted to write that 'in the last year or two so much has happened in the cinema [. . .] almost unawares one begins to expect a less precisely manipulated shape to the tale on the screen,' before concluding, presciently, that 'I fancy that presently we shall recognise a good deal of New Wavery as merely fashionable' (Powell 1961).

The Backlash

As the rest of the decade rolled out Powell was, to some extent at least, proved correct. While films from the likes of Truffaut, Chabrol, Godard and Malle continued to prove reliable draws at the art-house cinemas, the critics soon fell out of love with the *nouvelle vague*. Even as early as the time of Marienbad's release, *Time and Tide*'s critic John Ardagh was moved to write that Resnais had 'come a bit of a cropper', proclaiming that 'One aspect of the French so-called nouvelle vague is this failure of many of its best directors to sustain their early promise'. Chabrol, he claims, has 'collapsed'; Truffaut and Malle 'are not doing so well' (Ardagh 1961). While few would have agreed with his comments on *Marienbad*, the critics were nodding along in agreement by the time Resnais' subsequent film, *Muriel*, was given a first run at the Cameo-Poly in March 1964. Despite having won the British Film Institute's prize for the most original and imaginative film first shown at the NFT, the Sutherland Trophy, in 1963, *Muriel* was deemed a failure by its harshest critics, and simply a poor imitation of his earlier films by the kinder ones. Alexander Walker commended it only 'to morbid filmgoers who wish to see a talent seemingly in the last stages of decomposition' (Walker 1964).

Meanwhile, even Truffaut's second film, *Tirez sur la Pianiste*, released as early as 1960, had received lukewarm reviews ('not quite in the same class as his first', wrote David Robinson [1960]), and while the Curzon had run *Jules et Jim* for a 'phenomenal length of time' later films such as *La Peau Douce* and *Fahrenheit 451* failed to see similar success. By the time that *La Mariée était en noir* appeared at the Curzon in the August 1968, critics were united in their disapprobation. Alexander Walker described the film as 'one of the year's major disappointments' (Walker 1968); Robin Turner, in *The Sunday Express*, commented that it was 'so commercial that it is surprising that it was not considered worthwhile to dub in English dialogue instead of the sub-titles' (Turner 1968); and John Russell Taylor, in *The Times*, that, 'It is a lightweight film with no pretensions to doing anything but entertain, which it does very well, but in a safe, old-fashioned way' (Russell Taylor 1968). He sums up the sentiments of many when he writes, 'From anyone else it would be delightful, from Truffaut it is really not good enough' (Russell Taylor 1968).

Looking back to debates of the 1950s, and to Lindsay Anderson's heralding of these new young directors, we might well ask whether it was inevitable that Truffaut would come under criticism for turning his hand to more mainstream fare. And perhaps there is some truth in their accusations. But the British fate of the other directors associated with the *nouvelle vague* was similarly iniquitous. Louis Malle's *Vie Privée*, starring the usually reliable box-office draw of Brigitte Bardot, 'bombed' when it was released in 1962 in a dubbed version by MGM, causing *Sight and Sound*'s Arkadin to remark that neither stars nor directors were any longer a guarantee of success when it came to continental films (Arkadin 1963/64: 29). Godard's *Vivre sa Vie*, shown at the Academy at the end of 1962, was seen by John Coleman of the *New Statesman* as evidence that 'M. Godard seems dreadfully to have lost his way' (Coleman 1962) and by *The Daily Telegraph* as 'pretentious' (Gibbs 1962b) – a sentiment reiterated by *The Daily Worker*'s Nina Hibbin (1962) who adds 'phoney and abysmally dull' into the mix, and by Arthur Dent, in the *Sunday Telegraph* (Dent 1962) who notes that it is, moreover, 'nauseating' and 'ludicrous'. *Une Femme mariée* was more warmly received yet struggled at the Cameo-Royal as it had done in France. This despite a long wait while the well-documented controversy with the French censors who insisted on changing the original title from *La Femme mariée*, with the implied generalisation of the title, raged (the change, incidentally, was retained in the British translation) (Robinson 1965).

While the charges levelled at Truffaut – fairly or otherwise – have some foundation in the films themselves (it is widely acknowledged that

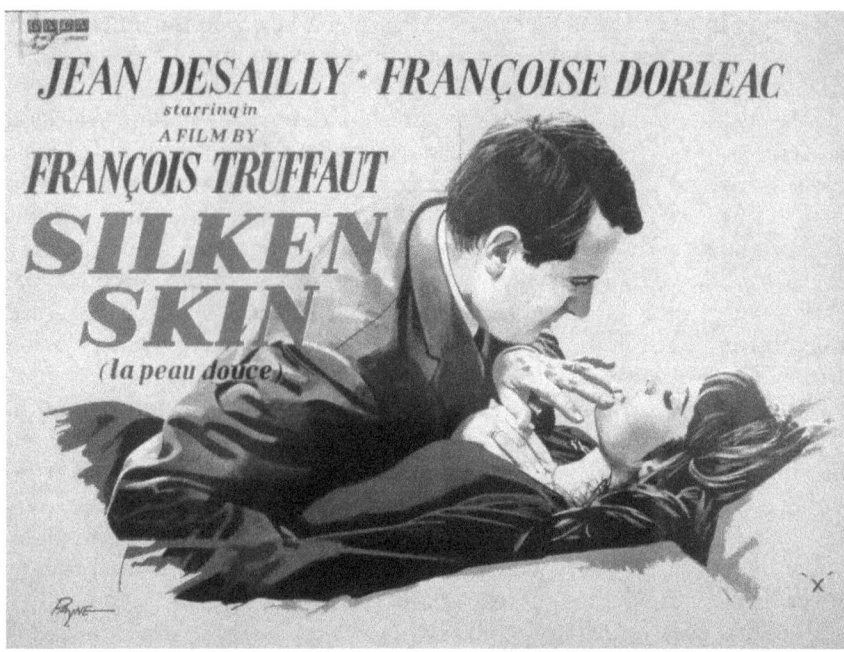

15. A UK poster for Truffaut's 1964 *La Peau douce*. The film was deemed a critical failure by the British Press, despite a typically racy advertising campaign. Image courtesy of the BFI stills department.

Truffaut's films grew more and more to resemble the quality French films which he had once criticised), neither of Godard's later films can justifiably be described as more 'old-fashioned', 'lightweight' or 'simple entertainment'. Far from it. And yet the association with the commercial is once more used to condemn him. Peter Graham, of *Films and Filming*, spat that Godard was a 'spent force', the *nouvelle vague* nothing more than a 'commercial ploy', and a failed one at that (Graham 1963). It's clear that for critics of the New Wave, commercialism was a dirty word; what's less clear is what exactly the rationale behind this is. In the case of *La Mariée était en noir*, it seems that the film itself is not 'bad'; but it is a crowd pleaser, and therefore is disappointing from a New Wave director such as Truffaut, who should be making more esoteric, artistic fare. Godard's later works, on the other hand, were not box-office hits, but they were disappointing films and this disappointment is expressed through a blanket dismissal of the *nouvelle vague* banner as a disingenuous scam to incite more interest in the films than they perhaps deserved. The paradox that pertained in the 1950s prevailed: French films should be artistic masterpieces and therefore seen by the many, but French films should not have commercial interests at heart, for this is not the artist's way.

A Thriving Film Culture?

For Penelope Houston, the dubious fortunes of the *nouvelle vague* directors were endemic to British film culture during the period. She writes that:

> There has never been a larger, more wide-awake, or more interested public for the kind of film which only a few years ago would have seemed desperately specialised. The distributors who acquired *l'Avventura* or *L'Année dernière à Marienbad* or *Shadows* knew what they were about: yesterday's defiant risk becomes today's cocktail-party talking point. This cinema has become fashionable – sometimes to an extent dangerous for its own good. Directors' reputations go up and down as rapidly as speculative shares. Buy blue-chip Bergmans in 1959 and Antonionis in 1961; watch the continental festivals for the next hot tip, the next director whose work will be talked up, written up, photographed for the glossies, before most people have even got around to seeing it for themselves. Film magazines all over the world weigh in with articles which uncover the same new trends at the same time: when the trends turn out to be not quite what was expected, the disillusionment comes as abruptly as the discovery. New directors are constantly being told that they are betraying a promise they never knew they had shown: behind them, the next New Wave is already thundering up the beach. In this atmosphere, which makes for liveliness if not for stability, the queues swing over from the Odeons to the specialised cinemas, the Hollywood talents are scattered to the winds of Europe, and Hollywood itself no longer looks like the capital of cinema, but the Park Avenue of the American television industry.
>
> (Houston, 1959/60: 13–14)

Houston recounts how, in the immediate post-war years, specialised cinemas were few in number and relatively regular in their clientele. By the 1960s, she claims, they were abundant and, 'the number of people who would never think of going to see a film in a foreign language falls away every year' (14). The reason for these shifts in attendance is perhaps, Houston speculates, not only that by the early 1960s specialised film was more readily accessible than ever before, but also that attitudes to cinema themselves had shifted. That is, that with a whole generation now taking colour, sound, and film language as a whole for granted, the old battles between art and industry, creativity and commerce, silence and sound, were abandoned, and spectators began to seek novelty elsewhere – namely (although Houston does not make this explicit), in the formal experimentation of the European film (14–15), which would account for the huge box-office success of films such as *Marienbad*, which, in addition to having played ten different cinemas in London, played some thirty-six other commercial, and thirty-one non-commercial venues across the country, reaching such outposts as Holt in Norfolk and Broughty Ferry in Scotland (*Sight and Sound* 1964a: 107).

But how was this apparent growth in the market for continental films reflected in the exhibition and distribution sectors? It is perhaps telling that of the 131 'foreign' films registered with the Board of Trade in 1962 (as opposed to seventy-one British and 117 American), only eight were given a general release by the circuits (six by Rank, two by ABC) (Baker 1964: 41). On the other hand the addition of smaller screens at the Academy and the National Film Theatre enabled a wider range of more esoteric films to be shown in London (Baker 1964: 41); and even foreign investors started looking to open showcase cinemas: a series of correspondences between Louis Malle's Nouvelles Editions de Films and Contemporary's Charles Cooper reveals a plan to join forces for the opening of another art cinema in London's Mayfair area, although in the end the plan seems to have come to naught (Bifi Malle Archive).

Gala meanwhile embarked upon what *Sight and Sound* referred to as both 'a gesture of faith' and an 'unusually ingenious venture in film marketing' – the operation of one of their cinemas for two days a week as a private members club (*Sight and Sound* 1960a: 55). This proved popular indeed – within a week, the club was reported to have acquired around 2,000 members at a guinea a head. What these members were paying for was, succinctly put, a way around censorship. Since clubs were exempt from the censorship laws which applied to commercial cinemas at the time, they were able to show films banned by the censor. It was a solution to a thorny problem which suited both Gala and the BBFC Secretary of the time, John Trevelyan. Famously proud of his reputation for liberalism, Trevelyan had loosened the ban on unpunished adultery on screen for the New Wave films, with the justification that 'when you're dealing with people of quality and integrity and artists there is practically nothing they can't do because they do it for valid reasons' (Robinson 1971: 71),[9] and was in fact present at the opening screening (of *The Wild One*). Of the club's first six screenings, three were from the U.S.A., one from Spain, and two were French – *Razzia sur la Chnouf* (1955) and *La Neige était sale* (1954) – both having been heavily cut upon their original releases (*Sight and Sound* 1960a: 55).

Sight and Sound was somewhat dubious about Gala's motives, suggesting that of the six films in question, the French pair were the only ones to have cuts of any real substance to them, and pointing out that only eight or nine films were usually banned in any one year. 'If Gala wants the sensation-seekers, it no doubt knows how to find them', the editorial wryly commented (*Sight and Sound* 1960a: 55). A later article in the Summer 1960 issue of the same magazine reiterates the sentiment, reporting that uncut versions of *Mamselle Striptease* and *Femmes de Paris* were subsequently shown (so, too, was Alexandre Astruc's *Une Vie*) (*Sight and Sound* 1960b: 116), and pointing out that other areas of the West End's cultural sector had caught on fast: at least two Soho striptease clubs had founded film clubs of their own already, and there were rumoured plans for a the first all-club cinema to be opened in a Soho basement – 'where, allegedly, experiments may be made with the 'glamour' films currently enjoying a boom among home movie enthusiasts' (116). Be this at it may, the experiment was a great success for Kenneth Rive and the Gala group, with the film clubs extending to cinemas outside the West End, operated by Gala in conjunction with their exhibitors. It would continue to run well into the 1970s, when, with the clubs foundering in the light of relaxed censorship policy, Rive would perhaps naturally enough call for the removal of Trevelyan's successor, Stephen Murphy, for being too liberal.[10]

The National Film Theatre was also moving beyond the capital. In Autumn 1965 *Sight and Sound* reported on the publication of *Outside London*, a survey prepared for the British Film Institute by its former director, James Quinn, proposing the inauguration of what would come to be known as the regional film theatres (RFTs): a chain of cinemas which would eventually roll out in 1967 and which were modelled on the National Film Theatre and run by the local authorities, with full-time RFTs at Brighton, Manchester and Newcastle and part-time operations elsewhere, presenting a mixture of public and private showings. 'The most interesting fact to emerge,' writes *Sight and Sound*, is that 'the old idea of the cinema as essentially a commercial enterprise, left to sink or swim at the box-office, seems to have been quietly dying' (1965: 159). The problem now, as the magazine saw it, was a shortage of cinemas outside of London showing quality films, both old and new, English and Continental. Outside the doors of the Academy, the Curzon and the Paris-Pullman, beyond the limits of London's West End,

> the specialised cinema represents an uneasy attempt to reconcile two irreconcilables. The audience for the latest nudist film, or tour of the European striptease joints, is not the audience for Godard or Antonioni. Yet there is neither enough sensationalism nor enough quality to sustain the average cinema; and the result is an unholy alliance, a policy which results in the optimistic selling of *Une Femme Mariée* as *24 Hours in the Life of An Adulteress*, or the pretence that films like *Mondo Cane* are art as well as sensation. A potential audience is lost because it would rather go without than join the sad, raincoated queues in their forever frustrated search for screen pornography.
> (*Sight and Sound* 1965: 159)

This is a view seconded by the chairman of British Lion Films. David Kingsley offers an intriguing take on what he perceives as the on-going lack of venues for continental films, claiming that any cinema which shows specialised films has to carve an identity for itself as a specifically art-house venue. The tendency of some cinemas to hedge their bets by dabbling in the continental market was, to Kingsley's mind, a crucial error: 'An exhibitor cannot chop and change', he insists (Baker 1964: 46).[11] Neither Kingsley nor Kenneth Rive however believed there was much of an audience outside the West End for foreign-language product, with the possible exceptions of large urban areas such as Edinburgh, Birmingham or Glasgow. Basil Clavering, Managing Director of the Cameo Cinemas, foresaw another problem with any attempt to roll an art-house chain beyond London. Since West End audiences refused, in the main, to watch dubbed pictures, and parochial audiences refused subtitles, it fell to the distributor who wished to roll a film out across the whole country to produce two separate versions of a film, at great expense to themselves. Sure enough, writing from Manchester, another area that Rive singled out as rather more amenable to foreign-language product, a youthful Geoffrey Nowell-Smith was able to see 'over half the Continentals but these came in various guises' and it was only by keeping alert that he was able to catch them (Nowell-Smith 1965: 60). Even in a city such as Manchester, 'The audience for continental and rep films is not large', Nowell-Smith writes, adding that Alain Resnais' *Muriel* 'lasted a bare three days at the Cinemaphone before taking off'. Perhaps, he suggests, echoing David Kingsley's view, the audience could be increased 'if the cinemas had a more determined and go ahead policy', but as it is the two art houses available to him at the time kept their cinemas full 'with sexies and X's' (Baker 1964: 61).

Low Tide

Despite the apparent growth in audiences, despite the *nouvelle vague* and despite the success of films as diverse as *Mon Oncle* and *Marienbad*, the outlook for French film in Britain might not have been as rosy as Houston had predicted at this point. In the early months of 1964, both the French and the Italians withdrew their official film bodies from London, Unifrance's Jean Néry leaving only a secretary to operate the London office with a substantially reduced budget, which was limited to financing publicity and organising visits to Britain by French artists and technicians (Baker 1964: 41). Commenting on Unifrance's decision to pull out of the UK, *Films and Filming*'s Paris correspondent Peter Graham remarked that on the whole, 'French producers of quality films feel that the British only want sex films. There is no enthusiasm here for the British market – costs are high (dubbing, titling and so on) and very little money can be made because they are often run as second features *if* they reach the major circuits, and the "art houses" are not numerous enough to be financially rewarding' (Baker 1964: 42). François Truffaut adds to this Gallic take on the British market:

> The feeling we have in France about the British market is a pessimistic one. It seems to us that the British film industry over-protects itself and does not

favour foreign films. To put things in perspective, the films I have made have been bought for less in England than they were in Switzerland, Belgium and Canada. This seems to me normal.
[...]
The British public regards the cinema as a show based on collective reactions, like the theatre. This does not help the career of intimate films in which the spectator absolutely must feel alone vis-à-vis the film. On the other hand, this favours family films, comedies, or spectaculars. A material proof of this theory is that while all over the world the spectator is plunged into darkness, in Britain cinemas are obliged by safety regulations to remain over-lit, almost like theatres.

(Baker 1964: 45)

For *Sight and Sound* meanwhile one set of stereotypes remained: 'The X-certificate and the carry-over of an attitude that holds that seeing French films (like reading French novels in the nineteenth century) is a slightly suspect activity' (*Sight and Sound* 1965: 159).

Disillusionment with the *nouvelle vague* came quickly: even as early as November 1960, the premières of the new crop of French films at the London Film Festival were, keenly awaited as they had been, deemed a disappointment. *Moderato Cantabile*, *Tirez sur la Pianiste* and *Les Bonnes Femmes* were frankly not, according to Peter John Dyer's festival report, up to par (Dyer 1960/61: 17–18). By 1964, distributors were realising that while the usual outlets provided steady audiences for films by the likes of Truffaut, these weren't crossover hits. And even compared to the average quality film (that did not get a circuit release), they weren't particularly profitable: David Kingsley estimated £10,000 to £15,000 was the usual return; Godard's *Le Petit Soldat* took, at £6,000, about half of that, and *A Bout de Souffle* only £8,300 from the 130 British cinemas that showed it over the course of approximately two years, which was slightly less than the James Bond movie *From Russia with Love* made in one week at the one West End cinema it was playing (Baker 1964: 41). Considering that the price of a 35 mm colour print of Godard's *Pierrot Le Fou* cost Connoisseur £1,250 (Pallanca 1977: 21), and that was not including charges for transport, censorship, the costs of marketing or of translation (roughly £300 for a subtitled print, £5,000 for a dubbed print – although this could stretch up to £20,000 – Baker 1964: 49), the profits for these films were marginal, if indeed there were any at all.

In fact the biggest art-house hits of the first half of the decade came not from France at all, but from Italy: these were Leopoldo Savona and André de Toth's *I Mongoli / The Mongols*, with Jack Palance and Anita Ekberg, and Federico Fellini's *La Dolce Vita* which, for comparison, had taken over £100,000 in 1964, despite having been released in a subtitled print (Baker 1964: 41). For the critics, too, it was the Italians, rather than the French, that best exemplified the new atmosphere and attitude of the period. Thus it is with a chapter entitled 'The Italian Experience' that Penelope Houston opens her classic study of the era, *The Contemporary Cinema* (1963), and by a comparison with 'Italian aesthetic feeling allied to a simple humanism' that John Ardagh dismissed the 'Clever French Theorising' of Alain Resnais. 'Too often, the nouvelle vague is callow, derivative, pretentious. Its worst fault is a wilful frivolity in choice of subject, a turning the back on reality. [...] By contrast, the hallmark of the great contemporary Italians – Antonioni, Visconti, Fellini – is their ability to look life squarely in the face' (Ardagh 1961). If the German and Soviet cinemas overshadowed their Gallic counterpart in the 1930s, and today it is world cinema which has assumed the status of the true cinephile's choice, even in the heady days of the New Wave, French cinema was seen as second choice for the arts crowd, or at least one choice among many. And as the advertising campaign for *Hiroshima*, for example, makes clear, in order to lure audiences beyond the cognoscenti it had to rely on the same old stereotypes: sex, style and sophistication.

Hardly a surprise, then, that one of the biggest French hits of the 1960s was the Bardot–Moreau collaboration *Viva Maria!*, directed by Louis Malle but about as far away in tone and style from the two works with which he introduced himself to these shores, *Les Amants* and *L'Ascenseur au Chauffaud*, as possible. A gala screening of the film, with Malle himself in attendance, reopened the Curzon in April 1966 after a three-year period of closure for renovations to the building. It was preceded by weeks of interviews and profiles of its two sexy stars and articles on how to recreate the *Viva Maria!* look: as early as January, *The Daily Express* was advising its readers on the best hairdressers to visit for a 'Bardot-do' (McSnarry 1966); in February *The Daily Mail*'s David Lewin introduced a profile of the pair that featured, amongst other things, their vital statistics, by stating that the two women 'represent(s) all that is most intriguing in French cinema and sex' (Lewin 1966). By March one or other of the two women was on the cover of most fashion and women's magazines. On the night before the première the *Evening News* reported that the film's 'exotic costumes have set new trends in fashions and in the accessories that women wear and use, ranging from new underwear styles to lipsticks', and that one fashion writer had published no fewer than eight separate articles on the film (*Evening News* 1966).

Viva Maria! was a smash and ran for weeks, first at the Curzon and then, in a dubbed print, on the circuits. The critics, for the most part, found the film 'amusing' and 'entertaining': unfortunately these very qualities proved somewhat problematic in the context of a French film. Patrick Gibbs, in *The Daily Telegraph*, expressed delight at the Curzon's reopening but some trepidation at the choice of film: '[The reopening] will certainly help to reduce the queue of foreign films of quality awaiting a London showing. But not immediately, I would say' (Gibbs 1966).

Richard Roud, of *The Guardian*, writes that the film is 'undeniably pretty' and 'reasonably enjoyable' – 'if one forgets about Louis Malle, white hope of the French cinema' (Roud 1966). *The Times* gives a glowing review:

> Louis Malle's new film is superlative entertainment. True, it is in French (mostly) with English subtitles, and that is generally supposed to mean that what we have before us is, or ought to be, Art, with entertainment perhaps lurking in the background. But this slight linguistic accident should not blind audiences to the sheer enjoyment M. Malle's wide-screen, tuppence coloured romp has to offer.
>
> (*Times* 1966)

But after praising Bardot and Moreau's beauty at length, the reviewer concludes that in fact, any people likely to be disappointed by the film 'are those who hoped that Louis Malle might turn out to be the great serious creator in the New Wave'. That, 'it becomes increasingly clear, he is not' (*Times* 1966).

In September 2009, *Viva Maria!* appeared once more on the Curzon Mayfair's 43 × 20 foot screen, part of a series of four screenings (the other films being *L'Atalante*, *La Ronde*, and *A Room with A View*) celebrating the cinema's seventy-fifth birthday. While it marked a seminal moment in the Curzon's history, however, Malle's film was not the most successful French acquisition of the 1960s for the Wingates. This honour fell instead to another film which watered down the great promise of the New Wave with a series of chintzy images of French chic. Claude Lelouch's *Un Homme et une femme* did not draw upon its stars for its pulling power – leads Anouk Aimée and Jean-Louis Trintignant were relatively unknown in Britain; what it did do was requisition the techniques of the New Wave filmmakers and package them in an accessible and attractive format. Once more, much mention was made in the press of the elegant costuming, painterly aesthetic and windswept French countryside. Penelope Houston describes it thus:

> Some of the beach scenes echo Boudin, trapping that cool light off a pale sea; back from the beaches it's more Sunday supplement, in the not unengaging area where the advertisements and the editorial content meet. Jean-Louis Trintignant zigzags a car in exuberant circles: a Ford Mustang for the getaway people. Anouk Aimée, on her film set, peers over the collar of her sheepskin coat at a property camel. He reads *Time* and *Nouvel Observateur*; she reads those luxuriously printed French editions of comic strips. They reach agreement on a quotation from Giacometti – about saving a cat rather than a Rembrandt from a fire.'
>
> (Houston 1967)

Many of the critics were disapproving: the general consensus was that here was a case of all style and no substance. Time and again the film was compared to a slick commercial, an advertisement for love, set to what Alexander Walker refers to as 'ingeniously bland' music by Francis Lai (also responsible for the theme from *Love Story*) that 'percolates insidiously into scenes like the tranquilising melodies pumped into shoppers ears at the supermarkets' (Walker 1967). Nonetheless, there was a grudging admiration for the sheer panache of the packaging and an acknowledgement that *Un Homme et une femme* was a film that, although disposable, was likely to run at the Curzon for a very long time. After all, as *The Times* put it, 'rarely does the cinema offer such a thoroughly nice, splashy, rosy, romantic treat of a film' (*Times* 1967). Or, as Basil Clavering would have it:

> [Sometimes] I crave a French meal with their wonderful sauces and the way it is served, the atmosphere of food in a French restaurant. You cannot get that atmosphere of sophistication in an English restaurant, or in an English film. The English language is a drawback compared with the French language, which flows beautifully and evenly, even if you don't understand it. It all adds up to the sophistication of France; the food, the films, the air, roads and trees, in the south that wonderful warmth, the way people dress.
> (Baker 1964: 46)

Legacies

The predictions of box-office success were sound enough, and *Un Homme et une femme* would become a model which distributors of French cinema would continue to ape throughout the coming decade: through it, The Curzon's Roger Wingate 'learned the nice way that British audiences often fall for French movies which depict the French behaving as the Brits would like to think of them behaving' (2010). It would also, to a large extent, be the final nail in the coffin of French cinema's critical standing in Britain for quite some time. The ambivalence surrounding it amongst the cognoscenti even extended to its Grand Prix at Cannes, with John Coleman somewhat sniffily referring to it in the *New Statesman* as 'the ideal festival film', since in any case, 'you can't tell one grand prix from another these days' (Coleman 1967).

While the individual films may have faltered, the *nouvelle vague* nonetheless left a dual legacy for British film culture, in terms of both film practice and film criticism. These two concepts are linked (possibly even inseparable), firstly since, to a lesser extent than in France, film-maker and critic was often one and the same; and secondly since it is hard to tell whether many of the films described by critics as somehow *nouvelle vague*-ish are genuinely derivative, or with the terms and concepts of the *nouvelle vague* circulating so widely and frequently in British film criticism were symptomatic of a tendency to 'read into' films that which was not there.

Moreover the relationship between British film-cultural figures such as Lindsay Anderson, Richard Roud and Gavin Lambert and their French equivalents, if we can see them as such – François Truffaut, Louis Marcorelles, and Jacques Siclier, for example – is complex, and it is difficult to know to what extent these people influenced and aided one another. Anderson, who had co-ordinated the Free Cinema programmes at the NFT during the late 1950s and arranged for the first screenings of *Le Beau Serge* and *Les Mistons* as part of this series, was, like Truffaut, a critic-turned-film-maker. He had previously written widely on film for the influential *Sequence* magazine (1947–52), which he co-founded with Lambert and Karel Reisz; later he wrote for the left-wing political weekly *The New Statesman* as well as *Sight and Sound*, where in 1956 he published his notorious polemic, 'Stand Up, Stand Up', in which he attacked contemporary critical practices, in particular the pursuit of objectivity. In the *Cahiers* group, Anderson found the embodiment of exactly the practices he had been calling for. His programme notes to the Free Cinema Five speak eloquently to this discovery:

> *Cahiers du cinéma* is sometimes described as the French *Sight and Sound* – but this is true only in that it is the leading 'serious' film revue in France. There is nothing institutional about its tone; and its one indisputable quality is an obsessive passion for the cinema. [...] their general attitude towards their own cinema is best expressed by a recent comment – 'The French cinema is a British cinema that doesn't know it...'.
> [...]
> The criticism in *Cahiers* is often unreadable. But its weaknesses appear in a new light now that its writers have actually started to makes films themselves [...] if there is one quality which has always been apparent in the writing of these young men, it is vitality. And courage too. For at least these critics have shown no inclination to use their influence to insinuate themselves into a system which they despise. Their first steps in filmmaking have been as independent as their criticism. And they are extremely promising.
> (NFT programme notes 1957)

The relationship between Anderson and Truffaut certainly seems to have extended beyond the professional, to a friendship of sorts. The former had, for example, written to the latter on 9 September 1958 to congratulate him on the success of *Les Mistons*:

> My dear Truffaut,
> The screening of *Les Mistons* went well yesterday; it was very well received, and I think that the Cahiers-cineastes movement has got off to a good start in England.
>   I'm happy to hear that you are filming at the moment. Really, everything that you, and the others are making in France at the moment is brilliant. And very important. In this land of dead cinema it all seems a miracle.

I could watch *Les Mistons* over and over. It's a very beautiful film. We're waiting impatiently for whatever it is you'll give us next.

Thanks again,
Yours,
Lindsay.

(Source: Bifi Archives, Truffaut Collection)

A subsequent letter from Gavin Lambert to Truffaut, dated 15 January, assures him that *Les 400 Coups* will be well-received in London (Source: Bifi Archives, Truffaut Collection). Along with Roud, Lambert was an occasional contributor to *Cahiers*; *Sight and Sound* meanwhile printed work not only by Marcorelles and Siclier, but also Bazin, Truffaut and Chabrol. In an unpublished interview with Geoffrey Nowell-Smith and Christophe Dupin, Penelope Houston, who was editor of *Sight and Sound* at the time, recalls how 'envious' and 'admiring' of *Cahiers du Cinéma* the *Sight and Sound* staff were. 'I think [English critics] are more phlegmatic; probably more literary influenced [than French ones]. I sometimes felt that the Cahiers critics were sort of floating above the surface of the film' (Dupin and Nowell-Smith, 2007).

Comparing the writing of the time, it seems unlikely that the *Cahiers* critics had a particular stylistic influence on British critical traditions. But the *nouvelle vague* – as both a method of industrial practice and a formal conceit – echoed throughout critical writing on British cinema. It was there in the opinion pieces bemoaning the lack of a Minister for Culture with the same breadth of vision as André Malraux, whose address to the *Assemblée Nationale* on 9 November 1963, stating the need to show 'films which we know to be seminal', was quoted at length in that Winter's issue of *Sight and Sound* with the postscript: 'No wonder that French films are so much more influential creatively than our own' (*Sight and Sound* 1963/64: 23). It was there in the commonly held assumption, neatly encapsulated by Hollis Alpert, that 'In France, serious young men take movies seriously' (Alpert 1959). And it was there most of all in reviews of all kinds of British films, from Joseph Losey's Anglo-Italian *Eve* (whose starring role for Jean Moreau perhaps made the comparisons unavoidable), through Jack Clayton's *The Pumpkin Eater* to Richard Lester's *A Hard Day's Night*. Houston perhaps puts it best when she claims that:

> It is British directors who have tried most resolutely to demonstrate that anything France can do we can do better. Long after it lost any meaning it ever had, the term nouvelle vague crops up everywhere, as a standard synonym for all that is casual, inconsequential, or in the vaguest sense up-to-the minute. *A Hard Day's Night*, on these terms, becomes 'a very nouvelle vague film'. Britain can hand-hold her cameras with the best of them. And it seems on the cards that the kind of stylistic influences apparent in *Tom Jones* will make their own indirect entry into Hollywood, like a ship of the French Line calling in at

Southampton on its way to New York. Recent British film-making has assimilated a good deal from across the Channel; and when the influences actually seem to work, as in the exuberant introduction to Julie Christie in *Billy Liar*, they can refresh and lighten the whole tempo of a picture.

(Houston 1964: 167)

Conclusion

By the end of the 1960s, the *nouvelle vague* had come to be disliked: too commercial for the critics yet not commercial enough for the exhibitors, it turned out to be something of a disappointment. But that first moment of excitement left its mark on film history: on the screen and in print, the enduring understanding of the term '*nouvelle vague*' is as a benchmark for quality, freshness, novelty. It is noteworthy in this respect that by the end of the 1960s the term's meaning had bifurcated. In one sense, it is synonymous with 'New Wave' – the British New Wave, the Czech New Wave, the Polish New Wave and so on – a term applied to any body of works from any country by young, hitherto unknown film-makers. On the other hand its meaning is interchangeable with 'the Cahiers group', a set of men (and perhaps one woman) including Truffaut, Godard, Chabrol and Rohmer, and sometimes Resnais, sometimes Malle. Its borders seem porous, but what it connotes is a moment in French film history which has acquired the status of legend: and it is in this sense that Joe Queenan uses it in the opening sections of this chapter. In both cases, the meaning has solidified, become something of a given. As the above history explains, this was not the case at the time of its introduction into British film culture. The *nouvelle vague* as it was only two years after it arrived on British shores in the early 1960s was not the *nouvelle vague* as we understand it now.

Today, the *nouvelle vague* is held up amongst critics and scholars of cinema as a standard bearer – this despite the fact that its influence far outweighs the critical reception of its time. In many ways, the temporality of the New Wave films is directly inverse to that of Lelouch's, which Richard Roud described as a 'Cinderella' film: popular, well-thought of, but ultimately forgettable. 'No revivals', he predicted (Roud 1967). The *nouvelle vague* films have however been, in Britain as in both France and the United States, the subject of countless revivals, reprints, anniversary screenings and so on. Once the initial ripple of excitement ebbed away, the British critics of the 1960s lost interest; but time has been kind to not only the works but the phenomenon: in hindsight the *nouvelle vague* appears bigger, better, grander, more seminal by half.

Where the *nouvelle vague*'s implications for French cinema's standing in Great Britain are most durable, perhaps, is in its insemination of a critical and commercial model, a manner of discussing and marketing French cinema to British audiences (and other export markets). Consider the comments of a certain G.G. in a 2002 issue of *Cinémaction*:

> The New Wave went beyond – sometimes well beyond – the traditional French cultural sphere of influence. One still catches the term, from time to time, amongst the very few expressions that the Americans have borrowed from the French. America and Britain – not countries who are particularly inclined to following the foreign example, for once paid attention, at least within their criticism, to these young filmmakers who were making so much racket.
>
> (G.G. 2002: 104)

Then think, perhaps of, subsequent film-making 'movements' such as the 'movie brats', Lars von Trier's 'Dogme '95' and most recently the French 'New Extreme', whose very title seems to mimic the semantics of the *nouvelle vague*. Clearly, this paradigm of definition and self-definition has had a lasting impact.

While its legacy has endured, however, its immediate impact was, as we have seen, negligible. Indeed, as the 1960s drew to a close, a survey of the habits and tastes of London film-goers revealed that only 1 per cent chose the films they saw because of an interest in 'the producer, director or author' (Houston 1965: 121–22): this compares to 11 per cent in France according to another survey conducted the same year (*Perspectives 1970: CNC Bulletin d'information* no. 91). As we will go on to discuss, the 1970s saw French cinema in Britain revert to earlier concepts and clichés in its marketing and reception as if the *nouvelle vague* had almost never happened. If the moment of the *nouvelle vague*'s arrival in the UK has become, with the passing of time, an imagined paradise for British fans of French cinema, then the 1970s undoubtedly saw French film's fall from grace. Perhaps it's appropriate to leave the last word to the woman who wrote most widely, most hopefully, and then most despondently about French cinema in the 1960s, the ubiquitous Penelope Houston:

> In the cinema, specifically, 1960 felt like the beginning of something; and at various moments during the decade filmmakers have been able to extend their own language to isolate and make tangible feelings previously only in the air. They have been ahead of us not merely in their silliness (perpetrating, for instance, the whole ghastly business of swinging London), but in their sensibility: films as varied as *The Eclipse* and *Muriel* and *Pierrot le Fou* have expanded consciousness. But, for the moment at least, that might seem to be over. Cinema had moved fast, and from the moment when filmmakers in the more conventionally minded industries began using the new languages, the publicists and salesman of change moved in to persuade us that it was still moving faster than ever. I am not so sure that it is; and 1970 feels rather more like the end of something, with clues and hints to another beginning still just out of sight.
>
> (Houston 1969/70: 3)

Notes

1. The same article wryly reports that Antony Balch, an executive of Mondial Films, the film's British distributors, leapt to the defence of culture: 'This is a tasteful picture of a great statue,' he argues, 'After all, The Kiss has been on public view in the Louvre for 50 years or more, and no one's objected to it there'. This despite the fact that the statue was actually held in The Tate at the time. (*News Chronicle* 1959a).
2. The possible exception to the overwhelming critical adulation of the film comes from Hollis Alpert in the *Saturday Review* (3 October 1959), who, while admiring the film, nonetheless writes that 'it hardly seems as impressive as *The Lovers* and *The Cousins*, made by two others of the New Wave of French directors'.
3. Figures compiled from the *Monthly Film Bulletin*, 1960–69.
4. A fascinating counterpoint to the praise the film received amongst the broadsheet reviewers comes courtesy of John Moynihan's society column in *The Evening Standard* (8 January 1960), published the day after Moynihan had attended the première of the film: ' At a party after the film I saw a man standing sipping white wine by himself. He looked remarkably like Vicky's conception of the Foreign Secretary. He was the Foreign Secretary. Mr Selwyn Lloyd was completely unmoved by the film. "It's rather on the heavy side. It slows down a lot near the end", he said. I turned to the French Ambassador, M. Jean Chanvel, who said: 'I prefer a film like *Gigi* myself. But I don't often go to the theatre or the cinema anyway'.
5. For the recurrent use of this visual trope in advertising French film in the U.K., see Wheatley (2010).
6. The film was banned in France until the end of the Algerian war.
7. Arkadin asked the three about specific titles that hadn't been picked up at all: *La Baie des Anges* (none of the three had heard of it); *Bob le Flambeur* (Rive didn't like it; Pallanca deemed it was already too late, Cooper thought it was not quite a competitive enough title in a saturated market place), and *Une Femme est une femme* (Rive thought someone else had already picked it up, Cooper thought it doubtful commercially and Pallanca thought it had been superseded by Godard himself). When asked why none of Michel Deville's films had been shown in the U.K., Mr Rive said they would need dubbing, since comedy was 'very dodgy' unless, as with Clair, it had a built-in cultural selling-point or, like Tati, had very little important dialogue (Arkadin 1964: 90).
8. Interestingly, a time lag of a different sort has restored *A Bout de Souffle* to its original status. Now a canonical classic, its re-release some twenty-five years later, in 1988, saw Geoff Brown compare it with contemporary French film, stating that 'Beside *A bout de souffle*, most recent French excursions into the same territory seem ponderous, over-calculated, and top heavy with chic' (1988), while Sheila Johnston, in *The Times*, was left 'uncertain whether to revere a venerable classic or marvel at the undimmed and insolent charm' (1988).
9. Trevelyan did, however, refuse to pass *Trans-Europe Express* in 1967 on the grounds of sadism (Robinson 1971: 72).
10. When it was pointed out that Gala were distributors of such Danish sex comedies as *Seventeen* (1965) and *Bedroom Mazurka* (1970), Rive replied

that he was opposed to excessive screen brutality but 'sex with a smile is permissible'. 'I would have bought *Emmanuelle* had I had the chance: that is the type of sex film that deserves the success it is having,' he said (Eyles 2003).
11. Interestingly, in the following passages Kingsley discusses the tendency to describe as 'Continental' films that are English language 'but which do not fit the commercial pattern' (Baker 1964: 46).

Bibliography

Alpert, H. 1959. 'Les Cousins', 19 September.
Anderson, L. 1958. 'French Renewal', *National Film Theatre Programmes*, September.
Ardagh, J. 1961. 'The Cinema's Poets', *Time and Tide*, 8 June.
Arkadin. 1962. 'Film Clips', *Sight and Sound* 31(4), Autumn: 189–190.
Arkadin. 1963/64. 'Film Clips', *Sight and Sound* 33(1), Winter: 29.
Arkadin. 1964. 'Film Clips', *Sight and Sound* 33(2), Spring: 90–91.
Arkadin. 1969. 'Film Clips', *Sight and Sound* 38(2), Spring: 106.
Baker, P. 1964. 'The Foreign Papers', *Films and Filming* 10(5): 41–61.
Basil, R. 1959. 'Les Amants', *Star*, 29 October.
Betts, E. 1962. 'Movie? It Never Gets Moving!', *People*, 2 February.
Billard, P. 1958. 'La Nouvelle Vague', *Cinéma 58*, February: 31–34.
Brown, G. 1988. 'A bout de souffle', *The Times*, 5 June.
Coleman, J. 1962. 'Vivre sa Vie', *New Statesman*, 14 December.
Coleman, J. 1967. 'Une Homme et une femme', *New Statesman*. 20 January.
Cowie, P. 1966. 'Art Cinemas in Alliance', *Sight and Sound* 35(3), Summer: 117–18.
Crewe, Q. 1962. 'L'Année Dernière à Marienbad', *Daily Mail*, 23 February.
Daily Record. 1960. 'The Four Hundred Blows', 6 March.
Daily Worker. 1959. 'France Takes Over from Italy . . .', 9 May.
Dehn, P. 1962. 'French Farce Gets a Face-lift', *Daily Herald*, 24 February.
Dent, A. 1962. 'No Nobility', *Sunday Telegraph*, 16 December.
Dixon, C. 1959a. 'Les Amants', *Daily Telegraph*, 31 October.
Dixon, C. 1960. 'The Four Hundred Blows', *Daily Telegraph*, 5 March.
Dublin Evening Press. 1959. 'Bird's Eye View', 24 September.
Dupin, C. and G. Nowell-Smith. 2007. Transcript of an unpublished interview with Penelope Houston.
Dyer, P.J. 1960/61. 'London Festival', *Sight and Sound* 30(1), Winter: 17–19, 46.
Evening News. 1966. 'Curzon Re-opening', 5 April.
Eyles, A. 2003. 'Kenneth Rive: Obituary', *Independent*, 2 April.
G.G. 2002. 'Flashback sur la nouvelle vague', *Cinémaction* 104: 114.
Gibbs, P. 1962a. 'L'Année Dernière à Marienbad', *Daily Telegraph*, 24 February.
Gibbs, P. 1962b. 'A Sort of Loving', *Daily Telegraph*, 15 December.
Gibbs, P. 1966. 'Viva Maria', *Daily Telegraph*, 7 April.
Graham, P. 1963. 'The Face of '63: France', *Films and Filming*, May: 13–20.
Guardian. 1960. 'Les Quatre Cents Coups', 5 March.
Guardian. 1962. 'Images of Marienbad', 20 February.
Hartley, L.P. 2004. *The Go-Between*. London: Penguin Modern Classics.

Hibbin, N.1962. 'Clever-clever', *Daily Worker*, 15 December.
Hill, D. 1958. 'Masterpiece – By Breaking All The Rules', *Tribune*, 19 September.
Hollingworth, A. 1959. 'Les Cousins', 3 March.
Houston, P. 1961. 'Critic's Notebook', *Sight and Sound* 30(2), Spring: 62–66.
Houston, P. 1962. 'The Front Page', *Sight and Sound* 31(2), Spring: 55.
Houston, P. 1963. 'The Front Page', *Sight and Sound* 32(2), Spring: 55.
Houston, P. 1963/64. 'Whose Crisis?' *Sight and Sound* 33(1), Winter: 26–28, 50.
Houston, P. 1964. 'Keeping up with the Antonionis', *Sight and Sound* 33(4), Autumn: 163–68.
Houston, P. 1965. 'In the Picture: Perspectives 1965', *Sight and Sound* 34(3), Summer: 121–22.
Houston, P. 1966/67. 'Monopoly', *Sight and Sound* 36(1), Winter: 15–16.
Houston, P. 1967. 'Un homme et une femme', *Spectator*, 20 January.
Houston, P. 1969/70. 'Seventy', *Sight and Sound*, 39(1), Winter: 3–5.
Houston, P. and D. Crow. 1959/60. 'Into the Sixties', *Sight and Sound* 29(1), Winter: 4–8.
Hunnings, N. 1969. 'Censorship: On the Way Out?', *Sight and Sound* 38(4), Autumn: 201–2.
Irish Press. 1959. 'Cork Film Festival Opens Tonight', 23 September.
Jacob, G. 1964/65. 'Nouvelle Vague or Jeune Cinema?', *Sight and Sound* 34(1), Winter: 4–8.
Johnston, S. 1988. 'A bout de souffle', *The Times*, 4 June.
Kael, P. 1961/62. 'Fantasies of the Art-house Audience', *Sight and Sound* 31(1), Winter: 5.
Kine Weekly. 1960. 'Gala-Films de France Deal', 21 April, A.
Les Echos. 1959. 'Les 400 Coups récompensés à Londres', 27 October.
Lewin, D. 1966. 'Bardot vs Moreau', *Daily Mail*, 23 February.
Libération. 1959. 'La nouvelle vague française à l'honneur au Festival du Film de Londres', 14 October.
Maclaren, C. 1960. 'Black Orpheus', *Time and Tide*, 4 June.
Macnab, G. 2009. 'From New Wave to Tedious Old Hat', *Independent*, 6 March. Available at https://www.independent.co.uk/arts-entertainment/films/features/from-new-wave
McSnarry, D. 1966. 'BB's Bullseye in Fashion!', *Daily Express*, 8 January.
Millar, G. 1962. 'L'Année Dernière à Marienbad', *Listener*, 8 March.
Mosley, L. 1960. 'Black Orpheus', *Daily Express*, 27 May.
News Chronicle. 1959a. 'Banned', 29 October.
News Chronicle. 1959b. 'Les Amants', 30 October.
NFT Programmes. 1977. '25th Anniversary. Connoisseur Films Season', September: 22–28.
Nice-Matin. 1959. 'Au Festival de Londres', 3 November.
Nowell-Smith, G. 1965. 'Chasing the Gorgon', *Sight and Sound* 34(2), Spring: 60–61.
Nowell-Smith, G. 2010. 'The Reception of the *Nouvelle Vague* in Britain', in Lucy Mazdon and Catherine Wheatley (eds.), *Je t'aime, moi non plus: Anglo-French Cinematic Relations*. Oxford: Berghahn, pp. 117–26.
Pallanca, W. 1977. 'The Connoisseur Criterion', *Screen International*, 24 September: 21.
Pilard, P. 2002. 'Nouvelle Vague' in English, *Cinémaction* 104: 115–22.

Playboy. 1960. 'The 400 Blows', April.
Powell, D. 1959. 'Les Amants', *Sunday Times*, 1 November.
Powell, D. 1961. 'Youthful Sinners', *Sunday Times*, 8 January.
Powell, D. 1962. 'L'Année Dernière à Marienbad', *Sunday Times*, 25 February.
Queen's University of Belfast Film Society, 1961. 'Les Tricheurs', October.
Queenan, J. 2009. 'We'll Always Have Paris', *Guardian Film and Media*, 27 March: 7.
Quigley, I. 1960. 'Orfeu Negro', *Spectator*, 3 June.
Quigley, I. 1961a. 'New Films: A Bout de Souffle', *Guardian*, 8 July.
Quigley, I. 1961b. 'Manifesto', *Spectator*, 14 July.
Quigley, I. 1961c. 'Paris, France', *Spectator*, 13 January.
Quigley, I. 1962. 'Some Time, Never', *Spectator*, 21 March.
Rhode, E. 1962. 'L'Année Dernière à Marienbad', *Listener*, 8 March.
Rive, K. 1960. 'Films To Fill The Cinemas', letter to *The Daily Cinema*, 17 June: 7.
Robbe-Grillet, A. 1962a. *The Voyeur*. London: John Calder Publishers.
Robbe-Grillet, A. 1962b. *Jealousy*. London: John Calder Publishers.
Robbe-Grillet, A. 1962c. *The Erasers*. London: John Calder Publishers.
Robinson, D. 1959. 'Les Amants'. *The Times*, 2 November.
Robinson, D. 1960. 'Tirez sur la Pianiste', *Financial Times*, 16 December.
Robinson, D. 1961. 'Turn of the Tide', *Financial Times*, 7 July.
Robinson, D. 1962. 'L'Année Dernière à Marienbad', *Financial Times*, 21 February.
Robinson, D.. 1965. 'The Physical Life', *Financial Times*, 8 April.
Robinson, D. 1971. 'Trevelyan's Social History: Some Notes and a Chronology', *Sight and Sound*, Spring: 70–72.
Roud, R. 1960. 'The French Line', *Sight and Sound* 29(4), Autumn: 167–71.
Roud, R. 1964. 'Lettre de Londres', *Cahiers du Cinema* 152, February: 45–46.
Roud, R. 1966. 'Viva Maria', *Guardian*, 7 April.
Roud, R. 1967. 'Un homme et une femme', *Guardian*, 19 January.
Roud, R. 1968. 'Andre Bazin: His Rise and Fall', *Sight and Sound*, Spring: 94–96.
Russell Taylor, J. 1968. 'Truffaut à la Hitchcock', *The Times*, 1 August.
Sight and Sound. 1960a. 'The Front Page', 29(2), Spring: 55.
Sight and Sound. 1960b. 'In the Picture: Questions of Censorship', 29(3), Summer: 116.
Sight and Sound. 1960c. 'The Front Page', 29(4), Autumn: 159.
Sight and Sound. 1963/64. 'In the Picture: Risk in Art', 33(1), Winter: 23
Sight and Sound. 1964a. 'The Front Page', 33(3), Summer: 107–8.
Sight and Sound. 1964b. 'The Front Page: The London Filmgoer', 33(4), Autumn: 161–62.
Sight and Sound. 1965. 'The Front Page', 34(4), Autumn: 159.
Summers, S. 1975. 'Beautiful, Violent, Controversial ... You Couldn't Wish for More', *CinemaTV Today*: 12–13.
The Times. 1962a. 'Film of Subtlety and Fascination', 20 February.
The Times. 1966. 'Viva Maria', 7 April.
The Times. 1967. 'Un Homme et une femme', 19 January.
Today's Cinema. 1953. 24 April: 19.
Today's Cinema. 1954. 'Continental Specialists Join Forces', 26 May: 5.
Turner, R. 1968. 'La Mariée était en noir', *Sunday Express*, 1 August.
Walker, A. 1964. 'Beyond a Guessing Game', *Evening Standard*, 19 March.

Walker, A. 1967. 'Un Homme et une femme', *Evening Standard*, 19 January.
Walker, A. 1968. 'Irritating Homage to Hitchcock', *Evening Standard*, 1 August.
Weightman, J. 1962. 'Masterpiece or Insoluble Riddle?', *Observer Review*, 14 January.
Wheatley, C. 2010. 'The Language of Love? How the French Sold *Lady Chatterley's Lover* (Back) to British Audiences', in L. Mazdon and C. Wheatley (eds.), *Je t'aime, moi non plus: Franco-British Cinematic Relations*. Oxford: Berghahn, pp. 81–100.
Wingate, R. 2010. 'A Short History of the Curzon Mayfair.' Online. Last retrieved 21 May from: *www.actproductions.co.uk/iabout_company.asp*

Filmography

A Bout de Souffle / Breathless (1960, Jean-Luc Godard)
Abysses, Les (1963, Nikos Papatakis)
Ah! Les Belles baccantes / Femmes de Paris (1954, Jean Loubignac)
Alphaville (1965, Jean-Luc Godard)
Amants, Les (1958, Louis Malle)
Amour à Vingt ans, L' / Love at Twenty (1962, François Truffaut)
Année dernière à Marienbad, L' / Last year at Marienbad (1961, Alain Resnais)
Ascenseur au Chauffaud, L' / Lift to the Scaffold (1958, Louis Malle)
Atalante, L' (1934, Jean Vigo)
Beau Serge, Le (1958, Claude Chabrol)
Billy Liar (1963, John Schlesinger)
Bonnes Femmes, Les (1960, Claude Chabrol)
Brief Encounter (1945, David Lean)
Chinoise, La (1967, Jean-Luc Godard)
Cousins, Les (1959, Claude Chabrol)
Dolce Vita, La (1960, Federico Fellini)
En effeuillant la marguerite / Mamselle Striptease (1956, Marc Allégret)
Enfant Sauvage, L'/ Wild One, The (1970, François Truffaut)
Eve (1962, Joseph Losey)
Fahrenheit 451 (1966, François Truffaut)
Femme est une femme, Une / A Woman is a Woman (1961, Jean-Luc Godard)
Femme mariée, Une / A Married Woman (1964, Jean-Luc Godard)
Gai Savoir, Le (1969, Jean-Luc Godard)
Goha (1958, Jacques Baratier)
Hard Day's Night, A (1964, Richard Lester)
Hiroshima, Mon Amour (1959, Alain Resnais)
Homme et une femme, Un / A Man and A Woman (1966, Claude Lelouch)
I Mongoli / The Mongols (1961, André de Toth, Leopoldo Savona)
Jules et Jim (1962, François Truffaut)
Jument Verte, La / The Green Mare's Nest (1959, Claude Autant-Lara)
Landru (1963, Claude Chabrol)
Liaisons Dangereuses, Les / Dangerous Liaisons (1959, Roger Vadim)
Main Chaude, La (1959, Gérard Oury)
Mariée était en noir, La / The Bride wore Black (1968, François Truffaut)
Mistons, Les (1957, François Truffaut)

Moderato Cantabile / Seven Days ... Seven Nights (1960, Peter Brook)
Mon Oncle (1958, Jacques Tati)
Mondo Cane (1962, Paolo Cavara, Gualtierro Jiacopetti, Franco Prosperi)
Muriel (1963, Alain Resnais)
Neige était sale, La / Stain on the Snow (1954, Luis Stavslasky)
Orfeu Negro / Black Orpheus (1959, Marcel Camus)
Parapluies de Cherbourg, Les / The Umbrellas of Cherbourg (1964, Jacques Demy)
Paris Nous Appartient (1961, Jacques Rivette)
Peau Douce, La / Silken Skin (1964, François Truffaut)
Petit Soldat, Le / The Little Solider (1963, Jean-Luc Godard)
Pierrot le Fou (1965, Jean-Luc Godard)
Pumpkin Eater, The (1964, Jack Clayton)
Quatre Cents Coups, Les (1959, François Truffaut)
Razzia sur la Chnouf / Chnouf (1955, Henri Decoin)
Repos du Guerrier, Le / Love on a Pillow / Warrior's Rest (1962, Roger Vadim)
Ronde, La (1950, Max Ophüls)
Room with A View, A (1985, James Ivory)
Scandale, Le / The Champagne Murders (1967, Claude Chabrol)
Tête Contre Les Murs, La / The Keepers (1959, Georges Franju)
Tirez sur la pianiste / Shoot the Pianist (1960, François Truffaut)
Tom Jones (1963, Tony Richardson)
Tricheurs, Les / Young Sinners (1958, Marcel Carné)
Vie Privée / A Very Private Affair (1962, Louis Malle)
Vie, Une (1958, Alexandre Astruc)
Viva Maria! (1965, Louis Malle)
Vivre sa Vie / My Life to Live (1962, Jean-Luc Godard)
Weekend (1967, Jean-Luc Godard)

5

'A NEW LOW IN FRENCH FILMS'
Changing Perceptions of French Cinema (1970–1982)

In an article published in the winter of 1979, Penelope Houston, the editor of *Sight and Sound*, looked back over the wreckage of the decade that preceded it and concluded that, if the view from 1970 had been bad, the outlook from here was much worse. 'It would be difficult to maintain that the cinema seems as significant, as relevant or as enlivening as it did ten years ago' (Houston 1979/80: 2), she writes, describing the 1960s as 'a remarkable decade for cinema', one whose glory seems all the greater compared with the poor fare available to the public at the time of writing. 'Half a dozen times in the past year', she writes, 'I have had more or less identical conversations with various friends who also earn their living writing and thinking about films, and who agree that they see fewer films than they used to and approach them with less sense of expectation' (2).

What happened to film in the 1970s? Or, to be more precise, what happened to the kind of French film so fervently championed by *Sight and Sound* some fifteen years earlier? Houston points to several possible explanations for the demise of art-house culture, the home of French cinema, as we have seen, for so much its of history. First was the upsurge of Hollywood spectaculars, from *Jaws* through *Star Wars* to *Saturday Night Fever*, which brought a new generation of film-goers into cinemas and revived the national box office (although takings dropped in the first half of the decade, 1977–78 saw a staggering leap in revenues); but which, as David Thomson puts it, were merely 'light-and-music trips for kids, a kind of environmental disco illusion' and whose audience 'is not assumed to be taking its mind into the cinema' (1979: 6). Houston underlines the coincidence of this increase in takings with a huge increase in advertising expenditure on film promotion (from £2.21 million in 1972 to £7.30 million in 1978), the vast majority of which came from the major studios (Houston 1979/80: 3). Smaller, niche distributors – those more commonly associated with foreign-language film – could not be expected to keep up, particularly given increases in the cost of importing prints; although she is unable to provide specific figures, Houston's impression from talking to those within the 'specialised' industry was that exhibitors and distributors were gaining more on their 'popular' films, but were otherwise losing money (3). A more pressing problem presented itself in the form of the increasingly fragmented audience for art-house film: 'In the 60s, anyone interested in the cinema at a certain level would have felt that he had to see the latest film by Godard or Antonioni or Bergman,' but 'not everyone feels the same need now to keep up with the Fassbinders' (3).

These factors go some way to explaining why audiences weren't attending art-house films in the same numbers; yet they do not explain Houston's perceived drop in the quality of the films being shown. If, to her mind, what was needed in European film at the beginning of the 1980s was 'a major new surge of creative excitement: not a New Wave, since that expression has been devalued by all the other old waves, but a shake-up of ideas and assumptions' that is 'long overdue' (4), tacit in this battle cry is the understanding that the old guard whose films had proved so exciting in the late 1950s and early 1960s had become creatively atrophied or stopped working altogether. 'The film-makers who manage to be always productive, incessantly on the go, like [. . .] Chabrol and Fassbinder, are the admirable exceptions' she laments (4). While serving as an excellent starting point for an investigation of French cinema's status in the U.K. during the 1970s, then, Houston's article needs further elucidation. What precisely is she referring when she talks of 'popular' and 'specialised' cinema – two notoriously thorny terms within the discourses surrounding French cinema in Britain? (3) If the decade was a period of 'disturbingly long hiatuses' and 'total absences' for the major European directors of the 60s, who or what was replacing them on British screens? (4) And, more crucially, how did this situation arise in the first place?

The End of the French New Wave, the Turning of the European Tide

The factors leading to the critical disappointment in French cinema within the 1970s are complex and multifarious, and it is essential to understand the developments that took place over the course of the decade in a pan-European context, if they are to be understood at all. For this is a decade when politics, in the form of the EEC and the changing cultural regimes of France and Britain, came to play a significant role in shaping both forms of and responses to national cinemas, and the second great era of co-productions and the battle with Hollywood: a conflict waged by France, Britain, and numerous other European countries at the level not only of production, but also of exhibition, distribution and marketing. As ever, the twin deities of Industry and Culture circled around one another within the discourses surrounding French film in Britain at this point. To determine precisely what status French cinema occupied within Britain in the 1970s, then, and the reasons for this, must entail a careful process of unpacking. It is just such a process that will unfold over the course of this chapter.

A good place to start is with the divergent fiscal and aid systems operating throughout Europe in the 1970s, and with the efforts of the EEC to bring these into line. Once again feeling the pressure from Hollywood and its dominance of the film market, the early 1970s saw Europe unified in its efforts to establish a firmer grip on its audiences through a series of pan-European initiatives: 1972 alone saw the inauguration of a European Commission aimed at establishing a system of multilateral co-production and co-financing, designed to lead to the harmonisation of aids and promotion of co-distribution within the EEC; a major study of co-distribution, conducted by the International Federation of Distributors (FIAD); a meeting of the *Union Internationale de l'Exploitation Cinématographique* (International Exhibitors Union) to discuss the construction of a European Film Industry; a meeting of the *Comité de l'Industrie Cinématographique Européene* (European Cinematographer's Committee); and a meeting of the English, French and Italian trade unions (Degand 1973). Then, in 1973, Britain joined the Common Market and the British quota was replaced by a 'British or Community' quota, intended to bring the U.K. into line with EEC competition policy: a seminal move which would have significant consequences for screenings of French films on this side of the Channel.

The quota had been introduced in 1927, one of three key protective devices of British film legislation, the other two being the national Eady levy and the National Film Finance Corporation. At its inception it was intended to ensure that British films were screened in British cinemas, but when Britain joined the EEC, the nationalist remit became a Continental one. With British feature production slowing in the 1970s (eighty long films were produced in 1973; a number that had almost halved to forty-two in 1977), vanquished by its long-standing enemy Hollywood and that young upstart, television, exhibitors turned to Continental film, whose numbers had remained more or less steady at approximately eighty-five registered features per year, to fill their quotas (Porter 1979a: 91). According to the 1978 report of the Cinematograph Films Council, cited by Vincent Porter in *Sight and Sound*, the evidence at the end of the 1970s suggested that while this should have been an advantage for the fate of French film in Britain, a not insignificant number of exhibitors were selecting poor quality, cheap, or 'unsuitable' product solely to achieve quota and therefore avoid penalisation by the Department of Trade

(Porter 1979a: 91). Quite what Porter means by 'unsuitable' is a question that we will approach in due course; for now, suffice it to say that the ultimate outcome of the confluence of Britain's entry into the EEC and its status as the only country in Europe other than Italy to deploy quota regulations may be that as far as French cinema was concerned, it was quantity, rather than quality, that determined the selection process for British exhibitors.

Changes in French cultural policy, meanwhile, had their own impact on the kinds of films available for selection by the British distribution and exhibition companies. In 1969, the responsibility for censorship in France transferred from the Ministry of Information to the Ministry for Cultural Affairs. This in itself had little impact on French film production or indeed on censorship practice, but in 1974 the newly elected President Giscard d'Estaing began to make statements about revising the French censorship system; and on 30 April 1975 the French Cabinet approved a Bill containing the reform proposals of M. Michel Guy, Minister for Culture, which restricted censorship to films which infringe human dignity (e.g. extreme violence or incitement to drugs), all political and pornographic censorship being excluded (Hunnings 1975: 158). At the same time, fiscal measures were introduced imposing a heavy tax on all foreign X-rated films, which led to a considerable drop in their importation (Hayward 2005: 34). The knock-on effect of these two measures was a surge in X-rated French-produced films, and in particular in films that could be loosely described as 'soft-core porn' films.

Until 1974, pornographic cinema in France had been very marginal. Now it had moved from being a cinema of the periphery to a very central one: according to Susan Hayward, during the period 1975–79 this cinema averaged 50 per cent of all French production screened (Hayward 2005: 241). However, as Neville Hunnings points out in a piece written for *Sight and Sound* in 1975, this is not quite the whole story (Hunnings 1975: 158), for while the door was being opened legislatively, the window was being closed economically. Following developments in censorship policy in Sweden and Denmark that had occurred in the preceding years, increased control was to be exercised over French publicity, which extended to blanket bans on *any* form of publicity 'for certain films' (Hunnings 1975: 158). Moreover, a form of financial censorship was simultaneously introduced, involving the abolition of all automatic financial aid to pornographic films 'which do not have manifest artistic quality' (158). Consequently, the practical difference that resulted from these legal changes was, as a report in *Le Monde* put it: 'aesthetic pornography, the erotic fantasies of the intellectuals, [was] accepted and subsidised, while the vulgar pornography for everyone [was] excluded' (cited in Hunnings 1975: 158). It was precisely this type of cerebral, aestheticised sex film (the quintessential example being Just Jaeckin's *Emmanuelle*, on which more in due course) which would flood the British market in the latter half of the 1970s (Castell 1981), and which would be dubbed by the British press as 'chocolate box pornography'.

While the government measures implemented in France during the early 1970s were giving rise to an indigenous porn business, other parts of the film industry were looking outside France for guaranteed box-office success. From 1948 to 1975 France was involved in a reciprocal arrangement with Italy to make co-productions, with the object of taking on the Hollywood majors on their own terms by producing big-budget, star-led, spectaculars, films which, like the major exports of the 1950s such as *Du Rififi chez les homes / Rififi* and *Le Salaire de la peur / The Wages of Fear*, were action driven, light on dialogue, and often took the form of the suspense-thriller. The most prolific amongst this category of films was the *polar*, otherwise known in the U.K. as the gangster flick. Examples of this type of film include, amongst others, *Le Clan des Siciliens* (1969, France), *Le Cercle Rouge* (1970, France/Italy), *Borsalino* (France/Italy, 1970), *Un Flic* (1972, France/Italy) and *Stavisky* (1974, France/Italy). A majority (and certainly the most successful films at the British box office) of these starred either Alain Delon or Jean-Paul Belmondo and in some cases both – by this time France's most exportable stars. Sometimes these products were filmed as MLVs (multiple language versions), a strategy that had fallen out of practice since the unsuccessful attempts of the 1930s: the same cast, for example, made French, Italian and English versions of *Le Clan des Siciliens*. In others, they were dubbed for or upon export. It's worth noting here that *Stavisky* was directed, somewhat surprisingly, by Alain Resnais. Once the epitome of all that was innovative, perplexing, and exciting about the French New Wave for British critics, like Truffaut and Malle he too had, by this point, moved from the experimental towards more populist work and in so doing had fallen from critical grace. *Stavisky*'s notices lacked the tone of haughty dismissal that characterised those for Truffaut's *La Mariée était en noir*, which as we saw in the previous chapter was widely berated by the same critics who had once championed the New Wave directors. But its arrival in the U.K. was hardly feted: a million miles away from the heady anticipation that surrounded *Marienbad*.

There were other genres that saw success around this time: Bernard Borderie's *Angélique* series (France/West Germany/Italy), adaptations of novels by Anne and Serge (Sergeanne) Golon, was perhaps the most successful of a slew of historical melodramas, many of which were inspired by nineteenth-century literary works. Following in the wake of Claude Lelouch's hugely profitable waterings down of the *nouvelle vague* came a steady flow of quotidian romances, watered down still further, Jean-Charles Tacchella's *Cousin Cousine* being perhaps the quintessential example. The visibility – and evidently marketability – of such co-productions was such that by 1978 Vincent Porter was led to comment that: 'the dominant film culture of Europe is that of the big budget picture, produced, financed and distributed by the multinational corporations' (Porter 1978: 135).

Second Features in the Circuits

What was the practical effect of these changes that took place in Europe during the 1970s on French film as it appeared on British screens at the time? Generally speaking, we can deduce from the above that France was producing two particularly successful types of film; the Euro-blockbuster and the artistic porn film. This dualism is rather reductive, of course, and as we shall see, there were indeed other categories and kinds of films making the transition from France to Britain's cinemas during the 1970s, some successfully, others less so. But a quick survey of what was screening in British cinemas reveals that these were indeed the two principal bodies of films being shown to the public during the decade. The outlets in which they appeared, and the ways in which they were marketed were, however, very different, as was the way in which their Frenchness was inscribed within their presentation.

Distributed by Columbia-Warner, one of the British majors, Jean-Pierre Melville's *Un Flic* was retitled *Dirty Money* for its U.K. release, and played as second feature to the Barbra Streisand feature *For Pete's Sake*. Typically for films of its ilk at the time, it was dubbed for its Anglophone release prior to export, so audiences were offered the bizarre spectacle of an American-accented Alain Delon and Catherine Deneuve. Despite the fact that Tony Rayns, writing in the *New Statesman*, described the film as being 'to gangster movies what Sam Peckinpah's *Pat Garrett and Billy the Kid* was to westerns: a muscular affirmation of its genre's strengths' (Rayns 1974), the film was not given a West End showing when it was released two years after its French première in August 1974, but was consigned to the Rank and Odeon circuits. Eric Shorter, writing in the *Daily Telegraph*, bemoaned having to travel from London to Tunbridge Wells in order to track down a screening of the film (Shorter 1974).[1] Worse still, Shorter complained, was the lack of publicity accorded to the film: Columbia-Warner gave no press showing; no posters were produced; the film was not even advertised at The Classic, where Shorter finally saw it – this despite the fact that it starred two of France's most exportable actors of the time. Worst of all, wrote Shorter, there was: 'nothing to suggest that this engaging thriller . . . contained one of the most exciting sequences in the history of train robberies on film' (Shorter 1974). This obscurity despite the fact that only one week prior to the release of *Dirty Money*, the London Film Festival had presented a retrospective of Melville's work, featuring *Les Enfants Terribles* and *L'Armée des Ombres*. Despite, too, the fact that the film fits the classic mould for crossover hits: much like *Le Salaire de la Peur*, a film which, as we have seen, had phenomenal success in the U.K., *Un Flic*'s dialogue is, according to Nigel Andrews, 'sparse and functional', while its narrative revolves around a silent yet 'enthralling' extended suspense sequence (Andrews 1974). 'One simply wonders if film distributors in this country are capable of recognising a good commercial prospect when they see one', sighs Andrews (1974).

Melville's *Le Samouraï (The Samourai)* had fared no better upon its release three years previously, after a lag of three years from the French release. Cut by some fifteen minutes (a fate spared *Dirty Money*), the film was badly dubbed: 'a character makes a quintessential Gallic gesture and speaks with an American accent', wrote Araminta Wordsworth in *The Times* (1971a), while *Time*'s Jay Cocks described the actors' accents as like those of 'waiters in a New York French restaurant' (Cocks 1972). Although it escaped the indignity of its American retitling as *The Godson* – a move calculated to capitalise on *The Godfather*'s huge success in the previous year – it was shunted onto the back of Robert Parrish's *A Town Called Hell*, starring Telly Savalas. Sadly the film received little coverage in the press and disappeared more or less without trace, a late night appearance on BBC2 in 1979 withstanding. Indeed, it was not until 1993 that the film, now heralded as a classic of art cinema, was shown uncut and undubbed on British screens.

This artistic bent to *The Samurai* and, to a lesser extent, *Dirty Money*, may have contributed to the distributor's difficulties in knowing what to do with them. In March 1972, between the two, Melville's *Le Cercle Rouge / The Red Circle* had a somewhat higher profile release, opening in the West End at the Columbia, Shaftesbury Avenue, and the Paramount cinema. It may be no coincidence that Arthur Thinkell sums up the responses of many critics when he states: 'Nothing arty-crafty in *The Red Circle* . . . this entertaining French-made film has no frills, but plenty of thrills' (Thinkell 1972). Yet again Melville's film was dubbed; however, the techniques employed – having the actors mouth their words in English before overlaying the voice track – jarred less. Thinkell, along with David Robinson in *The Financial Times* (1972), Dilys Powell in *The Sunday Times* (1972) and John Russell-Taylor (1972) in *The Times* are amongst the numerous critics to make mention of the high quality dubbing. Only Margaret Hinxman (1972) in *The Sunday Telegraph* and Cecil Wilson in *The Daily Mail* (1972) are critical – and both were, as we shall we in due course, notorious opponents of dubbing.

However, if *The Red Circle* saw greater popular success than Melville's other thrillers, it was not without its critical opponents. For Richard Roud, writing in *The Guardian* after a Parisian screening of the film (1971), Melville's attempt at a 'box-office smash' encapsulates all that he perceives as wrong with contemporary French film. It is worth quoting

Roud at length here:

> In many ways, the situation of the cinema in France has now become the same as in the rest of the world [...] as in America, films are either tremendous, colossal successes, or miserable failures. Gone are the days when a film could do just well enough to make its money back plus just enough to start the next one. This is depressing, because it means that the French cinema is bound to be affected by that hit-or-flop syndrome which has destroyed the Broadway theatre.
> One example of its deleterious effect, I should say, is Jean-Pierre Melville's newest film, *Le Cercle Rouge*. In the past Melville made a number of extraordinary films. [...] But he is a shrewd businessman as well as a fine director, and it would seem that, gauging the recent economic developments, he decided that this time he had to go for the big box-office smash.
> His calculations have proved to be exact: *Le Cercle Rouge* is a runaway success – but the price has been high. He seems to have carefully calculated which elements appeal most to today's audiences, which features of his previous films have been most successful, and come up with a formula; not so much a film as a piece of market research.
> [...]
> There is no denying that Melville has done supremely well what he has set out to do, but it is the lowering of sights that I persist in regarding as temporary.
> (Roud 1971)

The elements which Roud singles out for disapprobation – the lack of poetry or abstraction, the all-star cast and, most tellingly perhaps, the film's structural similarity to *Rififi* – are precisely those elements which, as we have seen, have accounted for some of the greatest French hits at the British box office. Not least of these is *Le Clan des Siciliens*, France's biggest export of 1970, and if not a roaring success, then at least a solid proposition for British audiences. Starring Delon (again!) and Jean Gabin, *The Sicilian Plan*, as it was known in England, was perhaps the most flagrant of European attempts to play the Dream Factory at its own game. As Virginia Dignam puts it in *The Morning Star*: 'With dubious morals and even more dubious dubbing it is calculated to capture the box office in most European countries and both North and South America' (1970). The Mafia theme and generational stardom are obviously inspired (to put it kindly) by Francis Ford Coppola's *Godfather*; while the multi-language filming – it was filmed several times over with the actors mouthing their lines in French, Italian and English then dubbed – shows an awareness already at the production stage of the importance of international audiences.

Released in Britain in July 1970, as Britain was contemplating joining the European Common Market, the film's international outlook is a key feature of several reviews. Dignam writes that the Sicilians all speak with American accents, 'but in these days of internationalism who cares' (1970), while Stanley Price, in *The Observer* (1970a), remarks that Gabin exudes 'such Gallic confidence', that 'in his company I feel one could successfully lift the Crown jewels, get them through Customs, and use them to blackmail Britain into joining the Common Market'. However, the unifying strand running through almost all the critical response to *The Sicilian Plan*, as through the reviews for the other films discussed above, is of course a commentary on the success or otherwise of the films' dubbing strategies.

Dubbed and Snubbed?

In the early 1970s, the question of dubbing versus subtitling became a key issue within the discourses circulating around French cinema in Britain, with distributors split between those who believed that dubbing a film would enable it to reach a wider, more 'popular' audience and those who, on the other hand, felt that dubbing alienated the longstanding devotees of foreign-language film who tended to prefer subtitles. In 1970 *Films and Filming* asked a number of distributors whether it might not be possible to play both dubbed and subtitled versions of a film in the cinema. While all but one of the interviewees concurred that the audience in any given area would not be sufficient to support such a practice, not to mention the expense involved, their remarks on the question of film translation are revealing. Here, for example, is the response of Michael Chivers, director of Amanda Films (the distributors of Godard's *Une Femme est Une Femme*, amongst other titles):

> Where possible we do try and obtain dubbed prints in addition to subtitled prints of the original version as more outlets are available where dubbed prints are in distribution. We find the more commercial cinema acceptable to dubbed prints and much more willing to show a film in English in preference to subtitles. Many areas would not be able to show subtitled prints due to adverse box-office conditions, for example, Hampstead, Bayswater, Notting Hill Gate and Chelsea are excellent areas in London for Continental pictures in their original version, whereas Tooting, Balham, Clapham and such like areas would not, but these areas would indeed accept dubbed pictures.
> (*Films and Filming* 1970: 20)

Director of Connoisseur Films, William Pallanca, takes quite the opposite point of view. 'In my opinion', he states, 'the British public does not accept dubbed pictures' (*Films and Filming* 1970: 20). Stressing that he is referring to 'quality films of the type shown in the respectable specialised theatres', Pallanca argues that 'the dubbing merely negates the artistic merits the film has' (20). On the other hand, he concludes dismissively, dubbing is perhaps preferable for films 'which depend entirely on action,

16. Connoisseur's poster for Claude Chabrol's *Le Boucher*, the type of 'quality' film that the company's director William Pallanca felt should be subtitled but not dubbed.
Image courtesy of the BFI stills department.

sensationalism, sex etc.', and which appeal to a 'quite different public' (21). Target's Ian R. Jessel is matter-of-fact: 'a cinema showing the o.v. [original version] will be classified as an art house and the cinema showing dubbed prints will be regarded as the "commercial" cinema' (*Films and Filming* 1970: 26).

Looking at the critical responses to the films discussed above, it is clear which side of the divide the majority of critics fall on. Where dubbing is discussed, whether films were judged successful depended a great degree on the extent to which its dubbing was apparently seamless: thus *The Samurai*, a film dubbed by its U.S. distributors subsequent to export, and in which the actors' gestures and lip movements were out of sync with its soundtrack, is deemed a 'failure', while *The Red Circle*, produced with an eye to its eventual dubbing, and still more *The Sicilian Plan*, 'successes'. By extension, we might say that the positive reception of these Euroblockbuster thrillers was dependent on the effacement of their Frenchness. As Thinkell puts it, 'they are "French-made" films, but they are not French' (Thinkell 1972). In fact, with location shooting common practice by this point, it was left to the stars to provide an indication of nationality. And even this was no guarantee – Delon and Deneuve may have been two of France's most celebrated stars, but they were also no strangers to working in other languages, with Delon having appeared in several Italian films (notably *L'Eclisse*, and *Il Gattopardo*, with Burt Lancaster) and Deneuve most familiar to audiences in 1970 from her appearance in Roman Polanski's English-language *Repulsion* (although in 1969 she was also to be seen at the Curzon in Luis Buñuel's notorious *Belle de Jour*).

But this is only half the story. It is true to say that critical disapprobation was levelled at films which were badly dubbed, but this is not to say that good dubbing was a guarantee of box-office success (as the iniquitous fate of *Dirty Money* testifies), nor that subtitling was equated with poor revenues. Indeed, in July 1970, the same month that *The Sicilian Plan* was attempting to win British audiences over with its highly evolved dubbing strategies, Paramount made what Derek Malcolm, in *The Guardian*, refers to as the 'brave' move of releasing the gangster flick *Borsalino*, starring Jean-Paul Belmondo and Alain Delon, at its own circuit of cinemas in an undubbed version (Malcolm 1970). The decision was met with unmitigated delight amongst critics. This is what *The Sunday Mirror*'s Madeleine Harmsworth had to say:

> Charming may seem an odd word to describe a gangster film, especially as there are so many gruesome killings.
> But *Borsalino* is charming! It must be because it's in French. Even gangsters in French have an elegance, a wit and a sophistication which make the rest of the world's criminal fraternity look clod-hopping.
> (Harmsworth 1970)

Ironically, given Paramount's decision if not to foreground, then at least not to disguise, the film's Frenchness (the poster features Belmondo and Delon in classic 1930s gangster garb, their names emblazoned over the title and the words 'The Gangsters of The Year' overlaid), *Borsalino* garnered arguably the most favourable comparisons to American product of the Euro-thrillers released in Britain. *The Sunday Express* describes it as 'evoking in atmosphere *Bonnie and Clyde* and *Butch Cassidy and the Sundance Kid*' (Errol 1970); *The Observer* places it alongside *Easy Rider*, *Midnight Cowboy* and *Butch* once more as a film about 'male relationships' (Price 1970b), and *The Sun* announces that its stars 'go together like Laurel and Hardy, Butch Cassidy and the Sundance Kid, Bonnie and Clyde, and George Raft and his flipping silver dollar' (1970). *The Daily Sketch* (Gillard 1970), *The New Statesman* (Coleman 1970) and *The Spectator* (Houston 1970) reiterate the comparison to *Bonnie and Clyde*, while *The Financial Times* sees it as a French remake of *The Public Enemy*. It is, according to the latter's David Robinson, 'A gorgeous film . . . And the dialogue (with sub-titles) is so nitty-gritty and economic that even those who failed the 11-plus will come out of this French film like it's home-time at the Sorbonne' (1970). Perhaps the relative critical success of *Borsalino* vis-à-vis its dubbed counterparts is best conjured by John Russell Taylor's relieved exclamation that: 'For once, one can understand why the film should have broken box-office records all over France' (1970).

Borsalino's success at the British box office was grist to the mill of a number of critics and commentators waging war on the dubbed film. Felix Barker of *The Evening News* remarked that: 'There's an ingrained Wardour Street belief that the public hates subtitles. But it's my contention that audiences dislike far more English and American voices superimposed on foreign actors' (1970). The debate that had been taking place since the advent of sound cinema had been gathering steam since the early 1960s and arguably reached its apex during the 1970s, when a number of key British publications were moved to publish polemics on the subject. Adrian Turner's piece for *Films Illustrated* in 1974 is the most detailed, not to mention the most vitriolic, of these. Turner describes how a fire was lit under the question when, in 1963, Luchino Visconti's *Il Gattopardo / The Leopard* opened in London. All the major critics hailed the film as a great artistic achievement, but they also wrote in no uncertain terms about the way the film was being shown to British audiences – which was in a severely cut (forty-four minutes had been shaved off its running time) and badly dubbed print. Visconti himself was suing 20th Century-Fox, the distributors, for their interference with the film; indeed such was the row that *The London Evening Standard* printed the banner front-page headline, 'Leopard Man Sues Fox' (Turner 1974: 382). Despite the furore, '20th Century-Fox weathered the storm, the critics calmed down, and Visconti's ravaged masterpiece disappeared from all but the most specialised cinemas who would rather show the film cut and dubbed than not at all' (382).

In 1974, Turner states, very few non-dubbed films were receiving general releases following a West End run (he cites *Un Homme et une femme*, *Seventeen*, and *Last Tango in Paris* as the few exceptions), and to his disturbance, films by even major directors were starting to be dubbed as standard practice. True, he admits, the three regular distributors of what he calls 'quality' foreign-language cinema – Connoisseur, Contemporary and Gala – had continued to subtitle their films; but increasingly, non-specialised distributors were picking up foreign product to sell as second features (back to the quota!): companies who were neither 'geared nor inclined to treat their product individually' (382). Prime amongst the culprits Turner lists is Columbia-Warner – the distributors, of course, of *Un Flic* (or *Dirty Money*) who he describes as treating their films as 'saleable commodities', and, 'if a French version doesn't sell in Bradford or Torquay [. . .] immediately assume that the citizens dislike foreign films per se' (382).

It was not the dubbing of genre pictures that had provided the impetus behind Turner's polemic though; like the majority of critics, he was happy to let the Euro-blockbusters slide. What prompted him to unleash his tirade was the fact that the previous year Columbia-Warner had picked up Truffaut's *La Nuit américaine / Day for Night* for British distribution. To be fair to Columbia-Warner, whereas in the United States, the film had been shown uniquely in a dubbed print,[2] in the United Kingdom they released the film in both a dubbed and subtitled print, and left the option of which to screen to exhibitors. At the time that Turner's piece was published, the film was showing in five London suburban cinemas, one of which, the Screen on Islington Green, was showing the original version, and another of which, the Golders Green ABC, had been showing the subtitled trailer only to mistakenly be sent a dubbed print (not insignificantly, the manager had to deal with a number of complaints). And while it is difficult to discern what version was being viewed by the press – or indeed in other, specific cinemas throughout the country – it is worth noting Derek Malcolm's comment that, 'It was sensible of the English exhibitors to realise this by planning a general release, sub-titles and all' (1973a). Of perhaps more note still is Michael Walsh's exhortation of his readers: 'You don't have to speak French to enjoy this film – you'll probably be ahead of the subtitles anyway' (1973).

17. UK poster for *La Nuit Américaine*, shown in both dubbed and subtitled versions as *Day for Night*.
Image courtesy of the BFI stills department.

Across the range of the print media, *Day for Night* was heralded as a resounding success, and was one of the most profitable films of 1973. The same could not be said however for Truffaut's subsequent release, *La Sirène du Mississippi / Mississippi Mermaid*. Made in 1969, *Mississippi Mermaid*'s U.K. release was delayed until 1974: although it had been purchased by United Artists (whose French subsidiary had also acted as co-producers on the film) as part of a bundle with Truffaut's *Baisers Volés / Stolen Kisses* and *L'Enfant Sauvage / The Wild Boy*, the film was not given a commercial release in Britain, despite the presence of Catherine Deneuve and Jean-Paul Belmondo (Dawson 1974). Following two one-off screenings at the Edinburgh Film Festival and the National Film Theatre it was picked up by that great stalwart of the art house, the Everyman, and shown for fourteen days as part of a Truffaut season (Dawson 1974), but since there was no subtitled print in existence and the cinema could not afford to title the film themselves, it was the American print that was shown: a version that had been cut by fourteen minutes and suffering from, as Turner puts it, 'insensitive translation and crude dubbing' (1974: 382).

According to Turner the 'more responsible' critics were scathing of what had been done to *La Sirène du Mississippi* (1974: 382) – Margaret Hinxman describes the dubbing as 'gruesome' (1974a); Jan Dawson calls it 'grotesque' (1974), and Alexander Walker describes it as 'vile' (1974). The film, admittedly not generally viewed as one of Truffaut's best in any case, was dismissed by all but the most generous or wilfully perverse critics as a resounding failure, but if the dubbing wasn't wholly responsible for the catastrophic reception of the film, to Turner's mind it at the very least made a bad film a good deal worse:

> We are perhaps ready to accept Truffaut's romantic agonies in French because we have been brought up to believe that this is how the French behave. It is certainly true to say that lines like 'I've always dreamed of marrying someone like you, so I don't mind if you kill me. I'm just glad to have known you', come over poignantly and meaningfully in French or Italian, but no Englishman would say a thing like that and keep a straight face. Unless we accept *Mississippi Mermaid* as a romantic fantasy, it will appear ridiculous when dubbed [. . .] less so, if at all, when seen in the original language. Dubbing not only destroys atmosphere, it undermines performances and can even corrupt plots and obscure a director's intention.
>
> (Turner 1974: 382)

For Turner the great failure of dubbing is not merely the technical ineptitude of the process in this instance: rather, in translation from spoken French to spoken (American) English, Truffaut's dialogue loses its cultural salience. That is, as an attempt to efface the film's French origins, dubbing fails because it only serves to call attention to its own artifice. It is a point of view echoed in the majority of critical responses to *Mississippi*

Mermaid: while many critics expressed gratitude to the Everyman for salvaging even such a flawed work of a major director (as Jan Dawson writes, 'dubbed Truffaut is better than no Truffaut at all') (1974) the general response was one of disconsolation that the situation had come to this. Writing in *The Observer*, Russell Davies puts it that 'there was a good case for making a generous assessment of the audience's intelligence and offering them the French without any linguistic interference of any kind' but that most likely, 'this, too, was unavailable' (1974).

Since Truffaut seems to have been something of a barometer for dubbing and subtitling trends in the 1970s, it's interesting to consider the case of his 1975 film, *L'Histoire d'Adèle H. / The Story of Adele H.*, released in 1977 at the Odeon Haymarket and distributed by Hemdale. The version that was shown in the West End was in English, but it was not dubbed; rather Truffaut, drawing on techniques that had been employed within popular genre cinema for some time now, shot the film simultaneously in French and English with the same cast. It's worth mentioning, too, that the person responsible for the English translation of the script was film critic Jan Dawson, one of dubbing's most outspoken opponents. Opinion on the finished product was mixed, however. By and large, this method of translation was seen as preferable to a dubbed version (Felix Barker describes the decision not to dub as 'merciful') (Barker 1977), but not wholly successful nonetheless. Barker for instance claims the English sounds 'stilted ... probably because the director's ear is not quite attuned to the subtleties of cadence and emphasis', but that, 'this "amateur" quality adds a feeling of documentary authenticity to this fascinating film' (Barker 1977). Alexander Walker of *The Evening Standard* on the other hand sees lead Isabelle Adjani as 'handicapped' by 'having to chew up and spit out mouthfuls of English', leading to 'over emphatic delivery' (1977).

To Walker's mind, the experiment had failed. Others thought it trod a neat line between subtitling and dubbing. Either way, it was not a strategy that Truffaut was to repeat; and nor did it catch on as standard practice amongst European auteurs.

Sexy Cinema

If *L'Histoire d'Adèle H*. was to prove an exception in regard to its linguistic strategies; there were other ways in which it stood out amongst French films screening in Britain during the late 1970s. Consider this quote from Douglas Johnson, writing in the *Times Literary Supplement* on the warm public reception to Truffaut's film:

> It is not to detract in any way from the qualities of *L'Histoire d'Adele H.* to note that [praise for the film] was marked by a certain relief that here was a film

which bore no possible relation to the pornographic cinema, a phenomenon which remains something of a national obsession in France. It is in this context that Truffaut has been acclaimed as having saved the honour of French cinema. Let the repressed and the imbecilic go and see O, proclaimed one critic; that is their problem. Let the rest of us go and see H. It should not be necessary to add, when writing about a director who has an almost legendary restraint and discretion in his treatment of sexual scenes, that the use of the letter H in the title has no echo at all of the 'films à scandale' Histoires d'A, or Histoire d'O.

(Johnson 1975)

Johnson's commentary may be sardonic, but it is a not-atypical British view of French film in the later stages of the decade. As previously mentioned, the coincidence of Britain's entry into the EEC (and the concomitant change in quota regulations) with the softening of France's censorship laws opened the door to British screens for a raft of French soft-core porn films from 1975 onwards. The first of these – or certainly the first to make a major impact on British shores – was Just Jaeckin's *Emmanuelle*, released in 1974 by SF Distribution, and advertised with the tagline: 'X was never like this. This movie has changed the meaning of X. It's the first film of its kind that makes you feel good without feeling bad'.[3] This catchphrase featured on radio advertisements as well as on posters featuring a large image of a topless Sylvia Kristel (the film's star), clad in a pearl necklace and staring sultrily out at the viewer, her nipples just covered by the n and the first l of the title. Meanwhile a press statement by Jaeckin announced that 'the difference between eroticism and pornography is the quality' (SF Films 1974). The film opened at the Prince Charles Cinema in London's West End in October, but by this point it had been long anticipated, with reports in July papers announcing the success of 'the sex film that has broken the French respectability barrier' (Webster 1974). *Emmanuelle* was heralded as evidence of a new era of permissiveness in France under Giscard d'Estaing. In August a series of interviews with Sylvia Kristel appeared in the papers and trades. *The Sunday Times* asks 'Who is Sylvia?' before launching into a detailed, if somewhat florid, description of the would-be star (Raven 1974). As for the film itself, author Susan Raven describes *Emmanuelle* as a 'chicly beautiful blue movie', tapping into two sets of national stereotypes – French elegance and Gallic sensuality (1974).

These twin preconceptions were to sculpt most responses to the work. Indeed, in contrast with the reception of the Euro-blockbusters, whose French identity was for the most part effaced in order to sell them to a mass audience, the 'Frenchness' of *Emmanuelle* was a key feature in its marketing and its reception – both positive and negative. Where these perceptions were positive, they associated Frenchness with eroticism, artisanship, taste and quality. Derek Malcolm describes it as 'better done than any others of its ilk' (1974), *The Daily Telegraph* calls it 'erotic, very prettily photographed' (P.G. 1974), while British *Playboy* claims it offers 'glamour, sensuality and softcore raunch without quite violating the impeccable good taste that remains true of all of France's major exports [. . .] On the subject of sex, French *savoir faire* is alive and well and still thrashing around in Paris' (1975). Where they were negative, Frenchness became synonymous with sleaze, gratuity, pretension and dullness. John Coleman, in *The New Statesman*, comments that 'only the French could make such a monumentally boring film about that interesting concern, sex' (Coleman 1974); Margaret Hinxman in *The Daily Mail* (Hinxman 1974b) describes it as 'posh tosh' while Dilys Powell in *The Sunday Times* (1974) describes it as 'the ultimate turn-you-off film'. Ian Christie claims that 'all that differentiates *Emmanuelle* from the other rubbish to be seen in sleazy sex cinemas around town is that it is glossily photographed [. . .] Rubbish still smells no matter how you wrap it up' (1974), while David Robinson veritably spits that it is 'the silliest type of soft-core striptease [. . .] dolled up with fashion magazine photography, exotic locations and ludicrous pretension in the dialogue [. . .] simply awful' (1974). Duncan Followell, in the *Spectator*, sums up the two-sided nature of the stereotypes being applied when he writes that it is 'the sort of piece that the French do very well, or if you do not like that kind of thing, do very badly, the intense sex film' (1974).

Apparently audiences did indeed like that sort of thing: *Emmanuelle* was a huge hit in 1974 at the U.K. box office. According to Penelope Houston, a report in November's *Cinema TV Today* listed *Emmanuelle* as the year's second biggest taker in the West End, after *The Odessa File* but before *That's Entertainment, Juggernaut, The Night Porter, Chinatown* and *Stardust*. 'No surprises in that list', Houston comments, which 'probably sums up fairly well the range and kind of pictures – thrills, disasters, nostalgia and sex – which currently draw the crowds' (Houston 1974/75: 23)

The version of *Emmanuelle* shown to British audiences was, it must be noted, a somewhat sanitised version of that shown to their French counterparts, having suffered cuts to its most provocative imagery – including the total excision of the film's now notorious sequence of a woman 'smoking' a cigar via her vagina. Two years later, however, newspapers reported the advent of the first uncut pornographic film to be shown to the general public. Jean-François Davy's *Exhibition*, which Susan Hayward describes debatably as 'hard core porn' (Hayward 2005: 242) and which shows copulation, full frontal nudity and a fifteen-minute shot of female masturbation, was released by distributors Oppidian in eleven West End cinemas in December 1976, including the Jacey, the Pigalle, the Classic and Studio One. It had in fact been refused a certificate by the BBFC, but given an X by the Greater London Council (GLC), on the grounds that rather than being a sex film, per se, this was a 'documentary about people who make pornographic films' (Lewis 1976).

Oppidian played a canny game on this front. Its press release for the film described it as 'an historical film [...] about what happened to the French film industry in 1974', before holding forth on the political and social context into which *Exhibition* had been released and upon which it proclaims itself a commentary (Oppidian 1976). 'If you are interested in Censorship, or just what is happening in the U.K. in 1976, then *Exhibition* is important', the distributors declared (Oppidian 1976). Pitching the film very much to a liberal leftist audience, the end effect is less of an advertisement and more of a rallying cry against censorship practices and the extreme conservatives:

> The British may be conservative but they are always fair ... We will give anybody the opportunity to say what they like and if a handful of non-going Cinema enthusiasts want to put the entire industry into turmoil, all they have to do, apparently, is stand up and shout Obscene – Disgusting – God never intended people to make love (well not on celluloid anyhow) and hey presto we all stop what we are doing and waste 18 months fighting the fight (that perhaps shouldn't and certainly wouldn't have happened elsewhere).
>
> (Oppidian 1976)

Interestingly, the polemic concludes: 'it's a pity *Exhibition* is French. It would have been so much more important if it had been a home grown film' (Oppidian 1976). Reading the piece, one would be forgiven for thinking then that *Exhibition* stands a world away from the art-house soft-core of *Emmanuelle*. But if Oppidian dressed the film up in political threads, it took care to make sure some of its sexual underlay peeped through, describing in great detail the exploits of the film's subject, porn star Claudine Beccarie, and billing the work as 'the most explicit film ever to be shown in public cinema'. Perhaps most tellingly, the majority of the press releases are emblazoned with the film's logo – a silhouette of a spreadeagled woman, viewed from a position beyond her feet, her hand sinking into the dark space somewhere between her thighs. It's an apt visual metaphor for this body of films in general: shocking, but hardly explicit.

The GLC may have been convinced by the distributor's rhetoric;[4] the critics however were less so. 'A licence for filth' was the verdict of *The Sunday People* (Brien 1976). 'Too many blue films are getting the green light nowadays' (Malcolm 1976a). Margaret Hinxman in the *Mail* laments that despite its historical status, it 'will be exploited as the ultimate – so far – in sex movies. One for the dirty raincoat mob' (Hinxman 1976). Nigel Andrews claims it is 'hardly less tame and plodding an essay in titillation than most of its current raincoat trade brethren' (1976). For Clancy Segal in *The Spectator* the film is hamstrung by the same problems as *Emmanuelle*, coming somewhere between porn film and intellectual art-house film and failing to fulfil either set of criteria: 'There wasn't enough talk to satisfy me, and probably too much to satisfy other would be patrons' (1976). Only the *Continental Film Review* – which having begun life as a highbrow publication for Europhiles, as we saw in Chapter Three, had by the 1970s descended into a cross between a film guide and a girlie magazine – greeted *Exhibition* with enthusiasm, listing it alongside several more straightforward sex films as part of the 'New French Cinema' and claiming that 'Since *Emmanuelle*, erotic films have become part of with-it middle-class filmgoing in Paris [...] Exhibition is made by the master of the genre' (*Continental Film Review* 1975). Otherwise, the general mood seems to have been one of ennui: *The People* aside, there was little moral comment on the film's sexual content; the major criticism levelled at the film was that it failed as either entertainment or art.

In some cases, however, the film opened up debates on censorship more largely. Pieces by Virginia Dignam in *The Morning Star*, Ian Christie in *The Daily Express*, and Felix Barker in *The Evening News* (all 1976) took on the GLC's decision to defy the BBFC and pass *Exhibition* uncut. 'With stubborn defiance, the Film Viewing Board of the GLC continue to let us see films as if we were responsible adults', Barker snipes. Dignam goes further: 'The BBFC operate in secret and never have to justify their cuts and prohibitions. [...] If it was not for this type of double-think and hypocrisy *Exhibition* would be recognised for the type of sexploitation film it is and not have to parade as a social document in order to dispel cast-iron prejudices' (1976) The double-bind in which many of these critics found themselves was neatly summed up by Jill Forbes when she wrote that: 'Opponents of censorship are in the position of having to go to the stake for *Exhibition*, which may be, as it has been claimed, a "social and historical document", though not at all because it is "a documentary on the public and private life of France's premier sex actress. If the documentary label helps the film to escape censorship, then it does so dishonestly' (Forbes 1976).

Bad Taste Film

Just as in the 1950s, distributors of numerous French films could thus be seen to play on the country's reputation for intellectualism in order to woo the censors; and on its reputation for sensuality to lure in audiences. Notably, at the time of the emergence of 'New Hollywood' and its aesthetic of ultraviolence, the association of the X category with French film primarily implied sexual explictness, rather than carrying violent or political overtones. This much was true not only of films that were conceived and marketed as part of the new sex cinema, but also of other genres. A case in point is Bernard Borderie's historical romance *Angélique, Marquise des Anges*, adapted from a series of novels that had been hugely popular with teenage girls both in France and in translation in the UK (340,000 paperbacks were sold in Britain alone) (Barker 1967). Distributed by Butcher's and receiving a circuit release in a dubbed version at the end of the 1960s, *Angélique*, which was, in the words of Penelope Mortimer 'about as depraving as an ice lolly', 'should have been a cinch for Christmas treats' (Mortimer 1967). However, although the film was a popular hit in Britain, it was marketed not towards family audiences, but as an X-rated bodice-ripper: its posters comprising a single shot of the naked torso of lead actress Michèle Mercier stretched out on a rumpled bed, and bearing the tagline 'Half angel, half devil, wholly woman!'.[5]

This packaging of films as sexy even in cases where the reality was quite different extended even to their titles. In 1975 Antony Balch sold Alain Jessua's suspense-thriller *Traitement de Choc* to cinemas as *The Doctor in the Nude*. In response to criticism of the decision, he wrote in *Sight and Sound*:

> It was suggested that had I been the distributor of *Nanook of the North* I would have called it *Come, Warm my Igloo*. Well I wouldn't. Commands seldom entice audiences. It's much better to say who, or what, or where. *The Doctor in the Nude* certainly states who and what, and since most of the critics carried on about the title it gave the film extra publicity. [...] The result was that over 100,000 people around the country have now seen a film which might have died a natural death with its modest credentials – [the film's stars and director] Delon, Girardot and Jessua are not enormous draws over here in spite of their talents.
>
> (*Sight and Sound* 1976: 211)

Charles Cooper, owner of Contemporary Films, reflects the distributors' position when he sighs that 'As there is a total availability of approximately 200 English speaking films (from the US and UK) each year, there are only limited possibilities for foreign films. The only possible release in this country is either the highly artistic and/or experimental film or the sex picture' (*Films and Filming* 1970: 22). Miracle's Phil Kutner is even more despondent: 'the future of foreign film distribution is not particularly bright. In spite of many years' hard efforts to popularise foreign films, very few succeed other than the sex oriented film' (*Films and Filming* 1970: 24).

The backlash against what one newspaper dubbed the 'pornography explosion' in cinemas was swift and sharp (Wilson 1971: 189). In 1971, Lord Longford launched an anti-pornography campaign in parliament, urging that at the very least, films should be considered liable to forfeiture under the terms of the 1959 Obscene Publications Act and that the BBFC should come under review (189). It is perhaps no coincidence that the number of films confiscated at Customs rose significantly around this time (189), while police raids were being carried out with alarming regularity on private film clubs – even, as in the case of Andy Warhol's *Flesh*, when the BBFC had given their blessing (Hunnings 1970: 82). With John Trevelyan retiring in 1971, pressure was on replacement Stephen Murphy to crack the whip – an expectation heightened by Murphy's background in the more cautious area of television (Wilson 1971: 189). Newspapers and trades alike speculated on what the outcome of this change of personnel might be, fearing more stringent censorship and the closure, or at least curtailing, of the private cinema clubs which made their profits by showing soft-core porn films – although in the end, this came to very little.

The scandals surrounding soft-core porn paled in comparison however to the outrage provoked by a distinct group of French films that were causing the censors problems for reasons other than their implied eroticism. Both *La Grande Bouffe* in 1973 and *Les Valseuses* in 1975 were banned by the BBFC but passed by the GLC, evoking much comment in the newspapers and, in the case of the former, leading Mary Whitehouse's Festival of Light to bring a private summons against the Curzon Mayfair under sections of the Vagrancy Act of 1824 and 1838. Whitehouse made complaints over scenes where a middle-aged man was masturbated by his elderly nursemaid, where anal intercourse took place and where a man had food shovelled into his mouth while being masturbated until he died – all scenes which she claimed clearly offended 'against recognised standards of propriety' (Birkett 1974). The case was ultimately dismissed because under the laws invoked the Curzon could not be recognised as a public place; nonetheless, the presiding magistrate showed sympathy with Whitehouse's cause, declaring the film an 'indecent exhibition' and stating that his feeling was one of 'sadness that accomplished actors and actresses should prostitute their manifest talents' (Shaw 1974).

The GLC had passed *La Grande Bouffe / Blow Out* for distribution by Gala film under the condition that any cinema at which it was shown provided a synopsis of the film outside the building, and that all publicity material would be examined by the GLC Film Committee before being posted, a move that was repeated for several French films throughout the decade (Birkett 1974). This intended concession to the anti-pornography brigade was however taken as an insult, with Whitehouse commenting that 'The very fact that they put outside a warning that the film is offensive is enough to bring in the very people it may affect' (cited in Birkett 1974), a response which – whether we view it as hysterical or not – reflects what the distributors knew only too well: that the X and the censorship controversies surrounding their films were often the best publicity they could ask for.

In the press, Gala Chairman Kenneth Rive was applauded for refusing the BBFC's offer of an X with substantial cuts; the GLC for passing the film at all; and the Curzon for showing it. All in all, it was taken as a victory against censorship. However, as was the case with *Exhibition*, the film's symbolic value was not perceived to have been matched by its realities: reviews were mostly lacklustre, comparing Ferreri's directorship unfavourably with Luis Buñuel's, and dismissing the film as 'tedious' (Hinxman 1973), 'too long' (Malcolm 1973b) and 'all wind' (Gibbs 1973). Interestingly, where almost all the reviews focused on the prestigious European cast, very little was made of it as a specifically French film, the exception being where food was concerned. Virginia Dignam, in *The Morning Star*, wrote that 'Napoleon once dismissed England as a nation of shopkeepers, with France as the epitome of culture, good food, and wine, but it is salutary to reflect that the French economy is built on alcoholism and that bourgeois attitude is all too often built on decadence' (1974). In *The Spectator*, meanwhile, Christopher Hudson commented:

> There has been no shortage of scenes in which food has been used with heavy symbolism to presage love making; especially for some reason in the French cinema where more decisions are taken between hero and heroine over coffee and croissants on a breakfast tray perched amid rumpled sheet, than were ever taken with them fully-dressed and walking arm in arm through the Bois du Boulogne. It is a French film, *Blow-Out*, which takes this to its logical apotheosis.
>
> (Hudson 1974)

Les Valseuses, meanwhile, also shown at the Curzon under the title *Making It*, was received as the apex of all that was distasteful and wrong with the contemporary French cinema. Russell Davies' review in *The Observer* is one of the least vitriolic: 'the film is well-calculated in the sense that it will satisfy the market that exists, I regret to say, for visions of social and psychological damage inflicted in ways so wanton that the French at least take them as comic' (1975). He promptly dismisses the film as 'Balderdash'. Arthur Thirkell, meanwhile, describes it as 'a new low in French films': 'unwholesome, tawdry, moronic entertainment. *Valseuses* is French slang for testicles. It's fair comment on the film' (1975). Even as late as 1993, the year in which it premièred on Channel 4, the Broadcasting Standards Council were receiving complaints about its 'offensive' content.[6]

It is worth noting that not all films perceived by the general public as being in bad taste were accepted as such by the critical and commercial establishment. Araminta Wordsworth relates a typical reaction to the publicity material for Louis Malle's tale of adolescence *Le Souffle au Coeur*, showing at the Curzon as *Dearest Love* in August 1971. Regarding the images of a young man in the arms of his mother (with whom he will commit incest at the film's climax), a woman was heard to comment to her friend: 'Disgusting! They shan't do that to our lads' (Wordsworth 1971b). Yet while Wordsworth agrees that 'on pictorial evidence it did seem that the unknown lady had a point', having watched the film, she is

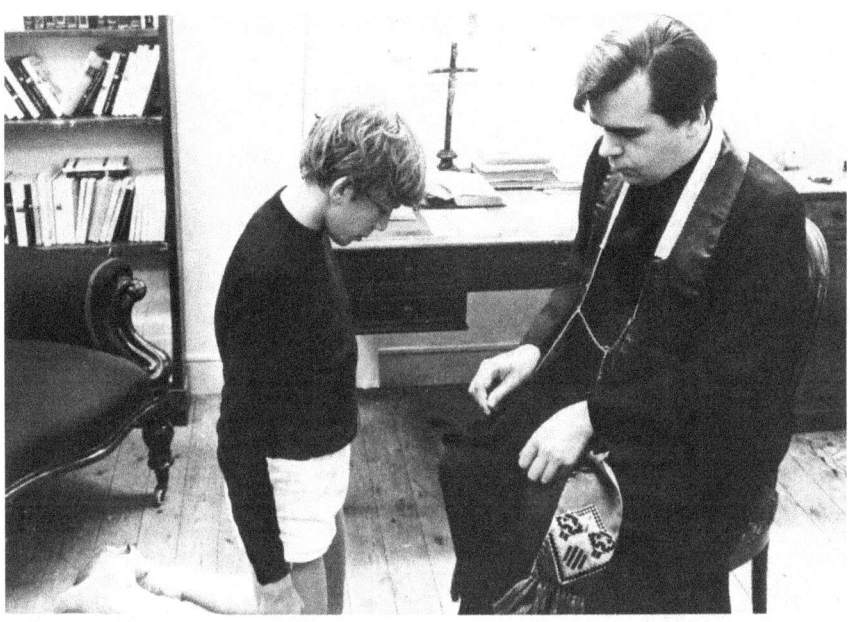

18. Gala's poster for Louis Malle's *Le Souffle au Coeur*, translated by Rive as *Dearest Love*.
Image courtesy of the BFI stills department.

typical of the critical majority in finding the scene of incest 'tastefully, tactfully done', and the film as a whole 'elegant and enjoyable. Its restraint tempers sensation' (Wordsworth 1971b). Cecil Wilson points out in *The Mail* that this is arguably one example of French film's lurid reputation being somewhat overexaggerated: 'Pernicious Foreign Filth! You may cry, but not, I fancy, after you have seen how delicately, and at times even lyrically, this director films it' (Wilson 1971). Indeed, concludes, Michael Walsh, if there's a lesson to be drawn from *Dearest Love*, it's 'how much more adult the French are about these things' (Walsh 1971). Mary Whitehouse may only have confirmed his suspicions when she attempted to sue the BBC for showing the film some eight years later in 1979.[7]

Be this as it may, the very fact that critics such as Eric Shorter were having to reassure their readerships that if on paper *Le Souffle au Coeur* 'all sounds rather French', on screen 'it is not shocking or sensational as one might expect' goes someway to suggesting how prevalent the stereotype of French cinema as bad taste cinema was, even at the beginning of the 1970s (Shorter 1971). The reputation of French film thus undergoes a double shift over the course of the 1970s: moving from the dominant association of French film with 'quality' and style which was put in place as early as the 1930s to a template of the glossy and artful (if rather banal) soft-core pornography films of the early to mid-1970s and finishing the decade as a cinema which is salacious, sleazy, and which sets out to shock. By 1976 and the opening of Jean-Charles Tacchella's *Cousin Cousine* (once more at the Curzon), this reputation had been firmly compounded. 'The decent French film, as opposed to the indecent, doesn't cross the Channel often these days' bemoans Patrick Gibbs in the *Daily Telegraph*, beckoning 'all the warmer welcome then, to *Cousin Cousine*' (Gibbs 1976).

Indeed, somewhat paradoxically for a film about adultery, *Cousin Cousine*'s success may be attributable in no small part to the fact that in a sea of X-rated French films, here was an AA film with no nudity, no explicit sex and very little to shock.[8] For Alexander Walker the film's appeal lay precisely in its 'likeability': for him, it looks back to an earlier class of French film:

> the ones about ordinary people doing ordinary things – but doing them in ways that are observed hilariously, truthfully, with sympathy, yet with ironic detachment. Films that have a common humanity – common that is, to the audience watching them. People the same as us, only different – French people.
> (Walker 1976)

Derek Malcolm echoes the sentiment: '*Cousin Cousine* [. . .] should be immensely attractive to those for whom any well-turned portrait of provincial life in France is manna from heaven' (Malcolm 1976b). He seems to have been proven correct, for subsequent to its showing at the Curzon the film received a circuit release, and despite having been shown almost exclusively in a subtitled print made good returns at the UK box office.

While the film's popularity was almost certainly due in part to its confluences with works by the canonical directors of the New Wave and its variants (Truffaut, Rohmer and Lelouch are frequent touchpoints across the range of reviews, in terms of the film's style and tone), it is not, with the benefit of hindsight, a particularly strong example of this kind of filmmaking and has not attained the canonical status of many of the works with which it is compared. As Richard Combs puts it in *The Times*, the film 'tends to suggest a whole spectrum of French filmmaking, without the distinctive gristle that some directors have brought to it: Eric Rohmer, perhaps, without the intellectual chat, or Claude Chabrol without any murder, or even Claude Lelouch without any soft focus' (Combs 1976). One suspects that had Tacchella's film been released ten years earlier, it would have been less rapturously received. As it is, Richard Barkeley sums up the majority of responses in *The Sunday Express*, when he characterises the work as being 'as stimulating and delightful as a holiday in France' (Barker 1976).

Whatever Happened to the Art Houses?

French film was not alone in being perceived as indecent, or in bad taste, by British audiences of the 1970s. Indeed, the following passage from the introduction to Robert Shail's book on 1970s cinema reveals profound similarities between perceptions of domestic product and those of French cinema as described above:

> The popular perception of the 1970s as 'the decade that taste forgot' unquestionably includes a broad critical consensus that British cinema of the period was generally of little interest apart from a few isolated films. [...] Major filmmakers like Lindsay Anderson, Tony Richardson, John Schlesinger, Jack Clayton, Karel Reisz and John Boorman either seemed to dry up creatively or found themselves driven to Hollywood in order to keep their careers afloat. The lively experimentation of the 1960s was forced to the margins, while popular mainstream cinema became dominated by cheaply produced exploitation horror films, tawdry sex comedies, and uninspired spin-offs from television sit-coms. [...] An air of desperation hangs over the period.
> (Shail 2008: xii)

And yet, Shail claims, there was simultaneously a 'lively independent sector' flourishing within 1970s Britain (2008: xvi), when the early work of Jarman and Greenaway sat alongside the quirky work of new auteurs such as Bill Forsyth and Barney Platt-Mills; punk cinema; documentary films of more politically radical groups such as the London Film-makers Co-op and the London Women's Film Group, and avant-garde and experimental work by theorists/film-makers like Laura Mulvey and Peter Wollen. Many of these films were being shown at the newly opened Other Cinema, an independent theatre opened by Nick Hart-Williams and Peter Sainsbury in August 1970 with Gilles Pontecorvo's *Battle of Algiers* as its inaugural screening (a film which had been shown only once before in the U.K. – during the 1966 London Film Festival). Run on a not-for-profit basis, the Other Cinema was also responsible, in the same year, for showing *Le Gai Savoir* and Straub-Huillet's *Chronicle of Anna Magdalena Bach*, both which saw great success at the box office and with the critics (Gillett 1971: 133). However, the cinema's focus on 'political, social and experimental work' (133) saw its directors turn from French cinema towards British and (Third) World Cinema (*Sight and Sound* 1976: 208). Derek Hill's Essential Cinema, meanwhile, was looking to similarly esoteric works to satisfy its audiences: Borowczyck, Makavejev, Oshima, Rocha and Warhol are amongst the directors that Hill lists as its more popular auteurs (*Sight and Sound* 1976: 208).

Even Contemporary pictures, the stalwarts of French cinema distribution, were seeing a shift in policy, announcing a new aim to 'promote films which involve a social and political need – films which say something of the reality of war (*Kanal, Unknown Soldier*); films which present an alternative point of view (*Inside North Viet Nam, End of the Dialogue, A Sense of Loss*); films which help to create a better sense of understanding between peoples (*China, Memories of Underdevelopment*)' (*Sight and Sound* 1976: 210). Having scored their biggest foreign-language hit of the early 1970s with Miklós Jancsó's Hungarian-language *Szegénylegények / The Round-Up*, Charles and Kitty Cooper told a *Sight and Sound* survey of independent distributors that: 'the cinema must change it if to remain vital and retain its relevance with the public [...] our audience is an informed audience, both socially and politically, and it is therefore always a challenge to us to satisfy its needs' (*Sight and Sound* 1976: 210) The implication appears to be that French film had fallen from fashion with the new, younger audience of '18–30 year olds' whom the Coopers, Hart-Williams and Hill describe as their target demographic. And it's true that a quick flick through the major film publications of the time – *Films and Filming* and *Sight and Sound*, for example – reveals a striking absence of French film coverage between their pages; instead, it is Eastern European, East Asian and American/English underground cinema which dominates the critiques within these magazines.

It is telling too that the directors of the much more mainstream art cinema, the Academy, George Hoellering and Ivo Jarosy, insist in the same survey that 'a film by a well-known French or Italian director stands a better chance of success than one, by, say, an unknown Albanian filmmaker' (*Sight and Sound* 1976: 211). They go on to note that while it is hard to generalise about their audiences, they comprise a core of long-standing regular attendees, some of whom have been patronising the Academy for many years. John Gillet thus describes the situation for foreign-language and independent film in the 1970s as follows: the Other Cinema, the ICA and other, small independents such as the Electric, the Gate, the Screen on the Green and the Essential in London, the Arts Lab in Birmingham and the Arnolfini in Bristol, dedicated themselves to political and world cinema; the BFI and the Regional Theatres to the making available of 'mainstream' continental productions, and the local film societies to classics and revivals (Gillett 1971: 133). In addition to these three categories, the larger art-house theatres tended to show new cinema from established auteurs or art cinema with a twist – the scandalous spectacles of *Les Valseuses* and *La Grande Bouffe*, for example – while the circuits stuffed co-produced dubbed genre pieces into their second feature slots.

There was, of course, one final outlet for French film in Britain, which was television. Much has been made of television's deleterious effect on Europe and America's cinema audiences in the 1970s (see for example Hayward 2005: 61–72), and one might expect that the BBC's scheduling of a weekly foreign-language film slot would prove similarly detrimental to the cinematic screening of French films in Britain. However, when, in a survey of independent distributors published in 1970 in *Films and Filming*, the following question was posed: 'Foreign films are shown regularly on BBC2, when in one viewing more people can see a foreign film than in many months of theatrical exhibition ... do you think this is helping to create a cinema-going audience for foreign films or is it direct competition for the specialised cinema?', the general consensus amongst the distributors interviewed was that competition from television was minimal, and that the increased visibility of subtitled films could only help to create a wider audience for it more generally. However, the caveats were twofold: firstly, it was perceived that BBC2 tended to show only 'artistic' types of film, and therefore it would only enhance audiences for this particular kind of product; secondly, there was a feeling that the television audience was of a different generation to the film-going audience (the view is reiterated that film-goers are younger than television viewers), and so the crossover potential was limited.[9]

There is also the question of how often French films were being shown on television, and what these films were. The weekly slot on BBC2 was given over to World Cinema from all nationalities, with French films making up a substantial proportion of these in most years of the decade. Yet only two French films were shown in 1970 (*Le Départ* and *À Double Tour*), with an average of twelve per year showing until 1978, when a Truffaut season which commenced in September contributed half of the eighteen films shown. In 1979, twelve of the twenty films shown were part of a Jean Renoir season. Take into account too that the slot moved between 9 and 11 pm on a Thursday or Friday night, and it is small wonder that the distribution companies were unconcerned with the question of whether French films on television would reduce cinema audiences – it was hardly a frequently occurring phenomenon. And this despite the fact that at the beginning of the 1970s, of the 1,750 cinemas in England, only fifty were estimated to be showing foreign-language films.

If the films themselves were few and far between, moreover, they were also limited in range. For the most part, the films shown fell into one of five categories: retrospectives based around a director or star (in addition to Truffaut and Renoir, Chabrol, Tati, Moreau and Bardot all had seasons dedicated to their works – the latter pair to coincide with the Curzon's release of *Viva Maria!*); 'classics' from the 1930s and 1940s; the more accessible works by the *nouvelle vague* directors; the more successful second-feature thrillers starring Belmondo and Delon, and the occasional première of a film that hadn't received a cinema release, such as Maurice Pialat's *L'Enfance Nue* and Claude Lelouch's *Un Homme qui me plaît*.

Note here the retention of the original titles. Where the BBC's screenings of French films make perhaps make an interesting contribution to the perception of the national cinema in the 1970s is in terms, once more, of dubbing and subtitling. For it appears, looking through the listings, that the BBC's policy was wherever possible to show subtitled versions rather than dubbed ones, even in cases, including *Day for Night* or *La Sirène du Mississippi*, where the dubbed versions had been used for the British cinema release. For the screening of *La Sirène*, they also showed the uncut version. The provenance of these uncut, subtitled prints is unclear, although in the case of Eric Rohmer's German-language *Die Marquise von O*, the *Radio Times* reviewer Philip Jenkinson states that the BBC subtitled the film themselves after the dubbed print received a terrible response in cinemas (Jenkinson 1976: 11). Jenkinson, who wrote a weekly round-up of films being shown, was prone to comment on the quality of the films' translation: discussing a 1977 screening of *Angélique* he describes the experience of being subjected to the film's poor dubbing as 'like listening to the radio and watching TV with the sound off while whistling Oh Mein Papa' (1977: 11); whilst previewing Rohmer's *Ma Nuit Chez Maud*, he advises the reader that 'there are lots of subtitles, so make sure your set is tuned just right' (1973: 9). The most interesting experiment with film translation came in 1972, when the BBC screened two versions of *Viva Maria!* – first a subtitled print, then a dubbed one. 'To dub or not dub, that is the question', wrote Jenkinson, inviting viewers to write to him with their opinions (1972: 19). Sadly, whatever responses Jenkinson received, they were not published.

The BBC's preference for subtitling was, for the most part, reflective of the product it was showing: canonical art-house hits. It was also, perhaps, suggestive of its audiences: the same middle-aged, middle-class, Sunday-intelligentsia that frequented the mainstream art houses and film societies, or, as one commentator describes them, 'the highbrow audiences of the Academy, Curzon [who] prefer sub-titled films' (*Films and Filming* 1970: 24). In this one context, at least, French film's primary appeal remained unchanged: these audiences are, then, a continuation of those very types who first frequented the Film Society in the 1930s and who flocked to the Continental cinemas in the 1940s.

Conclusion: Into the 1980s: French Films, British Tastes at the End of the Decade

And it is precisely this audience that would be targeted by exhibitors once again come the 1980s, and the arrival of a series of high-budget, glossy literary adaptations such as *Jean de Florette* and *Cyrano de Bergerac* on British shores, a film 'movement' that would once more have the chattering classes flocking to the art houses. Looking at the situation at the end of the 1970s, it is easy to spot the gap in the marketplace for this kind of product, and to see signs of a desire for a return to the 'quality' heritage drama so popular in the 1930s and 1940s, and in the frequently occurring and well-attended retrospectives of directors such as Pagnol, Clair, Renoir and Carné taking place at the larger art houses, in film societies and on the BBC.

When the 1980s arrived, they would be seen at the time as a second golden age for French cinema; the 1970s meanwhile have been historically dismissed as a black spot. And it is true that the decade was in many ways a difficult time for French film, both at the domestic box office and abroad. In the U.K., perceptions of French film altered significantly over the course of the decade: by its end, nostalgia for the vitality and innovation of the 1960s and the quality of the films made before that went hand in hand with a disdain for the 'poor quality' and 'bad taste' of the films that were now crossing the Channel. And yet to dismiss the 1970s as a nondescript, uninteresting period in the history of French cinema in Britain is to miss precisely what it is that makes it so interesting. For this is a period – perhaps the only period – in which British perceptions of French cinema are not dominated by one overwhelming trend, movement or genre. The sex film may have been the closest approximation, and yet it does not spring automatically to mind in the way that the *nouvelle vague* does when thinking of French cinema in the 1960s, or the heritage drama will in the 1980s. French cinema in 1970s Britain was a heterogenous entity, one that was both popular and artistic, mainstream and esoteric; which was the epitome of middle-class mores and the ultimate in bad taste; which was avant-garde and highly retro; and, in some cases, which didn't even seem to be French at all. If the 1970s was not a high point for French film in Britain in artistic or creative terms, then, it may well have seen the greatest diversity of national output available to U.K. audiences. Indeed the 'disappearance' of French cinema might in fact simply be a dispersal: if it lacks the homogeneity of previous eras, this is replaced by a multifaceted body of works, shown in various outlets and received in conflicting but often productive manners. It is telling, too, that what was once the *dernier cri* in bad taste has, over the course of time, become institutionalised: by the 1990s and 2000s, films such as *La Grande Bouffe*, *Les Valseuses* and even *Emmanuelle* have been the subject of numerous UK reprints or retrospectives. With time, the ambivalence levelled at them has disappeared, to be replaced with full-throated praise.

Notes

1. According to a former schoolfriend of Shorter's, Tunbridge Wells was in fact the town of his upbringing, to which he paid regular visits, so it is safe to assume that the implication that he'd searched the length and breadth of England to track down the film involves a little artistic licence.

2. Mark Betz writes that the film, a co-production between France, Italy and Great Britain, was partially funded by Warner Bros. through its London subsidiary (Columbia-Warner), and one of the stipulations of the agreement was that Warner Bros. would have worldwide distribution rights for the film, excluding France and Italy. Since they were a major studio whose business was 'to reach as large an audience as possible', Betz concludes, it was only natural that the film would be dubbed rather than subtitled. Moreover, he claims, Truffaut 'entered into production with full knowledge of this outcome' (Betz 2009: 47).
3. The first year of the decade had seen a revision of censorship categories, which was announced in July and intended to bring British categorisation into line with Southern European systems. The change saw films spread over four, rather than the previous three, categories, adding AA (over fourteens only) to the previous categories of X, A and U, with the age limit for the X being raised from sixteen to eighteen years (Hunnings 1970: 71). The implications for the industry were twofold: on the one-hand, fewer films would be placed in the X category; but on the other, those that were categorised as X were much more clearly marked as adult material.
4. The relationship of the BBFC and the GLC was not a particularly happy one in the 1970s. In the eyes of the latter, the BBFC was becoming increasingly obsolete (as Neville Hunnings points out, the impending development of cable and videotapes was to render it increasingly difficult to maintain control over who was watching what, bringing cinema into line with books and records – two forms of media subject to much less rigid censorship), and on 28 January 1975, the Greater London Council rejected by the narrowest of margins (fifty votes to forty-four) a proposal to abolish film censorship for adults (Hunnings 1975: 158), following a long battle by Mrs Enid Wistrich, then Chairman of the GLC's film viewing board, to persuade the Government to study the possibility of reforming its censorship laws – not significantly changed for over fifty years. The GLC appeared to have lost the battle, but it has been speculated that the number of those voting for the proposal shocked the BBFC into re-examining its methods: coincidence or not, two years later, in May 1977, Professor Bernard Williams was appointed to chair a new committee to review the laws on obscenity, indecency, and violence in publications, displays and entertainments and to review the film censorship system (Hunnings 1975: 158).
5. In a survey conducted in *Films in Filming* in 1970, Butcher's were one of a number of independent distributors asked the question: 'What has been the most successful foreign film you have distributed in the last three years ... is it possible to determine why the film was successful (eg. an original theme, controversial sexual content, a cult director etc)' to which their answer was *Angélique*. 'It has no sexual content', they added, somewhat disingenuously one might say (*Films and Filming* 1970).
6. This information comes from a Broadcasting Standards Council report located in the BFI microfiche for *Les Valseuses*, available from the BFI. The report, dated March 1993 and referring to excessive violence and pornographic elements in the film, notes that the complaint was not upheld.
7. This information comes from a report in *The Daily Mail*, dated 6 February 1979.

8. *Cousin Cousine* did not entirely escape commentary on Gallic morality: in *The Evening News* Felix Barker slyly comments that 'From Sutton to Woodford, I suspect, middle-class adultery would not be treated with the tolerance we observe on the outskirts of Paris [. . .] the comedy carries the message that when it comes to infidelity they obviously order things better in France (Barker 1976).
9. The distributors interviewed were Amanda Films, Butcher's, Cinecenta, Connoisseur, Contemporary, Darville, Miracle, New Realm, Planet, and Target (*Films and Filming* 1970).

Bibliography

Andrews, N. 1974. 'Un Flic', *Financial Times*, 6 September.
Andrews, N. 1976. 'Exhibition', *Financial Times*, 10 December.
Barkeley, R. 1976. 'Cousin Cousine', *Sunday Express*, 17 October.
Barker, F. 1967. 'Angélique, Marquise des Anges', *Evening News*, 28 September.
Barker, F. 1970.' Borsalino', *Evening News*, 30 July.
Barker, F. 1976. 'Exhibition', *Evening News*, 9 September.
Barker, F. 1977. 'The Story of Adele H', *Evening News*, 1 September.
Betz, M. 2009. *Beyond the Subtitle: Remapping European Cinema*, Minneapolis: University of Minnesota Press.
Birkett, P. 1974. 'Blow Out Sex Offended Mrs Whitehouse', *Daily Telegraph*, 9 April.
Brien, A. 1976. 'Exhibition', *Sunday Times*, 12 December.
Caskin, F. 1970. 'Borsalino', *Sun*, 30 July.
Castell, D. 1981. 'Lady Chatterley's Lover', *Sunday Telegraph*, 20 December.
Christie, I. 1974. 'Emmanuelle', *Daily Express*. 4 October.
Christie, I. 1976. 'The New Films', *Daily Express*, 10 December.
Cocks, J. 1972. 'Le Samouraï', *Time*, 2 October.
Coleman, J. 1970. 'Borsalino', *New Statesman*, 7 August.
Coleman, J. 1974. 'Emmanuelle', *New Statesman*, 11 October.
Combs, R. 1976. 'Cousin, Cousine', *Times*, 15 October.
Continental Film Review. 1975. 'The New French Cinema', 22(12): 14–15.
Davies, R. 1974. 'Mississippi Mermaid', *Observer*, 28 August.
Davies, R. 1975. 'Making It', *Observer*, 2 November.
Dawson, J. 1974. 'Mississippi Mermaid', *New Statesman*, 1 May.
Degand, C. 1973. '1972/3: A Turning Point for European Cinema?', *Sight and Sound*, Spring: 107–9.
Dignam, V. 1970. 'The Sicilian Plan', *Morning Star*, 24 July.
Dignam, V. 1974. 'Blow Out', *Morning Star*, 4 January.
Dignam, V. 1976. 'Sexpolitation Film Causes a lot of Hot Air and Hypocrisy', *Morning Star*, 10 December.
Errol, P. 1970. 'Borsalino', *Sunday Express*, 2 August.
Films and Filming. 1970. 'Foreign Films on British Screens: A Survey', 16(9): 18–26.
Followell, D. 1974. 'Emmanuelle', *Spectator*, 12 October.
Forbes, J. 1976. 'Exhibition', *Monthly Film Bulletin* 43(513), October: 213.
Gibbs, P. 1973. 'Blow Out', *Telegraph*, 28 December.

Gibbs, P. 1976. 'Cousin, Cousine', *Telegraph*, 15 October.
Gillard, D. 1970. 'Borsalino', *Daily Sketch*, 7 August.
Gillett, J. 1971. 'Towards Another Cinema', *Sight and Sound*, Summer: 133.
Harmsworth, M. 1970. 'Deadly Charm: Borsalino', *Sunday Mirror*, 2 August.
Hayward, S. 2005 [1993] . *French National Cinema*, 2nd ed. Oxford: Routledge.
Hinxman, M. 1972. 'The Red Circle', *Sunday Telegraph*, 12 March.
Hinxman, M. 1973. 'Blow Out', *Sunday Telegraph*, 30 December.
Hinxman, M. 1974a. 'Mississippi Mermaid', *Sunday Telegraph*, 28 April.
Hinxman, M. 1974b. 'Emmanuelle', *Daily Mail*, 4 October.
Hinxman, M. 1976. 'The Girl who Makes Skin Flicks Almost Respectable', *Daily Mail*, 11 December.
Houston, P. 1970. 'Borsalino', *Spectator*, 6 August.
Houston, P. 1974/75. 'Box Office', *Sight and Sound*, Winter: 23.
Houston, P. 1979/80. 'Onwards but not Upwards', *Sight and Sound*, Winter: 2–4.
Hudson, C. 1974. 'Blow Out', *Spectator*, 12 January.
Hunnings, N. 1970. 'The Film Industry and The EEC', *Sight and Sound*, Spring.
Hunnings, N. 1975. 'Censorship in France', *Sight and Sound*. Summer: 158.
Jenkinson, P. 1972. 'This Week's Films', *Radio Times*, 14 December: 19.
Jenkinson, P. 1973. 'This Week's Films', *Radio Times*, 24 May: 9.
Jenkinson, P. 1976. 'This Week's Films', *Radio Times*, 30 October: 11.
Jenkinson, P. 1977. 'This Week's Films', *Radio Times*, 28 August: 11.
Johnson, D. 1975. 'The Story of Adele H', *TLS*, 21 November.
Lewis, J. 1976. 'Bluest Film Yet Gets the Cinema Go-ahead', *Daily Mirror*, 9 July.
Malcolm, D. 1970. 'Borsalino', *Guardian*, 30 July.
Malcolm, D. 1973a. 'Day for Night', *Guardian*, 15 November.
Malcolm, D. 1973b. 'Blow Out', *Guardian*, 21 December.
Malcolm, D. 1974. 'Emmanuelle', *Guardian*, 3 October.
Malcolm, D. 1976a. 'Bottom of the Market', *Guardian*, September.
Malcolm, D. 1976b. 'Cousin, Cousine', *Guardian*, 14 October.
Mortimer, P. 1967. 'Angélique, Marquise des Anges', *Observer*, 1 October.
Oppidian. 1976. Exhibition pressnotes. Available from the BFI library.
P.G. 1974. 'Emmanuelle', *Daily Telegraph*, 3 October.
Playboy Magazine. 1975. 'Emmanuelle' [no month – source is available from BFI clippings unit] .
Porter, V. 1978. 'British Film Culture and The European Community', *Sight and Sound*, Summer: 135–9.
Porter, V. 1979a. 'End of the Road for Quota?', *Sight and Sound*, Spring: 91.
Porter, V. 1979b. 'Film Policy for the 1980s: Industry or Culture?' *Sight and Sound*, Autumn: 221–23, 266.
Powell, D. 1972. 'The Red Circle', *Sunday Times*, 12 March.
Powell, D. 1974. 'Emmanuelle', *Sunday Times*, 6 October.
Price, S. 1970a. 'The Sicilian Plan', *Observer*, 26 July.
Price, S. 1970b. 'Borsalino', *Observer*, 2 August.
Raven, S. 1974. 'Who is Sylvia?', *Sunday Times*, 15 August.
Rayns, T. 1974. 'Un Flic', *New Statesman*, 30 August.
Robinson, D. 1970. 'Borsalino', *Financial Times*, 31 July.
Robinson, D. 1972. 'The Red Circle', *Financial Times*, 10 March.
Robinson, D. 1974. 'Emmanuelle', *The Times*, 4 October.
Roud, R. 1971. 'The Red Circle', *Guardian*, 5 January.

Russell Taylor, J. 1970. 'Borsalino' *The Times*, 1 August.
Russell Taylor, J. 1972. 'The Red Circle', *The Times*, 10 March.
Segal, C. 1976. 'Exhibition', *Spectator*, 18 December.
SF Films. 1974. *Emmanuelle* pressnotes. (Available from BFI library.)
Shail, R. 2008. *Seventies British Cinema*. London: Palgrave.
Shaw, T. 1974. 'Mrs Whitehouse Loses Blow-Out Court Fight', *Daily Telegraph*, 27 April.
Shorter, E. 1971. 'Dearest Love', *Daily Telegraph*, 20 August.
Shorter, E. 1974. 'Un Flic', *Daily Telegraph*, 6 September.
Sight and Sound. 1976. 'Other and Essential: A Survey of Independent Distributors/Exhibitors', 45(4), October: 207–11.
Thinkell, A. 1972. 'The Red Circle', *Daily Mirror*, 9 March.
Thinkell, A. 1975. 'Making It', *Daily Mirror*, 24 October.
Thomson, D. 1979. 'A Look Back', *Sight and Sound*, Autumn: 5–7.
Turner, A. 1974. 'Dubbed and Snubbed', *Films Illustrated* 3: 382–83.
Walker, A. 1974. 'Mississippi Mermaid', *Evening Standard*, 25 April.
Walker, A. 1976. 'Cousin Cousine', *Evening Standard*, 14 October.
Walker, A. 1977. 'The Story of Adele H.', *Evening Standard*, 1 September.
Walsh, M. 1971. 'Dearest Love', *Daily Express*, 18 August.
Walsh, M. 1973. 'Day for Night', *Daily Express*, 15 November.
Webster, P. 1974. 'Emmanuelle', *Guardian*, 16 July.
Wilson, C. 1971. 'Dearest Love', *Daily Mail*, 19 August.
Wilson, C. 1972. 'The Red Circle', *Daily Mail*, 9 March.
Wilson, D. 1971. 'Waiting for Murphy', *Sight and Sound*, Autumn: 189–90.
Wordsworth, A. 1971a. 'Le Samourai', *Times*, 4 June.
Wordsworth, A. 1971b. 'Dearest Love', *Times*, 17 August.

Filmography

À Double Tour / Web of Passion (1959, Claude Chabrol)
A Sense of Loss (1972, Marcel Ophuls)
Angélique, Marquise des Anges (1964, Bernard Borderie)
Armée des Ombres, L' / Army of the Shadows (1969, Jean-Pierre Melville)
Baisers Volés / Stolen Kisses (1966, François Truffaut)
Battaglia d'Algeri, La / The Battle of Algiers (1966, Gilles Pontecorvo)
Belle de Jour (1967, Luis Buñuel)
Bonnie and Clyde (1967, Arthur Penn)
Borsalino (1970, Jacques Deray)
Butch Cassidy and the Sundance Kid (1969, George Roy Hill)
Cercle Rouge, Le / The Red Circle (1970, Jean Pierre Melville)
Chung-Kuo – Cinema / China (1972, Michaelangelo Antonioni)
Chinatown (1974, Roman Polanski)
Chronik der Anna Magdelena Bach / Chronicle of Anna Magdalena Bach (1968, Jean-Marie Straub / Danièlle Huillet)
Clan des Siciliens, Le / The Sicilien Plan (1969, Henri Verneuil)
Cousin Cousine (1975, Jean-Charles Tacchella)
Cyrano de Bergerac (1990, Jean-Paul Rappeneau)
Départ, Le / The Departure (1967, Jerzy Skolimowski)

Easy Rider. (1969, Dennis Hopper)
Eclisse, L' / *The Eclipse* (1962, Michelangelo Antonioni)
Emmanuelle (1974, Just Jaeckin)
Enfance Nue, L' / *Naked Childhood* (1968, Maurice Pialat)
Enfant Sauvage, L' / *The Wild Boy* (1973, François Truffaut).
Enfants Terribles, Les (1950, Jean-Pierre Melville)
Exhibition (1975, Jean-François Davy)
Flesh (1968, Andy Warhol)
Flic, Un / *Dirty Money* (1972, Jean-Pierre Melville)
For Pete's Sake (1974, Peter Yates)
Gai Savoir, Le (1969, Jean-Luc Godard)
Gattopardo, Il / *The Leopard* (1963, Luchino Visconti)
Godfather, The (1972, Francis Ford Coppola)
Grande Bouffe, La / *Blow-Out* (1973, Marco Ferreri)
Histoire d'Adèle H., L' / *The Story of Adele H.* (1975, François Truffaut)
Histoire d'O / *The Story of O.* (1975, Just Jaeckin)
Histoires d'A (1974, Charles Belmont / Marielle Issartel)
Homme et une femme, Un / *A Man and a Woman* (1966, Claude Lelouch)
Inside North Viet Nam (1967, Felix Greene)
Jaws (1975, Stephen Spielberg)
Jean de Florette (1986, Claude Berri)
Juggernaut (1974, Richard Lester)
Kanal (1978, Erden Kiral)
Ma Nuit Chez Maud (1969, Eric Rohmer)
Marquise von O., Die / *The Marquise of O.* (1976, Eric Rohmer)
Memorias del subdesarrollo / *Memories of Underdevelopment* (1968, Tomàs Gutiérrez Alea)
Midnight Cowboy (1969, John Schlesinger)
Nanook of the North (1922, Robert J. Flaherty)
Il Portiere di notte / *Night Porter, The* (1974, Liliana Caviani)
Nuit Americaine, La / *Day for Night* (1979, François Truffaut)
Odessa File, The (1974, Ronald Neame)
Pat Garrett and Billy the Kid (1973, Sam Peckinpah)
Phela-ndaba / *The End of the Dialogue* (1974, Anon.)
Public Enemy, The (1931, William A. Wellman)
Samouraï, Le / *The Samurai* / *The Godson* (U.S. title) (1967, Jean-Pierre Melville)
Saturday Night Fever (1977, John Badham)
Sirène du Mississippi, La / *Mississippi Mermaid* (1969, François Truffaut)
Souffle au Coeur, Le / *Dearest Love* (1971, Louis Malle)
Star Wars (1977, George Lucas)
Stardust (1974, Michael Apted)
Stavisky (1974, Alain Resnais)
Szegénylegények / *The Round-Up* (1966, Miklòs Janscó)
That's Entertainment (1974, Jack Haley Jr)
Town Called Hell, A (1971, Robert Parrish)
Traitement de Choc / *Doctor in the Nude* (1973, Alain Jessua)
Ultimo Tango à Parigi / *Last Tango in Paris* (1972, Bernando Bertolucci)
Un Homme qui me plait (1969, Claude Lelouch)
Valseuses, Les / *Making It* (1974, Bertrand Blier)
Viva Maria! (1965, Louis Malle)

6

VIDEO SAVED THE FRENCH FILM?
(1982–2002)

Flicking through the pages of the various specialist film journals published in the 1980s, the standing of French film in 1980s Britain is not immediately discernible. To a large extent, this is because there is a major shift in the subjects being discussed within their pages and headlined on their covers. Once magazines such as *Sight and Sound* and *Films and Filming* were replete with studies of the latest auteurs and film movements – with the odd retrospective or nostalgia piece thrown in for good measure – and so it was easy to spot the Renoirs, Renais, the New Waves and the Avant-Gardes. During this decade, however, their pages were increasingly occupied with industrial surveys and 'think pieces' on the nature of contemporary film-consumption, making it altogether more difficult to trace the reputation of specific national cinemas. If French film in Britain during this period can be discussed, it has to be situated within a context in which film as a whole was undergoing substantial changes.

For while the focus of these articles ranged from television programming strategies to the varying attitudes of Britain's political parties to film and the arts, the most recurrent subject is best summed up by a five-page feature jointly authored by David Docherty, David Morrison and Michael Tracey: '?Who Goes to the Cinema?' (1986). The unconventional punctuation and the striking, soviet style font of the title, which spans a full half-page, conveys something of the urgency with which this question was posed: for the British film industry, this was arguably the key question of the 1980s, one which resounded throughout the decade. The search for an answer to it was arguably the key concern.

Docherty, Morrison and Tracey's article was based on the findings of a Broadcasting Research Unit (BRU) project, *The Entertainment Film in National Life*, which itself drew on a questionnaire administered for the BRU by the National Opinion Polls, between 7 and 10 December 1984, using a representative quota sample of 795 people at sixty-seven points throughout Great Britain. The imperative behind it speaks for itself. By 1981, cinema admissions had dropped to 86 million, from 107 million in 1976. The years 1980–84 saw a further decrease in audiences, witnessing the biggest percentage drop in cinema-going since the five-year period between 1955 and 1959 (Docherty et al. 1986: 82), with 1982 being the worst ever year for British cinemas (Murphy 1983/84: 8). During this period several of the leading independent distribution houses – Alpha, GTO, Barber International Entertainment – had switched from film to video distribution, while the majors struggled in their own way: no longer profitable as individual concerns, Universal, Paramount and MGM/UA had amalgamated to form a larger, umbrella company, UIP, while Rank was jettisoning unprofitable cinemas at break-neck speed, dropping down to 88 cinemas compared with a peak of 600 in the 1940s (Murphy 1983/84: 8).[1] The bleak mood was summed up by Artificial Eye's Andi Engels when he commented in 1984 that: 'There's no question in my mind that the commercial cinema here is doomed – and don't talk about the year 2000. It's finished, washed up, forget it' (Murphy 1983/84: 11). Viewed in retrospect, Engels' position was somewhat pessimistic, to put it mildly, and in fact Artificial Eye was one of the decade's success stories, as we shall see in due course. But in the early 1980s his perspective was one that many would have concurred with. Clearly, this was an industry in crisis.

Quite what had happened was a question that the press, along with the various sectors of the industry – film-makers, exhibitors, distributors, marketers – and even the British government, were struggling to answer. Competing theories abounded, and even today making sense of the state of British cinema in the 1980s involves a certain amount of speculation. However, if we are to understand the peculiar place of French films on British screens during the period in question, we need first to understand the context into which they were arriving. What will immediately follow, then, is an attempt at synthesising the various forces structuring the British film industry during the decade, and the responses to them, before we turn our attention once more to the position of French film upon screens in the U.K.

An Industry in Crisis

Much has been written about the perceived crisis in the British film industry that took place during the 1980s. The primary cause is most frequently cited as lying in competing technologies: on the one hand the advent of VHS (in 1975) and laser discs (1978); on the other the continued rise of television, in both its network and cable forms. However, cinematic attendance had been gradually declining for some thirty years. And as Docherty et al. point out: 'the discussion of the decline of cinema is often wrapped in half truths, excuses and genuine mistakes' (1986: 82). The authors suggest that two myths inform much of the thinking in Britain about the decline in audiences during the 1980s, myths which they term the 'myth of technological evolution' and the 'myth of the universal audience':

> The first myth states that cinema inexorably gave way to television as part of the development in the technology of delivering visual entertainment, and that cinema has therefore been fighting a losing battle ever since. The second myth states that once upon a time everyone went to the cinema, and that the way forward is an indiscriminate attempt to lure them all back.
> (Docherty et al. 1986: 82)

So just as television was blamed in the 1950s for the sudden drop in audience, VCRs (videocassette recorders) were frequently being held responsible for the decline in cinema attendance in the 1980s. Yet, as Docherty and his co-authors point out, neither of these technological developments is an adequate explanation of why the long-term decline in attendances was so much worse in the U.K. than in any other country. In 1980s North America, for instance, 'television is watched at least as much as it is in Britain, and the use of VCRs is increasing'; however, the American film industry was comparatively stable, 'with a ratio of population size to ticket sales of about 1: 5 [per year] ', compared with the British figure of 1: 1 (82). The authors of this article claim that what needs to be taken into account then are the different kinds of audience going to the cinema – their social background, income and lifestyle – a topic that makes explicit the questions of class and taste that, as we have seen, have so long circulated around the exhibition, promotion and consumption of French cinema in the U.K., and a manner of analysing the situation in 1980s Britain that can shed a clear light on its status at this specific juncture.

The article offers a very detailed analysis of the principal cinema-going demographic viewed through the lens of age, income, and even marital status. While we cannot reiterate every one of its fascinating revelations, a number of salient facts are worth reproducing here. Firstly, that 80 per cent of the population agreed that, 'If a film is good, I don't mind where I watch it' – and that those who went to the cinema were slightly more likely to agree that the setting doesn't matter than those who did not. Secondly, that only 31 per cent considered cinema to be the best way to watch feature films, with 22 per cent choosing VCR and 42 per cent television. Forty per cent of the general public considered that there were too few feature films shown on television. From this, Docherty et al. conclude that 'one can love film separately from loving cinema', and that the decline in cinematic audiences was not so much attributable to a disaffection with feature film, as with the cinematic space. 'For most of those who go', they write, 'a visit to the cinema is a social activity, and the cinema itself is only part of an evening out'. By contrast, 'when a film is hired on video, it is the film pure and simple that is enjoyed and not some experience wider than the home can provide' (85).

Given that the audience for French films in Britain has historically been shown to demonstrate a tendency for cinephilia, one might expect this statement to have some pertinence for the French cinema being consumed within the United Kingdom at this point. All the more so since those audiences who had been consuming a certain kind of French film not for reasons of cinephilia but salaciousness – the dirty raincoat brigade, as Ian Christie so kindly dubbed them – were one of the first audiences to disappear from cinemas. If nothing else, video certainly killed the sex cinema. However, the specific impact of VHS on French film is a little more complicated that the BRU's findings might suggest, as we shall come to see.

Exhibition and the RFTs

Docherty, Morrison and Tracey's conclusions put the onus on the exhibition sector: succinctly put, the problem was not one of convincing potential audiences to watch films, but convincing them to watch them in cinemas. One further interesting finding: according to the survey, the most frequent cinema attendees were the low-income eighteen to twenty-four age group, who went to the cinema for social reasons (often to be with their boyfriend or girlfriend; to escape the parental home; or to exercise some choice over their viewing – bear in mind that at this point most households still only had one television). This is paradoxically the same demographic that, according to Simon Perry (1980) represented the bulk of the home video audience. The implication for Perry is that 'the main categories of selling to home audiences will be thriller pictures, kung-fu, sexploitation, TV comedies and sport', while 'difficult films and foreign material won't flourish [. . .] until the market has developed sufficiently to support loss leaders and unprofitable prestige programmes' (1980: 82).

So young, lower-class people were still watching films at this point, both in the cinemas and in the home. But what of the middle-class audiences who had tended to constitute the primary audience for French films in earlier decades? One year on, the BRU conducted a further survey, this time looking into the audience for the regional film theatres; Docherty once more reported on its findings in the pages of *Sight and Sound* (writing solo this time around), in the Summer edition of 1987. The results were telling. According to the survey, the RFT audience was, as one might expect, primarily middle class; one-third was comprised by students; another fifth lecturers and teachers. Ninety per cent left school later than the minimum age; indeed approximately 25 per cent had some form of vocational or post-graduate training after university or college. 'Not only is the audience middle class', concludes Doherty, 'but it is only a small section of the middle class' (1987: 163). No surprises there. However, although 'it might seem that RFT audiences would have more positive reasons for seeing films [than the more generalised cinema-going public], and that attendances would therefore be less affected by social forces – marriage, childcare etc – that cause a steep falling-off [in ages] in the commercial sector', fully 80 per cent of the RFT audience were aged between fifteen and thirty-five, exactly the same as for the commercial cinema (193).²

The major implication that emerges from the BRU surveys is that cinemas, both commercial and state-run, were struggling to bring in a broad audience. Neither were able to successfully attract middle-aged audiences as regular attendees; while the younger audiences who were visiting adhered fixedly to a pair of determinate social types. As Tim Pulleine puts it: 'with "habit" filmgoing effectively dead, and with the number of cinemas diminished, 'the "town-and-gown" division between general and discerning viewers seems paradoxically to have become wider' (1982: 175). The question facing the industry was therefore how to appeal to a wider cross-section of society.

The solution as both sides saw it lay with the cross-fertilisation of discrete elements of these two audiences. For the BFI, who ran the RFTs, the imperative was a cultural one: to maintain a vital cinema culture by whatever means necessary; to 'put to use as broad and flexible a notion of film culture as possible'; to move away from the elitist image that had been built up, the perception that these were 'weird student places'; and, crucially, 'to construct an audience, persuading them to see a wider range of stuff' (Doherty 1987: 163). Thus the Tyneside Film Theatre in Newcastle might, in addition to running highly specialised events such as a Q&A with Marguerite Duras on *India Song*, couple a circuit film such as *Coming Home* with the little-known *Cuba* in order to entice a wider audience for the smaller film (Pulleine 1982: 176). By the end of the decade, the policy had reached a natural, if somewhat depressing apex. As Tony Kirkhope of the Other Cinema comments in 1989:

> The foreign product they show is a distillation of the more commercially successful art house movies in London. They run them for very short periods of time and they're not bothered about films which haven't entirely succeeded. There's not the commitment to this area that there used to be, and they tend to offset the more 'difficult' films with ones that could easily be at a Cannon around the corner.
>
> (Petley 1989: 225)

Meanwhile, taking a similarly scatter-gun approach to programming, the circuits experimented with Hollywood blockbusters and European 'specialised' product in turn. To some extent, this had been the standard, albeit inadvertent, practice for some time. As we discussed in the last chapter, the 1970s saw few nascent European talents make a marked impact on the British box office; Continental fare, and French film in particular, had ceased to be synonymous with quality and come instead to be associated with sex, scandal and second features. During the same period, North America had produced succeeding generations of innovative talent. The result was a rather confused booking policy whereby, as Guy Phelps describes it, 'the circuit cinemas, booking in the regular American product, frequently found themselves playing what could only be described as "art" films', usurping the art houses without even trying (Phelps, 1983/84: 14). But with the likes of Scorsese and Coppola having been replaced by Spielberg and Lucas, *Easy Rider* by *E.T.*, the integration of art and entertainment became a deliberate strategy. So it was that Rank was among several circuits to introduce a weekly evening dedicated to the screening of the latter type of product – films such as *Diva*, *The Marriage of Maria Braun*, *La Ronde*, *The Tree of Wooden Clogs* – programmed by the BFI. For Ian Christie, head of BFI distribution, this mix-and-match approach was deemed crucial to the survival of the cinema as a whole: 'Specialised cinemas can operate at very low profit levels', he claims, 'but they can't survive by themselves. There simply aren't enough of them to secure a regular supply of films – the sort of revenues they generate wouldn't make it worthwhile to release a film in Britain' (Murphy 1983/84: 9–10). The specialised exhibition sector in Britain had shrunk to the extent that for producers and distributors of what in Britain might be termed art house, or else non-mainstream (non-Hollywood) product, it made little sense to release a film in the U.K. without securing exhibition deals with the circuit cinemas. Thus the specialised cinemas found themselves in the paradoxical situation where in order to book specialised films they had to rely on a commercial cinema also wanting to book it. The commercial gain for the circuits lay less in the box-office take for a single night, but in the long-term luring back of the middle-aged 'respectable' audience to the circuits: those parents who would bring their children to see *E.T.* on a Sunday morning but who no longer visited by themselves on a Saturday night (1983/84: 10).

The London Scene

If the RFTs and the circuits were growing ever closer in their programming policies, the situation for the London-based 'art-house' or 'independent' exhibitor was however somewhat different, if no less complicated. On the one hand, the numbers of foreign-language 'art' films imported into Britain had dwindled: from sixty-five in 1962 to forty-two twenty years later, for example (Phelps 1983/84: 14). On the other, with the number of screens outside the capital decreasing rapidly, and the RFTs turning to less specialised product, the capital had become more important than ever in ensuring the success of a foreign-language film. According to Guy Phelps, writing at the end of 1983, distributors were estimating that as much as 85 per cent of rentals for 'art' films came from London (1983/84: 14).

Despite the despondent tone taken by Artificial Eye's Andi Engel in the quote cited earlier in this chapter, he appeared unruffled by the prospect of the circuits' encroachment onto the art houses' turf, contending that a mixed programming policy came at the price of a coherent identity:

> That's where the circuits fall down – one week you see a terrific movie, next week you see a piece of grab. They think that's normal. I see that as abnormal because it destroys your audience. If you go to a cinema like the Academy, you never see a bad movie.
>
> (Murphy 1983/84: 10)

For Engel, the threat facing the art-house sector was financial, not competitive. Ever the pessimist, he went on to complain that 'There's no future for me. My costs are too high. I need a good 2–3,000 people a week in each cinema and I won't get that' (Murphy 1983/84: 10). But the fact that in 1983 alone Artificial Eye expanded from one cinema in Camden Town to Chelsea and Covent Garden belies such curmudgeonliness, while his major competitor, Romaine Hart's chain of Screen cinemas, the exhibition wing of her umbrella company Mainline pictures, had recently added another three outlets (Phelps 1983/84: 12).

It is interesting that Engel cites the Academy as the epitome of art-house culture, for the 1980s saw something of a changing of the guard in London's film exhibition and distribution, and while Engel's Artificial Eye and Hart's Screen were making inroads, the Academy was on its way out. The first and foremost of London's Continental cinemas, it had, as we have seen, been programmed by Elsie Cohen since its opening in 1929 and, a couple of brief closures occasioned by war and refurbishment notwithstanding, had been a constant outlet for French film for over fifty years. But following the death of Cohen in 1972, and then of both her long-term colleagues George Hoellering and Peter Strausfeld in 1980, the cinema closed its doors for the last time on 2 April 1986 (the last films shown were the Swiss *Dangerous Moves*, the Japanese *The Empty Table* and a rerun of the French film *The Wanderer*). A generation younger and somehow exemplary of the film culture of the 1960s and 1970s, distributor Tony Balch had passed away in the same year as Hoellering and Strausfeld, as had the critic, scriptwriter and subtitler Jan Dawson, two more key champions of French film in Britain. Reading through their obituaries and through interviews with Engel and Hart, the two figureheads of the next era in art-house film culture, there is a sense of an abrupt break with the past. Romaine Hart's description of the Screen cinema's birth in 1970 is enlightening:

> Until the early 70s the London cinema could be seen in terms of a polarity between the commercial cinema, namely the Rank/EMI duopoly, and the 'serious' cinema, characterised by the Academy and the Curzon, archetypal art houses. The Screen on the Green [Hart's first opening] created a new kind of cinema for people who didn't much want to go to either of the existing types. Thoughtful programming and good atmosphere created a place where watching films was fun.
>
> (Hart et al. 1981: 254)

Fun, maybe, but profitable too: between them the Screen Group and Artificial Eye, along with David and Barbara Stone's Gate cinemas, inaugurated a new business model, one aimed at a new generation of art-film audiences. Initially, the Screen's programming relied heavily on American independent production; by the early 1980s, it was relying for its major commercial successes on British films such as *Prostitute* and *Gregory's Girl* (on which more in due course). The Gates focused primarily on German cinema. Artificial Eye was rather more esoteric: the German-born Engel's move into British distribution came about through a request from the directing team Straub and Huillet; the resulting distribution company, named Politkino, merged with the Other Cinema in 1973 to form Artificial Eye, whose acquisitions strategy initially tended towards the avant-garde. The three companies shared a common desire to move away from the increasingly standardised programming of the high-end Curzon and Academy; but more significantly perhaps they had a new vision for the cinema-going experience.

Throughout the 1960s and 1970s, the specialised (and to some extent the commercial) cinema's response to an audience which was no longer large enough to pack out the picture palaces was to split cinemas up into multiple screens. Unfortunately, this was often done hurriedly, with the result that, in Robert Murphy's words, most conversions were 'shoddy and unimaginative'. 'Though stories of slapdash projection, spill-over sound from adjoining screens, broken seats, dirty toilets, accumulations of litter are often unfair generalisations, they reflect that disenchantment with the cinema by those who work in them as well as by the public', he writes (Murphy 1983/84: 10). By contrast, Hart and Engel were spending time and money on creating exhibition spaces that proved draws in themselves to audiences, rather than obstacles to be overcome. As Hart put it in a 1984 interview with Sue Summers, of *The Sunday Times*: 'People will go to the cinema – but there are provisos. First, it has to be in the right area. Then you have to give them a really good environment to see a film.

You have to give them really comfortable seats, a bar, food, good service and a nice atmosphere' (Summers 1984: 10). Summers describes Hart's venues in glowing terms: the 'exceptionally big, luxurious seats (imported from France)', the 'big screens', and even 'the canopy with lots of lights'. Sue Norris, in the *Hampstead and Highgate Express*, coos too over the 'plush, roomy seats' and 'elegant bar' (1993: 28). If the formula sounds somewhat run of the mill to the modern reader, Hart having set the model for the majority of contemporary art cinemas, including the Picturehouse chain, the Curzon-Artificial Group and of course the revamped BFI, it is testament to the originality of her strategy that in 1986 she was awarded a unique BFI award for 'putting much-needed dynamism into cinema exhibition' (Summers 1984).

It was indeed a model that was to be much imitated, contributing in an unquantifiable, but inarguably significant manner, to a sea-change in the art-house exhibition sector in London during the early 1980s. In the decade following the Screen's opening, ten more independent cinemas appeared in London, including Artificial Eye's inaugural cinema and the first Gate. In 1970 the landscape of foreign-film exhibitors comprised the three Academies, the Berkeley, the Cameo-Poly, the Cinecenta, the Continentale, the Gala Royal, the Curzon, the Institute for Contemporary Art (ICA), the Classics, the Golders Green Ionic, the Paris-Pullman, the Prince Charles, the Times at Baker Street, the Venus at Kentish Town, the Hampstead Everyman and the first Screen cinema (the Screen on the Green). Twenty years on, in 1989, the number of exhibitors had stayed roughly the same but the venues had changed. Now one had the Lumière, the Renoir, the Chelsea, the Camden Plaza, the Premiere Centre, the Cannon screens at Baker Street, the Prince Charles, the ICA, the now four Screens, three Curzons, the Minema, the Metro and the Gate (Petley 1989: 224).

It might not quite have been all change, but it wasn't far off. The one remaining stalwart was Roger Wingate's Curzon, which had not only weathered the storm that had felled the Academies, but had actually expanded to the newly opened Curzon West End (now the Curzon Soho) on Shaftesbury Avenue, and the Curzon Phoenix in Charing Cross Road, in addition to the original Mayfair theatre. Wingate was a qualified chartered surveyor and full-time property developer who had inherited the business from his father and who, according to one of his staff members, ran the cinema as a sideline (Summers 1984: 55). Like Hart and her contemporaries, he took a businesslike approach to the running of the cinemas, which extended not only to the buildings but to the programming itself. Like the Screens, the Curzons prided themselves on their comfortable screening environments, operating a no-smoking policy well before it became standard practice and refusing screen advertising of any sort. Unencumbered by the cinephilia of Hart or Engels (or Cohen,

Hoellering and Jarosy before them), however, Wingate eschewed the term art house for his product, referring to it instead as 'the heavy end of popular movies', films such as *Heat and Dust, A Room with A View, The Bostonians, The Return of Martin Guerre*, which he described as 'middlebrow'. Some idea of Wingate's rather mercenary approach to the business can be gleaned from his admission, in a 1984 interview, that he had 'little interest in the cinema' and that, 'If I didn't have a large and successful company like [property business] Chesterfield behind me, I'm not sure I'd still want to be part of a business as horrendously risky [. . .] if the three cinemas start to look like expensive playthings, my board will make me think again' (Summers 1984: 55).

The Critical Issue

There were shifts taking place, too, amongst the critical fraternity, shifts that offer further evidence of the widening gap between British film culture in general and what was happening in London. The changes taking place were somewhat more subtle than those snaking through the exhibition and distribution sector, however. After all, as Gilbert Adair quite rightly commented in 1982, film reviewing in Britain had 'hardly budged over three decades' (Adair 1982: 248). The critical voices that had resounded throughout the 1960s and 1970s had all held on to their seats: Dilys Powell at *The Sunday Times*, Philip French in *The Observer*, Derek Malcolm in *The Guardian*, David Robinson at *The Times*, Gavin Millar at *The Listener*, the prolific Penelope Houston who in addition to editing *Sight and Sound* popped up in various papers to weigh in on the state of all things cinematic with disconcerting frequency. And of course there was Alexander Walker, who as the critic of London's sole remaining evening newspaper, *The Evening Standard*, had hitherto reigned over the capital's film scene with an iron fist. 'He has written more books about the cinema than any other British newspaper columnist', wrote Adair. 'He has been an unflagging castigator of what he perceives as the left-wing bias of the *Monthly Film Bulletin*. He sneered at its contributors as "mutants" and took one of them to task for writing a negative review of a film which he, Walker, did not deny was "meretricious" but whose director, Jules Dassin, he just happened to have interviewed on the stage of the National Film Theatre'. And yet, he was 'not only a sometimes perspicacious, sometimes infuriating, critic of the middle ground [. . .] a catalyst' (Adair 1982: 255).

'To be sure', Adair comments, 'sensibilities have been refined (we are all auteurists now), and there has been a more generous acknowledgement of the cinema's essential eclecticism, but these adjustments have almost always been preceded by theoretical shunting in magazines like *Sequence* and *Sight and Sound* and *Movie*, and by the audience's own supply-and-demand response to public taste' (248). What's most striking about the consistency of the critical establishment, and possibly most invidious, he feels, is the widening gulf between those writing about film and those both making them and, as statistics have shown, viewing them:

> What makes it all the more amazing is the number of skins the cinema itself has sloughed off during the same period. To a generation which regards *Le Mépris* as an old film, the early 50s [when many of these critics assumed their positions] must seem remote beyond words. Especially as movies that have long since assumed a near classic status, rich, potent fare by Ray and Sirk and Aldrich and Fuller, were actually being released on a quite regular, bizarrely non-revival basis in ABCs and Odeons up and down the country. Instead of European movies, there were quaint things called Continental films, where for each work of art, such as *La Ronde* or *La Terra Trema*, there was *Le Mouton à Cinq Pattes* with Fernandel or *Femmes de Paris* with Robert Dhéry and Colette Brosset.
>
> (Adair 1982: 248–49)

Adair's reference to *Le Mépris* was prompted by a review speculating on the 'original audiences' of Godard's film by Chris Auty, film editor of *Time Out*, the only challenger of the critical status quo and a publication which was crucially bound up with the developments taking place in London's art-house exhibition sector. Founded by Tony Elliot in 1968, it began life as little more than a pamphlet, listing cinemas, theatres, rock concerts, sports events, 'alternative' nightlife and poetry readings; there was no commentary, criticism or editorial copy as yet. Over the course of the subsequent decade, however, it evolved to incorporate reviews, becoming, according to Adair, 'a magazine you would read, not merely consult' (1982: 254). Correspondingly, its readership expanded slowly but surely: 'catering to the same growth market as the independently run cinemas which were beginning to dot gentrified suburbs of London' (254). By 1981, its circulation was running at over 80,000; what's more, a readership survey disclosed that some 30 per cent of purchasers bought the magazine for its film coverage alone (Pulleine 1981: 223).

The symbiotic relationship between *Time Out* and the new cinemas is nicely articulated by Romaine Hart, who claimed in 1981 that the existence of *Time Out* had been 'crucial' to the Screen group's growth, stating that: 'Film journalism is closely related to the question of whether the independent cinema educates the public or not [. . .] the continued existence, and one hopes the growth, of an independent, broadly based and generally popular film journalism will be essential to the development of the independent cinema' (Hart et al. 1981: 254). Testament to the magazine's influence came in Autumn of the same year, when a pay dispute between the staff and its publishers resulted in a four-month hiatus in its publication. The May–September period of this year coincided with a substantial dip in the takings of several London art cinemas, including the ICA (which reported a 50 per cent cut in audiences), the Ritzy in Brixton, the Scala in Tottenham Street and the Electric in West London, whose manager, Peter Howden, expressed grave concern about the extent to which the absence of a tacitly but specifically recognised publicity forum might dictate an element of playing safe in future (Pulleine 1981: 223). That specific danger was averted: *Time Out* was, eventually, revived. But by this time, many of its staff had been sacked, moving on to set up alternative magazines based on a similar format, such as *City Limits*, and the short-lived *Event*.

British Films on British Screens

This confusing and conflicting period, during which two papers could print stories on the same day, one of them bemoaning the spate of cinematic closures, the other heralding a cinematic boom time, is one which is hard to navigate. Loosely speaking, however, there seem to be three dominant counter-trends running throughout the decade. Firstly, there was future-facing embrace of new technologies and technological developments, led primarily by Hollywood and the multi-national companies which relied heavily on its product. This had little impact on French films on British screens, and so we need not discuss it at length here. Secondly, there was the old guard, still with one eye firmly on what Roger Wingate referred to as the 'middle-brow', or, perhaps better put, 'the middle way': the Curzon and its 'heavy end of popular movies', the RFTs and regional branches of the circuits with their mixed programming (Summers 1984: 55). Thirdly was the new generation, spearheaded by the likes of *Time Out*, Romaine Hart and Andi Engels, forging a new film culture for a new generation: young, cine-literate audiences armed with disposable incomes but with arguably little knowledge of film history, seeking a comfortable, sociable night out of which the film was but one part. There is however a fourth contextual factor which needs briefly addressing before we can assess the status of French cinema within 1980s Britain, and that is the role of the British industry.

For this was a heavily interventionist time. The year 1985 saw the launch of the British Film Year campaign, one-third funded by the government. The project spanned exhibition, promotion and production, and was aimed at stimulating all three sectors. Prior to this, in 1982, Channel 4 had been launched, under the auspices of the Conservative government and programmer Jeremy Isaacs, with a statutory mission 'to encourage innovation and experiment in the form and content of programmers' (Ellis 2007: 137). While initially it provided an outlet for interesting, often uncommercial films, it was not long before it branched into production, funding (at least in part) domestic art films such as *The Draughtsman's Contract, Another Time, Another Place* and *The Ploughman's Lunch*. British Screen followed suit, as did Roger Wingate, whose company contributed £50,000 to *The Europeans*, £25,000 to *The Bostonians*, £250,000 to *A Room with a View*, and underwrote the cost of *Heat and Dust*'s screenplay, therefore enabling the film to get off the ground in the first place (Sutherland 1987: 14). By 1987, producer Simon Perry was moved to comment that, together, Channel 4, British Screen and Curzon formed a tripod on which more and more small British films were being made (Sutherland 1987: 14). Little wonder then that the Curzon's prestige launches during the 1980s were very often these precise films, leaving the French fare which had for so long been the Curzon's staple product to take second place, showing on second and third screens and receiving little in the way of publicity. It may be more surprising to learn, however, that the most successful film of 1981 for Romaine Hart's Screen was *Gregory's Girl*, closely followed by *Prostitute* (Hart et al. 1981: 254). After trying for so long to compete with the U.S. for screen space, the British industry of the 1980s took a different tack, and started knocking Continental films off the screens. Interesting to note here is Wingate's comment that his turn to British cinema at the end of the 1970s was motivated by the fact that during the previous decade, the French cinema had become 'more and more commercial and less and less like the kind of films I was interested in' (Sutherland 1987: 14). As we turn to look at which French films were showing on British screens, where they were being played and how they were being discussed, there is a question of cause and effect that must be posed: did British independent film usurp French film, or did the exhibitors turn to British film because French film was no longer deemed 'suitable' product. And if it was the latter, what was unsuitable about it? Certain developments within the French industry during this period bear relevance to this question. But let's look first at the films themselves.

French Films on British Screens: The Hits?

In 1988, *Time Out* celebrated its twentieth anniversary with a special edition looking back over the previous two decades, surveying the key events, artistic and political, which had shaped the period, listing the big cultural hits of each year (*Time Out* 1988). It's informative to note that during the years 1980–90, although the magazine listed ten key films for each year, out of a total of eighty only two French films appear. These are Jean-Jacques Beineix's *Diva*, in 1982, and Claude Berri's *Manon des Sources*, in 1987 (there is a third contender for a 'French' film which makes the list, but we will come to this in due course). *Diva* and *Manon* were inarguably the two biggest French-language hits of the decade, and they are representative of the two principal types of French film that appeared on British screens during the 1980s. As in the 1970s, the exhibition, marketing and reception of two categories of French films, and the way in which their Frenchness was inscribed within these practices, was polarised. But whereas in the 1970s French films on British screens could be split into two types which appeared simultaneously in different outlets, the divide between the two categories of French film in the 1980s is temporal. As one iteration of French film is replaced by another over the course of a ten-year period, the transition reveals as much as about the changes taking place in the British film industry at the time as it does about French film.

We shall begin with *Diva*. Purchased for distribution by Romaine Hart's Mainline Pictures, the film had its first showings at the flagship Screen on the Hill and the more commercial Odeon in Kensington, a circuit cinema which nonetheless had the benefit of being located in an upmarket area of London with a large French community.[3] It was released in a subtitled version, although what use the translation was at all was questionable: both *The Scotsman*'s William Parente (1982) and *The Glasgow Herald*'s Alan Fielding (1992) criticised the shoddy job the subtitlers had done; however, a more commonly held view amongst the press was that the subtitles were by-the-by since the film lacked any narrative meaning in any case, being a clear example of style above substance. This in itself was not necessarily a negative quality: while Ian Christie (1982) in *The Daily Express* condemns the film's 'silly confused plot' which 'says nothing at all', the majority of critics lined up with Keith Nurse, of *The Daily Telegraph*, who comments that 'the film may be bursting with improbabilities, but the story is told with style and elegance' (1982). Most telling however is Alan Brian's review in *The Sunday Times* (1982a):

> Jean-Jacques Beineix's Parisian thriller-fantasy, *Diva*, has been elevated to cultdom as the most successful foreign-language film to rush the US box office in decades. And it's not difficult to see why.
> The vocabulary of its visual style is instantly understandable everywhere as ad-man's Esperanto – the lingua franca of the flash telly commercial, the glossy magazine double spread, the front cover of the Marvel comic, the pop-art record sleeve, the surreal iconography of the wall poster.
> (Brian 1982a)

One might be reminded here of the slick commercialism of Claude Lelouch's *Un homme et une femme*, so roundly condemned by the British critics for its distinct whiff of superficiality. There is however a key difference: where Lelouch's film was consistently referred to in terms of the Frenchness of its look – resembling nothing so much as a chic ad for Gauloises – the glossy surface of Beneix's film becomes, in Brian's words, a lingua franca: a visual language whose most distinctive trait is its lack of national specificity. He continues:

> Paris is omnipresent, brilliant and sinister, but somehow always uninvolved as if imprinted on top of the people like a theatrical back projection. There is the obligatory black fretwork of the Eiffel Tower but also, inexplicably, a lonely white lighthouse. Whenever invention flags, Beineix inserts another vast, indoor set – a bedsit in a loft amid the lift machinery of a multi-story parking block; a one-room cavernous flat, painted entirely in blue, the size of a Cunarder ball-room; a confrontation between antagonists, miles apart in a glass-walled warehouse that recalls the Crystal Palace.
>
> (Brian 1982a)

Indeed, in some ways, *Diva*'s success at the U.K. box office echoed the popularity of Jacques Tati's films in the 1960s: if not a silent film, it was a film that transcended language. Time and again, the references critics make are to Hitchcock and Welles; for John Coleman in *The New Statesman* (1982), the film's strongest resemblance is to Ridley Scott's *Blade Runner*.

Two years later Romaine Hart would release another film by a young French director which, like *Diva*, would garner comparisons with American independent science fiction of the time (in this case Carpenter's *Dark Star* and Aaron Lipstadt's *Android*) and which take this principle of a universally comprehensible style to its logical extreme, drawing explicit comparisons with Tati. Luc Besson's debut feature, *Le Dernier Combat / The Last Battle*, had no dialogue at all – ostensibly as Besson felt that 'without speech, emotion is laid bare, and the action is in a general way reinforced' (Johnstone 1984). Potentially it was also a canny way of appealing to international audiences, a major preoccupation of Besson's in his later career. Either way, the film was well received. Although its low-budget effects and monochrome aesthetic confined it for the most part to art houses, the press welcomed it as 'a lesson to Hollywood that biggest does not often mean best' (Malcolm 1984). Indeed, for Derek Malcolm its very lack of dialogue was a 'comfort': 'You've no idea what a relief it is not to have to listen to some dialogue-writer, like the ones employed on those two recent *American* nuke-operas, *The Day After* and *Testament*, putting into inadequate words a situation that's beyond even imagining' (Walker 1984; our emphasis).

Both *Diva* and *The Last Battle* (billed by *The New Statesman* as 'this year's *Diva*' – Wheen 1984) were thus welcomed as antidotes to trite Hollywood fare. As such, they fall into a tradition of French film as representative of an 'alternative' to North American studio product that has been discussed throughout the previous chapters. There are certain factors that trouble this categorisation, however, marking a deviation from earlier practice. First is the signal role of America in the promotion and reception of the films. *Diva* and *The Last Battle* are both trumpeted as having been 'big foreign language hits in America', as exemplified by Keith Brian's review of the former. With Unifrance making a significant effort to capture the American market during this period, French films were frequently being released some six months after they had been tried and tested across the Atlantic. And a success in the States was apparently not only an incentive for buyers, but also audiences, judging by the frequency with which the fact was underlined in press releases. More significantly, perhaps, while *Diva* and *The Last Battle* were all the more welcome for being not-American, it was this quality, rather than their Frenchness, which defined them across reviews, in marked contrast with the likes of *Manon des Sources*, to which we will turn shortly. The films that these two directors were producing during this period, along with the work of several other young French directors, has subsequently been ringfenced by both French and British film historians alike as part of a critical moment: the *cinéma du look*, whose gallic nomenclature is indicative of its tethering to the national. At the time of their release though, *Diva* and *The Last Battle*, along with subsequent films such as *Subway*, *The Moon in the Gutter*, and Didier Grousset's *Kamikaze*, were referred to most often as European, rather than French films.

The notable exception to this tendency was Beineix's *37,2 degrés le matin* (1986), shown as the inaugural film of the fortieth Edinburgh Film Festival in August of that year and released by Hart's Mainline in the same month under the title *Betty Blue* (opening in three prints at the Screen on the Hill, the Gate, Notting Hill, and the Cannon, Tottenham Court Road – indicative of a growing trend to 'spread release' films across several cinemas rather than hold them over as exclusives). *Betty Blue* was once more viewed as an antidote to the American fare circulating at the time ('the sort of film that restores your faith in cinema and makes you despair all over again that English language movie makers will ever be as comfortable dealing with sex as the Europeans' – Totterdall 1986), and readers of the *Daily Mirror* were once more assured not to worry about the subtitles, 'you'll still get the drift' (McLeod 1986). However, in the large it was received by the press as a distinctly French film; indeed, as Nick James would put it some six years later, when the film was released in an extended director's cut, it was for many: 'the ultimate French adolescent sex fantasy movie' (James 1992). Facetious as James's description may be, it is underpinned by the old, unwavering association of French films and sexy films. It can be no coincidence that *Betty Blue* is both the most sexually explicit of the 'cinéma du look' films, and, apparently, the most 'French', being full of 'highly erotic Gallic rumpy pumpy' (Heal 1992); a 'smouldering ... whimsical-sexy romance' (Usher 1986), featuring Beatrice Dalle as 'a Bardot for the eighties' (Christie 1986).

It seems old habits die hard. Indeed while Mainline were monopolising the stylish gloss of the 'European' (European having seemingly been sub-

19. UK poster for *Betty Blue*, starring Béatrice Dalle.
Image courtesy of the BFI stills department.

stituted by now for Continental to imply 'not American or British') films made by these young French directors, one of Artificial Eye's biggest crowd-pullers of the early 1980s drew on just the combination of 'visual luxuriance ... erotic and gastronomic extravagance' (Pulleine 1985) that had characterised the French fare popular with audiences in the late 1970s. Michel Deville's *Peril en la demeure / Death in a French Garden* (note the English title) was repeatedly described by critics such as *The Daily Mail*'s Shaun Usher as 'very Gallic' (24 January 1986). It was also a suspense thriller. Interestingly, many critics, including Minty Clinch of *Girl About Town* magazine – a sort of *Time Out* for Women – felt that like so many of Hart's releases, it was a film that went heavy on style, light on content (1986). 'Nevertheless', she writes, 'a French film, almost any French film, is welcome'. In fact astonishingly, in the light of *Diva*'s huge acclaim and substantial box-office takings, Mansel Stimpson seemed to see *Death in a French Garden* as the 'first' important French film to have hit British shores for some time:

In the early 1980s, French cinema was going through one of those phases when it seems to have become unfashionable here. But then along came a film which was such a success in London that a new vogue for French films quickly built up. That film was *Death in A French Garden* and its director was Michel Deville.

(Stimpson 1989)

Never one to pass up an opportunity for the exploitation of stereotypes, Roger Wingate premièred Deville's subsequent film at the Curzon Mayfair. *La Lectrice* was described by Derek Malcolm as being about 'reading and sex ... which in the hands of anyone but an intelligent French director, would seem either prurient or just plain silly' (1989). As it is, he claims, its international (read North American) success is due to the reason that it is 'very French, very funny and very erotic' (1989). The film's reception is surrounded in nostalgia for a period that perhaps never was, succinctly encapsulated by *The Sunday Times*' evocation of the film as a work which 'takes you back to the days when one never seemed to be disappointed in the civilised pleasures of the French cinema' (Johnstone, 2 April 1989), marking a shift back to earlier British stereotypes of French film.

Such words are an apposite starting point for a discussion of the second selection of French films which flourished on British screens during the 1980s, the most widely shown and discussed of which was Claude Berri's *Manon des Sources*, and its prequel, or companion film, *Jean de Florette*. If ever a pair of films were to encapsulate the 'civilised pleasures' of French cinema, this is it. As discussed earlier in the book, there is a long history of British taste for Pagnol adaptations; set in Provence in the 1920s and inspired by material dating back to the early 1950s – a heavily cut film, released in 1952, and a pair of novels based on the original screenplay, all authored by Marcel Pagnol – Berri's diptych looks to 'the great tradition of French rural epic that goes back to André Antoine's *La Terre* and the Provençal films of Marcel Pagnol' (Robinson, 1987a). That booming mouthpiece of the conservative, middle-brow film-going public, Alexander Walker, set the tone for the film's reception in his review of *Jean de Florette*:

> Once upon a time French films had stories with beginnings and middles and ends – in that order. They also had stars who acted parts and didn't just flash their screen images in front of us. And passions that took hold of you and had you laying emotional bets on the outcome.
>
> And best of all, the experience of being in France and watching the French embody their own folkways and lifestyles without giving a damn for the impression they made at home or abroad.
>
> What ever happened to that kind of vintage French film? The good news is that it has just booked into the Curzon Mayfair, the one London cinema (next to the late lamented Academy) where pre-war film-goers might have expected to find it going strong.
>
> *Jean de Florette* will be a back to the future treat for French film buffs who remember what full-bodied value the classic French cinema of Clair and Carné

and Renoir and Pagnol used to give them. For those to young too know, it'll be a revelation.

(Walker 1987a)

Within this remarkably dense introduction to Walker's review are a number of important revelations and assumptions about French cinema and the British public which require some unpacking. Firstly, and most prosaically, we should note that the two Berri films were opened at Curzon's flagship cinema, the bastion of the prestige heritage dramas of Merchant-Ivory which Roger Wingate so often funded. Perhaps unsurprisingly then, reviews of *Manon* in particular are haunted by the spectre of British literary adaptation – from the 1985 *A Room with A View*, set against a similarly picturesque European backdrop, to Roman Polanski's 1979 *Tess* (based on Thomas Hardy's *Tess of the D'Urbervilles*), which Berri had produced and which put the British countryside to similar use as a starring character within the film. For Walker, it was a natural fit: he points to the Curzon's historical links with quality French films, well documented in the preceding pages of this book. It is easy to infer from his comments that Berri's films were not for young upstarts such as Hart and Engels, who championed the young directors that Walker, by implication, associates with opaque narratives, lack of characterisation, and an atmosphere of emotional disaffection: a comparison made explicit in Philip Bergson's review of the film for *What's On*, in which he states that 'after the irritations of such enfants terribles as Leos Carax, what a pleasure it is to settle down for Claude Berri's lush but beautifully-observed adaptation', proof positive for Bergson that contrary to indications, 'the French *can* make films' (Bergson 1987). It is curious that suddenly Carax, Beineix and Besson are described within these reviews as French, no longer European. Yet by comparison with *Jean de Florette*, they become examples of what French film should not be – that is, insufficiently 'French', out of sync with the historical models that British audiences associate with the national cinema. (Little matter that, as Derek Malcolm [1987] points out, the *Jean de Florette* films are 'exactly the kind of cinema which the French New Wavers tried to overthrow and succeeded in eclipsing for over twenty years'.)

Implicit in both Malcolm's and Walker's comments too, then, is the matter of generational difference. Berri's film is a 'vintage', whose appeal is primarily for those old enough to remember and value the great French film-making traditions of the 1930s, 1940s and 1950s. There is almost a sense that these critics are inciting the middle-age, middle-class audiences so conspicuously absent from theatres during the 1980s to reclaim the cinema from the young pretenders, who may think they know about cinema but in reality are 'too young'. And indeed, although no information is traceable about the composition of the audiences for these films, they certainly saw great success. In an unusually long holdover for the period, *Jean de Florette* played for four months at the Curzon Mayfair, only moving to the Shaftesbury Avenue branch (as well as opening in a second print at the Cannon Premier) when *Manon des Sources* bumped it off screens in November. And the latter was still showing in the West End seven months later, when in June 1988 the Barbican opened a season of French film classics, spanning the years 1930–59, the precise era that Walker so wistfully invokes (Hutchinson 1988). Linked to this nostalgic appeal is the appearance of Yves Montand within the film, who, amongst a cast of contemporary stars and soon-to-be stars including Gérard Depardieu, Daniel Auteuil and Emmanuelle Béart – whose full lips, girlish demeanour and often semi-clad state in the film invoked another spate of comparisons with Brigitte Bardot – receives the most frequent and the most fulsome praise for his performance: his very persona iconic of a lost era of quality French film.

Perhaps the most significant subtext within Walker's review is not, however, to do with the film's narrative, performances or even aesthetic, but with its representation of Frenchness. Think of Walker's description of 'being in France' then recall, if you will, Malcolm's review of *Cousin Cousine* some ten years earlier as a 'portrait of French provincial life' which is 'manna from heaven'; or Richard Barkeley's exclamation that the film was 'as stimulating and delightful as a holiday in France'. The reception of *Jean de Florette* and *Manon des Sources* both reiterates a form of cine-tourism which as we have seen has been in place since the 1930s ('the tale dunks us deep in the French countryside', writes Nigel Andrews [20 November 1987]; it 'paints an utterly precise portrait of Mediterranean peasant life', according to William Parente [1987]), and takes it to its logical apotheosis: *The Sunday Times* ('The Romance of Two French Villages', Wickes 1988) and the *Independent* ('The Region that Ruined *Jean de Florette*', Barrett 1991) were amongst numerous newspapers whose coverage of Berri's films extended beyond the screen and into real life. '[The two films] should do for tourism to Provence what *Crocodile Dundee* did for Down Under', writes *The Sunday Times*' David Wickes, noting that at least one Paris entrepreneur has commenced construction on a hotel in the area. He gives details of the 'utterly seductive' locations in which the film was shot, which offer France 'at its most rural, baked and blanched', awash with 'pine, oak, and the silvery leaves of olive trees, the scent of wild rosemary and thyme', before listing sources from which British tourists can hire a 'Florette-like gîte' from whence to view the area (1988). Three years later, Frank Barrett wrote a two-page travelogue describing his visit to La Treille, the village which inspired *Jean de Florette* and 'the principal destination for Pagnol pilgrims', where one can take a guided tour 'In the footsteps of Marcel Pagnol' for only £4' (Barrett 1991).

Barrett draws a direct connection between *Jean de Florette* and 'the glib rose-tinted view of Provençal life to be found in the Peter Mayle books' so popular in late 1980s and early 1990s Britain (and which would later take on a screen life of their own in a 1993 television series starring John Thaw and a 2006 film featuring the unlikely Russell Crowe). Mayles' first Provencal-set book, *A Year in Provence*, was however not published until 1989, two years after the Curzon premièred *Jean de Florette* (in July 1987) and *Manon des Sources* (in November of the same year), so it is important to see the popularity of Berri's films with U.K. audiences as presaging, rather than following, the success of that work: the films whetted an appetite for an exoticised image of lavender-hued fields and living off the land.

Barrett makes the point that the tragic narratives of the films – which see the eponymous hero driven to his death by his inability to run his farm successfully (unbeknownst to him, a result of sabotage), and his daughter wreak a fatal revenge on the villagers who had brought about his demise – stand in counterpoint to the trifling stumbling blocks Mayle encountered when trying to build his swimming pool. Yet although the engaging plot and characters are commended in reviews of both films, the focus rests firmly with the picturesque landscapes replete with 'splendour and threat' (Robinson 1987b). As Richard Mayne puts it, describing *Manon des Sources*: 'To Britain's bleak November it brings a breath of summer in Provence, tingling with the scents of thyme and pine-trees, subject to sudden downpours but otherwise parched and chalky, stones and brushwood crackling underfoot. Dogs bark; goat-bells ring flat and hollow; the local patois twangs with the accent du terroir' (1987b). (Never has such poetic language been deployed with such abandon across such a wide range of film reviews!) Evidently, the film's impact lay primarily in its sun-drenched, azure and lemon portrait of Southern France, as Robert Dunkley speculated some six years later, in yet another travel piece (this time for *The Sunday Telegraph*) inspired by the film:

> If nothing else, watching Claude Berri's 1986 of *Jean de Florette* and *Manon des Sources* is a diverting experience. The masterful performance of Gérard Depardieu, the well-aired charms of Emmanuelle Béart, but most of all the scenery, serve to steer the unwary viewer's attention away from Marcel Pagnol's plot of Provençal perfidy.
>
> To a new generation, the film hinted at the reason why this region of France ranks second only to Tuscany in the English literary imagination as a place where a distant rural idyll can still be glimpsed.
>
> (Dunkley 1994)

The films were an enormous success: as late as 2007 *Manon des Sources* still featured in the list of the top ten grossing French films at the U.K. box office, in ninth position (Gant 2007: 9). And if further testament to the durability and dominance of the Provençal portrait that Berri painted were needed, it could be found in Stella Artois' 'Reassuringly Expensive' television advertisements, which began with a series based on *Jean de Florette* directed by the British duo Anthea Benton and Vaughan Arnell that ran throughout the late 1990s and early 2000s and that incorporated the film's visual aesthetic as well as its distinctive soundtrack, Verdi's fate theme. The series moved onto other genres, including war movies, silent comedy and even surrealism, but maintained the aim of portraying the drink in the context of sophisticated European culture. Moreover, from 1994 onwards Stella Artois courted an association in the U.K. with film through sponsorship of screenings – in cinemas and on television. Most recently, its British relaunch as Stella Artois La Nouvelle 4 drew on the iconography of the *nouvelle vague*, featuring a conspicuously Bardot-esque figure in print and television adverts alike. Its aping of the Berri films is thus bound up with a projection of exotic 'Frenchness' (although the beer is in fact Belgian), quality, and sophistication: words which all feature regularly in contemporaneous British reviews of Berri's films.

The View from France

The commercial exploitation of the imagery of *Jean de Florette* and *Manon des Sources* leads us onto a final point emerging from Walker's review, one which takes us on a brief detour into the French production context of the time. It may appear to Walker that *Jean de Florette*'s film-makers 'do not give a damn for the impression they made at home or abroad' – a point of supposed distinction from the marquee names of the cinéma du look'. However, Berri's diptych was conceived as a calculated attempt at conquering domestic and foreign audiences in the face of Hollywood's perceived dominance of Western screens.

Under a (relatively) new Socialist government, French cultural policy came to focus once more on national culture, its international role and its protection from external – namely North American – threat. As Lucy Mazdon has pointed out elsewhere, these priorities were made apparent by Jack Lang's notorious speech in Mexico in July 1982 when he decried 'a certain invasion, a certain influx of images produced elsewhere' calling for 'a veritable cultural resistance. A veritable crusade against – let's give its true name – this financial and cultural imperialism' (Mazdon 2000: 7). Berri himself likened European film-makers to 'redskins', thus invoking a history of American imperialism, and in many ways his Pagnol adaptations served as a call to arms, in which he led by example. The most expensive films in French history at the point that they were made, they marked the beginning of a concentration of big-budget, heritage films designed specifically to reinforce cinematic prestige and to appeal to both domestic and foreign markets. These films emphasised famous stars and the lavish reproduction of history as grand spectacle, and presented themselves as identifiably, indeed, uniquely, French, trading on its historical and cultural specificity (read exoticism). Both Berri and Lang saw the heritage film as a means to differentiate French cinema from Hollywood's action spectacles, but also to trade on the same production values and deployment of stars, and therefore, to some extent, to beat Hollywood at its own game, regaining France's market share of the domestic box office in addition to infiltrating the higher end of the popular film market abroad. Contrary to Walker's contention, there may not have been in the history of French cinema a film-maker that cared more about the impression he made at home and abroad.

If then, as we have argued elsewhere in this book, the Franco-British cinematic relationship can only be viewed as part of a triangular configuration in which the United States (principally – though not exclusively – Hollywood) figures as the third point, the Franco-American relationship has one further resonance here. For *Jean de Florette*'s extraordinary cultural specificity allowed it to avoid a fate to which French films of the 1980s were frequently falling victim: the remaking of French films by Hollywood. This is by no means a practice exclusive to the 1980s of course: it commences with the very advent of cinema and extends through to the present day (at the time of writing remakes of French films as divergent as Michael Haneke's *Hidden* and Pascal Chaumeil's *Heartbreaker* were slated for production). Nonetheless, as Lucy Mazdon has detailed in her dedicated study of North American remakes of French films, it was particularly rife during the 1980s (Mazdon 2000). And the implications for French film in Great Britain were not negligible.

It is beyond the scope of this study to reiterate Mazdon's arguments here, as it is to cover in detail the gamut of French films and their American remakes released in the U.K. during the period. Nonetheless, one particular example stands out. The third 'French' film to make *Time Out*'s pick of films released in the 1980s is listed within their pages as *Three Men and a Baby*. Cited as it is in the selection for 1988, one has to suppose that the film they are referring to here is Leonard Nimoy's film, made for Touchstone Pictures with Ted Danson, Tom Selleck and Steve Guttenberg as the titular trio and released in the U.K. in that year. However, only twelve months before the American version was released, Coline Serreau's original version arrived in England, two years after its French release. Nimoy's imminent English-language remake casts a shadow across all the reviews: hardly one fails to mention its in-production status. Serreau's film does not seem to have been reviewed by the popular press; across the range of broadsheets, however, an interesting accord emerges: the remake is intended 'for the purposes of American consumption' (Brown 1987). British audiences, meanwhile, were urged to either ignore the film entirely ('an instance of a Gallic brand of whimsy that proves not to travel too well' – Pulleine 1987) or to 'wade through the subtitles and see the original' (Brown 1987). No doubt a vein of anti-Americanism (or reverse snobbery towards popular American cinema, at least) runs through such exhortations; but be that as it may, the distinct preference for the French 'original' over the American 'imitation' reveals a continuing critical distinction between, as Lucy Mazdon describes it, French cinema's (even popular French cinema's) status as 'art' and Hollywood's production of mass cultural artefacts (2000). As Mazdon has demonstrated, this rather reductive division has a longstanding history in both French and American cultural policy; it would appear that much the same could be said of British critical thinking: 'Jack Lang used to speak of the success of French films in the United States', Alexander Walker sniffs, 'but it's a strange way of paying a compliment' (1987b). And yet it speaks volumes about the still-marginalised status of the subtitled film that despite largely lukewarm attitudes to the remake, at least where it is compared with the original, Nimoy's Hollywood production would turn out to be one of the decade's box-office sensations, while Serreau's French-language film disappeared after a run of only a few weeks.

French Film on British Screens: The Misses?

If *Diva* – a French film passing as a European film, distinctive primarily for its non-Americanness and its encapsulation of a slick superficial youth culture – and the Pagnol diptych – 'vintage' French films, dripping with nostalgia and with idyllic images of bucolic Provence, appealing to an ageing critical fraternity longing for the heady days of the past – were the major French successes on British screens during the 1980s, to what extent were these extremes reconcilable? How were they representative of French film in Britain more generally during the period? And how successful were the programming strategies of the various institutions promoting them in the long term? A first glance at an article rounding up the situation for subtitled films at the end of the 1980s suggests that the experiments of the period were largely failures: if the title of David Docherty's article, with which we opened this chapter, spoke volumes, Julian Petley's 'Where Have All the Foreign Films Gone?' appears to say it all. Published in the Autumn of 1989, Petley's article is not, however altogether negative in tone.

At the end of the 1980s, there were forty-six independent distributors in the U.K., of which fifteen had a policy of regularly handling subtitled films. Of these, seven had their own cinemas, with a total of twenty-three screens. These were Artificial Eye, Pathé, Electric Pictures, the ICA, Mainline (otherwise known as Hart's Screen group), the Other Cinema and Recorded Releasing (Petley 1989: 225). The number of subtitled prints being distributed had dropped from fifty in 1980 to thiry-nine in 1988, but had risen to fifty-five in 1985; and in terms of the percentage of total releases the figure had remained relatively constant at around 18 per cent since the beginning of the decade – a 6 per cent increase on 1965, a supposed golden age for French film in Britain. Most of the foreign-language films were released in only two prints, with up to four being made for more commercial releases such as *Jean de Florette*. According to Petley, the most popular foreign-language films could expect up to about 15–20,000 admissions in the first week (although such hits were rare).

The situation doesn't seem dire, then, although as Petley comments, the total market share of admissions for subtitled films boiled down to about 1 per cent of the whole. And yet a series of interviews with the key distributors of French-language film paints a rather different picture. Complaints centre on rising costs, audiences' general lack of adventurousness, the depressing state of much of what passes for film criticism and, for those distributors not lucky, or astute, enough to have their own theatres, the difficulty of finding theatres that will take their product and promote it thoroughly. 'Few working in the field seem to find much cause for cheerfulness in the present situation,' the author summises (Petley 1989: 225).

Significantly, in the light of how much has been made in accounts of the decade of the competition from television, almost all the interviewees agreed on the complementary nature of contemporary television programming, claiming that both Channel 4 and, under a newly-appointed appointed Alan Yentob, BBC2, were doing 'useful' work in this area (Petley 1989: 225). Whereas in the 1960s and 1970s the 'use' of television lay in its broadening of audiences for foreign-language film, its importance at this point was of a rather different nature. As Joe d'Morais, of Blue Dolphin explains, in order to make a foreign-language film profitable at this point: 'Television rights are absolutely vital. I wouldn't be interested in taking on a film without them' (Petley 1989: 225). D'Morais continues: 'What you get from selling the film to TV goes towards covering you if the film doesn't do anything theatrically' (226). What television got out of the arrangement was, of course, publicity for the films it had bought. Rather than a relationship of competition, therefore, television and theatrical exhibition stood as one of mutual benefit, with several distribution companies entering into standing agreements with television channels: Rive's Gala with the BBC, Artificial Eye with Channel 4.

Within this financial context, however, French cinema proves particularly problematic. According to d'Morais, whose Blue Dolphin distributed *Kamikaze*: 'It took ages to get [the film] because [the producers] were asking unbelievable prices. [. . .] Unlike the Germans, the French just don't seem to want to do deals. There have been five or six films from France that I would have liked to buy, but they have never opened here because nobody, quite rightly, has been prepared to pay those prices' (Petley 1989: 228). His words are echoed by Contemporary's Charles Cooper: 'At Cannes this year some [of the French] were asking for $100,000 for the theatrical rights alone. It's better to come back with nothing than pay too much, see the film flop and have your business go under. With interest rates as they are today, you just can't afford large debts. If you put a foot wrong, you can go out of business very easily' (228). While Cooper sees the British economy as a key factor in the 'play-safe' policies of many distributors, Rive however blames the proliferation of festivals: 'Once a film is in a festival, and particularly if they think it's in the running for a prize, producers tend to get cocky and start thinking in terms of telephone numbers' (228). On the other hand, Petley sagely adds, too long a wait for prices to come down and a film loses its topicality: people forget the festival reports, the prizes, the interviews.

However, cost was not the sole, nor perhaps the primary gripe levelled at French film. D'Morais adds that 'the most interesting films are coming from the third world at the moment [...] Africa and India and New Zealand' (Petley 1989: 228). According to Kenneth Rive, meanwhile: 'The French are certainly making a lot of movies, but many of them are simply unplayable rubbish. I think the public over here gets to see the best of them, such as, *La Balance, La Lectrice, Camille Claudel, La Petite Voleuse*' (228). An interesting choice of films: certainly not the most profitable of the decade, nor the most critically acclaimed, they are in fact a rather retrograde selection. *La Lectrice*, as was discussed, was sold as a stylish piece of Gallic eroticism. *La Balance*, distributed and exhibited by Mainline, was a violent, fast-moving policier made by an American ex-pat, Bob Swaim, and which garnered repeated comparisons with the likes of *Pépé le Moko* and *Rififi*. The main selling point of *Camille Claudel* and *La Petite Voleuse*, meanwhile, was the Truffaut connection: the former starring *Adele H*'s Isabelle Adjani; the latter adapted by Claude Miller from Truffaut's script (the presence of the coltish Charlotte Gainsbourg and a rites-of-passage – read loss of virginity – narrative an added bonus). It is worth noting that Truffaut's *The Last Metro* had been a rare French success for Curzon in the early years of the decade, picked up on the basis of its extraordinary success in the States, despite, or perhaps because, of its similarities with pre-war French film: *Rolling Stone* magazine denounces it as 'sharing all the flaws of the French tradition of quality that the young Truffaut hated' (30 April 1980). Indeed, some twenty years after its arrival on British shores, the *nouvelle vague* and its film-makers continued to constitute a not-insignificant proportion of the French films appearing on British screens: Resnais' *Mon Oncle d'Amérique / My American Uncle*, Godard's *Passion* and *Sauve qui peut (la vie) / Slow Motion*, Rohmer's *Le*

Rayon vert / The Green Ray and Chabrol's *Le Chevel d'orgueil / The Proud Ones* were all successes for their respective distributors, while Godard was the subjective of retrospectives at the Scala and Everyman in May 1983, as well as a Channel 4 season later in the same year. Given the critical disappointment in the New Wave at the end of the 1960s it is interesting that already by this point its directors had been revived and reinscribed into the critical canon, by dint of a process of nostalgic revisionism which has been taking place in Britain ever since.

Intriguingly, reviews of Chabrol's film, released in 1982, and Rohmer's, in 1987, rehearse much of the commentary surrounding *Jean de Florette* and *Manon des Sources*. Praise is heaped upon Chabrol's 'exhibition in picture-postcard folklore' (Brian 1982b). 'We are led to believe the peasants are poor, ignorant, superstitious, honourable and exploited', comments Alan Brian, 'But in their spotless national costumes, in their quaint, lovely cottages, against wild but eye-catching landscapes, it is difficult not to envy rather than pity them' (Brian 1982b). Sue Lermon puts it best in the *Times Literary Supplement*: 'One of the attractions of France and Italy to us urbanised English is their being closer to a rural past, the pastoral bliss that supposedly preceded the motor car and mechanisation [. . .] *The Proud Ones* disturbs our facile preconceptions, yet, in its rhythms and settings, evokes that for which we yearn' (Lermon 1982). And if the manner in which the oft-times bleak outlook of Chabrol's film is overwhelmed within British reviews by its picturesque evocation of the Gallic rural idyll in a manner that prefigures Berri's films quite astonishingly, then it seems Rohmer's *The Green Ray*, coming in the wake of the diptych, compounds the standing of the late-1980s French film as a piece of visual tourism. Saskia Baron (1987) lauds the film for 'its portrayal of a hazy, toasting France – brown bodies bobbing like flotsam on the waves at Biarritz'; while Richard Mayne, writing in *The Sunday Telegraph*, makes the explicit claim that Rohmer's film appear to be made 'with one eye on the French Tourist Board'. 'Most of them are made in idyllic postcard scenery. Who could forget the summer sparkle of the Lac D'Annecy in *Claire's Knee*, or the Normandy Coast of *Pauline at the Beach*?' (Mayne 1987a).

The success of the rather anachronistic works that Rive lists; the enduring popularity of a somewhat softened set of *nouvelle vague* directors; the huge popularity of the French heritage and the ubiquity of the cine-tourism trope in reviews of some very diverse works is suggestive of a growing conservatism in the tastes of audiences for French film. Which in itself engenders a conservatism in film importers. Which leads to a restrictive selection of French films for U.K. audiences. Which leaves audiences with only conservative films from which to choose. And so on and so forth: there's a perverse circularity operating within film culture at the end of the 1980s that is hard to pin down or indeed break down. For Andi Engels, the contemporary audience is at fault:

> The problem is not really to do with the actual number of films imported, but that those which are imported don't seem to be reaching audiences. When we started, we could bring in a film like Marguerite Duras' *India Song* and people would go to see it – not in vast numbers, I admit, but enough to cover our costs. If we showed a Duras film now, I'm convinced that many fewer people would come, and in the meantime our costs – prints, salaries, advertising, rates etc. – have shot up. People seem to have lost their curiosity about foreign films. The term art cinema has become a dirty word to people, something to be dismissed as bourgeois rubbish. Anything which is not genre cinema must be automatically bad – either it's entertaining or it's boring, there's nothing in between. It is not so much that people aren't interested in certain kinds of cinema and lack any cinematic curiosity. It's like going to a library and deciding you will only ever look at one part of it. It doesn't mean you can't read; it means that you are not prepared to consider everything that is on offer, even out of curiosity.
>
> (Petley 1989: 226)

D'Morais on the other hand looks to the critics, pointing to the paradox that at the end of the 1980s, there were more pages devoted to cinema in newspapers and magazines than ever before, but that there was less in the way of substantial criticism and informed analysis. For D'Morais, the younger generation of critics were simply ignorant, lacking historical perspective: 'for them, cinema doesn't seem to exist before 1970' (Petley 1989: 227). Derek Malcolm however points out that the papers were becoming increasingly 'obsessed with star interviews, listings, gobbets of pre-digested information, two lines on the best films at the London Film Festival. The last thing we ever get is any analysis of the films themselves. And some weeks there are twelve new films which have to be dealt with in about 1,200 words. Analysis is out of the question' (227).

Finally, and most intriguingly, Petley himself suggests that television might not be as benign as thought. The problem now is not that it is luring audiences away from the cinema, rather that since television rights are crucial to these art-house distributors, a French film – indeed any foreign film – will only be purchased if it will subsequently be shown by the BBC or Channel 4 (who across them screened an average of two or three new subtitled films a week). In which case the real arbiters of what French films appeared on British screens in the late 1980s were the people in charge of buying at Channel 4 and BBC 2. And as a part of a channel not dedicated solely to film, it was natural that their choices should be more oriented towards audience ratings than the state of specialised exhibition. John Ellis' explanation of the ultimate demise of *Visions*, Channel 4's specialised film magazine which ran fitfully from 1982 to 1985 and which, in its final series, was a co-production with France's Canal +, is instructive here. With a remit to 'centre on other cinemas [than Hollywood], covering some of the new releases on the art-cinema circuit, neglected or recently discovered cinemas', *Visions* took an authorial approach, running specials on such directors as Chantal Akerman and Raul Ruiz. If, as Ellis claims, *Visions* never 'quite caught on', for him the explanation lies in the seriousness of its approach to film (Ellis 2007: 142). 'Criticisms of the series at the time tended to include the word wilful, as in "wilfully obscure" or "wilfully eccentric"', writes Ellis, stating that the series 'simply failed to communicate the pleasures of the large screen' (Ellis 2007: 142) – in contrast, presumably, to the BBC's Film Magazine (*Film 1982*, *Film 1983*, etc.), which still covers in the main commercial, U.S. product, and which is still running on BBC1 at the time of writing.

Into the 1990s: Cyrano, Video, and Sleeping with l'enemi

It's hard to discern what exactly caused the turn away from the avant-garde and the art-house and towards the more popular end of French film amongst British audiences in the late 1980s. One is tempted to point the finger at the socio-political climate. In the throes of recession, 1980s filmgoers were perhaps seeking escapism in the sunny climes of the cinematic hexagon. But probably this, too, is a reductive view of things.

If it was Andi Engel who summed up the view from the early 1980s with his prediction of the cinema's imminent demise, however, then the fate of Artificial Eye come the end of the decade offered an altogether more hopeful outlook, albeit one that may be wrought with compromise. Following a moderate success with Volker Schlondorff's French-language Proust adaptation, *Swann in Love*, a film that tapped into the dominant trend for literary adaptation and costume drama, in 1990 Artificial Eye picked up the rights to the most expensive French film made to that date: Jean-Paul Rappeneau's *Cyrano de Bergerac*, starring Gérard Depardieu. This is the film that, twenty years later, remains the second-biggest grossing French film at the U.K. box office ever, taking £2,458,175 over the course of its run: despite the fact that the film was subtitled – and in verse, no less (particular care was taken over the film's subtitling, with the author Antony Burgess providing the translation). It was released on 11 January 1991 on eight screens throughout the country, taking £250,000 in its first ten days and going straight to number one. Three weeks after its release it was appearing in multiplexes across Britain, at UCI complexes in Swansea and Telford, Sheffield and Poole; Warner outlets in Bury, York and Basingstoke; Showcases in Leeds and Peterborough and Odeons in Hull and Exeter. Despite unanimous acclaim, critics were baffled by the film's breakout success, with Pam Engel's vague supposition that 'it's touched a current mood' providing little tangible explanation. Undoubtedly the familiarity of Depardieu following his role in *Jean de Florette* helped: shortly after *Cyrano* he was to star in his first Hollywood film, *Green Card*, an indication that his star had become international. Derek Malcolm simply puts it down to the fact that 'the specialist circuit works in exactly the same way as the commercial one: there are hits and there are flops, and the hits like *Cyrano* work in precisely the same way as movies like *Batman*' (1991).

For Malcolm, the crucial importance of a film such as *Cyrano* is that it creates opportunities for other films: allowing Artificial Eye to take chances on smaller, more edgy films that they might like to show but might otherwise not dare to do since the financial risk would be too high. It also, of course, goes some way to convincing the multiplexes that subtitled films could do good business: when the Warner West End opened in 1993, it announced its aim to programme more art-house fare – starting with *Les Visiteurs*, a popular comedy which can only be deemed art house by dint of being French, but the intention was there.

And for Artificial Eye it had the further bonus of funding the launch of a video label – on which the first film to be launched was another Depardieu film: *Trop Belle pour toi*. That year its French catalogue comprised another forty-eight titles from directors such as Jean Vigo, Claude Chabrol, Robert Bresson, Maurice Pialat, Eric Rohmer, Jean-Pierre

20. UK poster for *Cyrano de Bergerac*, starring Gérard Depardieu.
Twenty years after its release, it remains the second-biggest grossing French film at the UK box office.
Image courtesy of the BFI stills department.

Melville, Jean-Luc Godard, Claude Miller, Luc Besson, Bertrand Blier, Eric Rochant and Leos Carax. Speaking to *Le Film Français* (and therefore possibly flattering a little), Engels stated that although they carried a huge breadth of titles from across Europe and the rest of the world, French film occupied a privileged position as the bedrock of the business. 'Over the course of the years, France is the only country to have been a constant source of new and talented filmmakers', he states. 'If Italy offers a limited choice, Germany and Scandinavia are currently in crisis; France on the other hand has always offered us a cinema on which we could count' (Pham 1991).

The French government recognised Pam and Andi's efforts, making them *Chevaliers dans l'Ordre des Arts et des Lettres* in 1996. Rewards of a more lucrative kind came in 1994, when Artificial Eye merged with Curzon to form what the *Independent*'s Ralph Ludemann referred to as 'a powerful force – some would say a monopoly' on the art-house distribution scene (Ludemann 1994). A marriage of Curzon's money with the Engels' expertise, the deal created a network of eleven art-house cinemas across the capital. Ludemann was ambivalent about the implications, expressing concern that it would make it difficult for smaller distributors such as Electric or Joe d'Morais' Blue Dolphin to secure films and find cinemas in which to release them. The second problem he perceives is however more fundamental, having wider implications for art-house culture as a whole:

> This will mean more European films, more Japanese high culture-schlock such as Beat, more American independents such as Hal Hartley and better quality pictures which would have been too risky to show before. It might also mean that they will no longer bother with the quirky and eccentric films that make the art-house cinema. There is a danger that if they start paying more they will want a guaranteed return, which is understandable – cinema is commerce as well as culture. But if we lose the chance to see experimental or difficult films just because they don't make money, we will miss out on the gems that become cult classics and just be fed pseudo-mainstream middle-brow fare tailor-made for the urban middle class cineaste.
>
> (Ludemann 1994)

In 1997, upon the release of Gilles Mimouni's *L'Appartement*, another huge hit for Artificial Eye, Engels was still insisting that such large scale releases were a means of allowing them to present 'more difficult films' (A.C.P. 1997). If this is indeed the case, then the business model that Artificial Eye inaugurated with *Cyrano* offers a fascinating example of how French film might best infiltrate the UK market in its variant forms. The end of the 1980s was indeed a time of conservative tastes, but by exploiting this conversatism, Engel was able to take more risks, to diversify, screening a variety of French films, many of which were overshadowed by the larger releases, but which at least were there, present, on U.K. screens in the 1990s and the decades that followed in a manner that, to judge from the distributors' comments cited above, seemed impossible in the late 1980s.

Notes

1. Although with 222 screens.
2. It is worth noting that although, as we have discussed, the RFTs originally had an educational, archival and entertainment remit, by 1987 their status had changed somewhat: with the closure of so many regional screens (for instance, Scotland, lost almost two-thirds of its screens in the period between 1965 and 1985; the North-East over half), in some areas they had become the only remaining place to watch a film in public.
3. A fascinating note in the *NME* in September 1982, the same month that the film was released, announced that it was to receive a simultaneous video release (25 September 1982), although whether this was in fact the case has proved impossible to discern. However, a press release from Palace Pictures, Mainline's VHS distribution arm, dated August 1982 suggests that this was indeed the case. Since *Diva* went on to become one of the biggest-grossing foreign-language films of the decade, the implication is that theatrical audiences were not too badly affected by this direct competition from home viewing.

Bibliography

A.C.P. 1997. 'Pam et Andi Engel: les Croises anglais du cinema francais', *Le Film Francais*, 7 November: 16.
Adair, G. 1982. 'The Critical Issue', *Sight and Sound*, 51(4), Autumn: 248–57.
Andrews, N. 1987. 'Manon des Sources', *Financial Times*, 20 November: 19.
Baron, S. 1987. 'Throwing the Script Away', *Independent*, 12 March: 12.
Barrett, F. 1991. 'The Region that Ruined Jean de Florette', *Independent*, 14 September.
Bergson, P. 1987. 'French Country Matters', *What's On*, 23 July: 91.
Brian, A. 1982a. 'Murder in the Soap-Opera House', *Sunday Times*, 5 September: 34.
Brian, A. 1982b. 'The Proud Ones', *Sunday Times*, 23 May: 42.
Brown, G. 1987. 'And Baby Makes Four', *Times*, 2 May: 23.
Christie, I. 1982. 'Diva', *Daily Express*, 3 September: 22.
Christie, I. 1986. 'Betty Bardot Goes Potty', *Daily Express*, 12 September: 26.
Clinch, M. 1986. 'Death in a French Garden', *Girl about Town*, 27 January: 86.
Coleman, J. 1982. 'Diva', *New Statesman*, 10 September: 28.
Docherty, D. 1987. 'Who goes to the RFTs?', *Sight and Sound* 56(3), Summer: 161–64.
Docherty, D., D. Morrison and M. Tracey. 1986. '?Who Goes to the Cinema?', *Sight and Sound*, 55(2), Spring: 81–85.
Dunkley, R. 1994. 'On Location: Riboux, Provence', *Daily Telegraph*, 20 February: 24.

Ellis, J. 2007. 'Visions: a Channel 4 Experiment 1982–5' in L. Mulvey and J. Sexton (eds.), *Experimental British Television*. Manchester: University of Manchester Press, pp. 136–45.
Fielding, A. 1982. 'Diva', *Glasgow Herald*, 8 November: 6.
Gant, C. 2007. 'French Connections', *Sight and Sound*, 17(9), September: 9.
Hart, R., P. Dally and S. Whitaker. 1981. 'Independent Audiences', *Sight and Sound* 50(4), Autumn: 254–55.
Heal, S. 1992. 'Betty Blue', *Today*, 21 February: 27.
Hutchinson, T. 1988. 'Revelations Sprung from a Well of Glory'. *Hampstead and Highgate Express*, 10 June: 115.
James, N. 1992. 'Betty Blue', *City Limits*, 20 February: 25.
Johnstone, I. 1984. 'The Last Battle', *Sunday Times*, 12 August: 47.
Johnstone, I. 1989. 'La Lectrice', *Sunday Times*, 2 April: 89.
Lermon, S. 1982. 'The Rural Treadmill', *Times Educational Supplement*, 28 May: 24.
Ludemann, R. 1994. 'One Wedding and a Deal', *Independent*, 25 May: 7.
Malcolm, D. 1984. 'Samurai in a World Laid Waste', *Guardian*, 9 August: 11
Malcolm, D. 1987. 'Gerard's Cross to Bear', *Guardian*, 23 July: 13
Malcolm, D. 1989. 'La Lectrice', *Guardian*, 30 March: 25.
Malcolm, D. 1991. 'Sub-titles Spell Success', *Guardian*, 8 February: 91.
Mayne, R. 1987a. 'A Solitary Searcher', *Sunday Telegraph*, 15 March: 17.
Mayne, R. 1987b. 'All about Yves', *Sunday Telegraph*, 22 November: 19.
Mazdon, L. 2000. *Encore Hollywood: Remaking French Cinema*. London, BFI.
McLeod, P. 1986. 'French Affair is a Sizzler', *Daily Mirror*, 12 September: 46.
Murphy, R. 1983/84. 'The Public Has a Brain', *Sight and Sound* 53(1), Winter: 8–11.
Norris, S. 1993. 'Film, the Recession's "Happy Medium"', *Hampstead and Highgate Express*, 26 February: 28.
Nurse, K. 1982. 'Diva', *Daily Telegraph*, 3 September: 82.
Parente, W. 1982. 'Diva', *Scotsman*, 4 September: 3
Parente, W. 1987. 'Well and Good', *Scotsman Weekend*, 25 July: 5.
Perry, S. 1980. 'A Scan of the Video Industry', *Sight and Sound* 51(2), Spring: 82–83.
Petley, J. 1989. 'Where Have All the Foreign Films Gone?' *Sight and Sound* 58(4), Autumn: 224–28.
Pham, P. 1991. 'Portrait d'acheteurs de films francais – Grande Bretagne', *Le Film Francais*, 12 April: 7.
Phelps, G. 1983/84. 'Art-house', *Sight and Sound* 53(1), Winter: 12–14.
Pulleine, T. 1981. 'Time Out', *Sight and Sound* 52(4), Autumn: 223.
Pulleine, T. 1982. 'Who Only the West End Know', *Sight and Sound* 51(3), Summer: 173–77.
Pulleine, T. 1985. 'Gory of the Garden', *Guardian*, 28 November: 23.
Pulleine, T. 1987. 'Wait Till Your Fathers Get Home', *Guardian*, 2 May: 13.
Robinson, D. 1987a. 'Jean de Florette', *The Times*, 23 July: 21.
Robinson, D. 1987b. 'Classics and Cons', *The Times*, 19 November: 20.
Stimpson, M. 1989. 'Words and Images', *What's On*, 5 April: 68.
Summers, S. 1984. 'Star of the Silver Screens', *Sunday Times*, 5 February: 10.
Sutherland, A. 1987. 'Why Does Roger Wingate Invest in Film?', *The Producer* 1, May: 14–15.
Time Out. 1988. *Time Out 20: 20th Anniversary Supplement*, 5 October.

Totterdall, A. 1986. 'Behind the Joy Lurks a Fear', *Financial Times*, 12 September: 23.
Usher, S. 1986. 'Betty Blue', *Daily Mail*, 12 September: 30.
Walker, A. 1984. 'Too Awful for Words', *Evening Standard*, 9 August: 18.
Walker, A. 1987a. 'Opening a French Vintage', *Evening Standard*, 23 July: 30.
Walker, A. 1987b. 'Three Men and a Cradle', *Evening Standard*, 21 May: 23.
Wheen, F. 1984. 'Surviving in Style', *New Statesman*, 10 August: 26–27.
Wickes, D. 1988. 'The Romance of Two French Villages', *Sunday Times*, 8 May: 56.

Filmography

A Room with A View (1985, James Ivory)
Al-ard / La Terre (1969, Youssef Chahine)
albero degli zoccoli, L' / The Tree of Wooden Clogs (1978, Ermanno Olmi)
Amour de Swann, Un / Swann in Love (1984, Volker Schlöndorff)
Android (1982, Aaron Lipstadt)
Another Time, Another Place (1983, Michael Radford)
Appartement, L' / The Apartment (1996, Gilles Mimouni)
Arnacoeur, L' / Heartbreaker (2010, Pascal Chaumeil)
Balance, Le / The Balance (1982, Bob Swaim)
Bostonians, The (1984, James Ivory)
Caché / Hidden (2005, Michael Haneke)
Camille Claudel (1988, Bruno Nuytten)
Cheval d'orgueil, Le / The Proud Ones (1980, Claude Chabrol)
Coming Home (1978, Hal Ashby)
Cuba (1979, Richard Lester)
Cyrano de Bergerac (1990, Jean-Paul Rappeneau)
Dark Star (1974, John Carpenter)
Dernier Combat, Le / The Last Battle (1983, Luc Besson)
Dernier Metro, Le / The Last Metro (1980, François Truffaut)
Diagonale du fou, La / Dangerous Moves (1984, Richard Dembo)
Diva (1981, Jean-Jacques Beineix)
Draughtsman's Contract, The (1982, Peter Greenaway)
E.T. (1982, Stephen Spielberg)
Easy Rider (1969, Dennis Hopper)
Ehe der Maria Braun, Die / The Marriage of Maria Braun (1979, Rainer Werner Fassbinder)
Europeans, The (1979, James Ivory)
Femmes de Paris (1954, Jean Loubignac)
Genou de Claire, Le / Claire's Knee (1970, Eric Rohmer)
Grand Meaulnes, Le / The Wanderer (1967 Jean-Gabriel Albicocco)
Gregory's Girl (1986, Bill Forsyth)
Heat and Dust (1983, James Ivory)
India Song (1975, Margaret Duras)
Jean de Florette (1986, Claude Berri)
Kamikaze (1986, Didier Grousset)
Lectrice, La / The Reader (1988, Michel Deville)

Lune dans le caniveau, La / The Moon in the Gutter (1983, Jean-Jacques Beineix)
Manon des Sources (1986, Claude Berri)
Mépris, Le (1963, Jean-Luc Godard)
Mon Oncle d'Amérique / My American Uncle (1980, Alain Resnais)
Mouton a Cinq Pattes, Le (1954, Henri Verneuil)
Passion (1982, Jean-Luc Godard)
Pauline à la plage / Pauline at the Beach (1983, Eric Rohmer)
Peril en la demeure / Death in a French Garden (1985, Michel Deville)
Petite Voleuse, La / The Little Thief (1988, Claude Miller)
Ploughman's Lunch, The (1983, Richard Eyre)
Prostitute (1980, Tony Garnett)
Rayon vert, Le / The Green Ray (1986, Eric Rohmer)
Retour de Martin Guerre, Le / The Return of Martin Guerre (1982, Daniel Vigne)
Ronde, La (1950, Max Ophuls)
Sauve qui peut (la vie) / Slow Motion (1980, Jean-Luc Godard)
Shokutaku o nai ie / The Empty Table (1985, Masaki Kobayashi)
Terra Trema, La (1948, Luchino Visconti)
Tess (1979, Roman Polanski)
37,2 degrés le matin / Betty Blue (1986, Jean-Jacques Beineix)
Trop Belle pour toi / Too Beautiful For You (1989, Betrand Blier)
Homme et une femme, Un / A Man and a Woman (1966, Claude Lelouch)
Visiteurs, Les (1993, Jean-Marie Poiré)

Conclusion

Describing his journey into the academic discipline of French Studies in an article published in *French Cultural Studies* in 1999, John Stokes recalls his adolescent forays to the State Cinema on Leytonstone High Road in East London:

> It was at the State that my dreams of France were born, giving me first of all a taste for a film culture that was already slightly out of date and yet, in comparison with the life surrounding, seemed excitingly alien. Even the comedies of Fernandel had a raw, raucous quality, while romantic dramas starring, say, Michelle Morgan or Charles Boyer possessed a satiny erotic style that was distinctly unEssex. Later, around 1959, came the *nouvelle vague*: *Les Cousins*, *Hiroshima mon amour*, *Les Amants*, *A bout de souffle*, *Les 400 Coups*, *Tirez sur le pianiste* and visions of a different France, in its way equally unreal, but so much livelier, so much younger, than the films I had seen before that it was as if the two or three whole generations had been and gone in the space of a very few months.
>
> (Stokes 1999: 307)

Stokes' remarks recall a film culture described in Chapters Three and Four: a time when French films escaped the confines of the Continental movie theatres and were found in mainstream picture houses such as the State; a time when the great works of the past sat alongside and were then gradually replaced by the new cinema emerging from France; a time when trips to see French films were motivated both by a highbrow Francophilia and a rather more commonplace search for titillation. Stokes looks back at the State's weekly advertisements in the contemporary press and remarks:

> When my mother reproached me for going to see sexy French films in a seedy part of town I told her that the films were art and despised her ignorant prejudice. Now I see, as I read the *Stratford Express* for 1958, that the State regularly

advertised 'art films' of a dubious kind. So we were both right. The films may have been art, but they were certainly sexy too.

(Stokes 1999: 308)

Stokes' recollections provide us with an eloquent summary of some of the key discourses which have shaped French cinema's place in the United Kingdom over the last eighty or so years: Francophilia and cinephilia, sex and art. Yet particularly striking is Stokes' confession of the role French films played in nurturing his desire for France and, more importantly, in his sense of his own identity. Watching French films took him away from the humdrum streets of Leytonstone and transported him to a culture in which he sensed he could achieve his ambitions and become the man he wanted to be. His confusion over that infamous scene in Malle's *Les Amants*, described in Chapter Four, only reinforced that belief as he felt sure that French audiences would have had no difficulty at all in interpreting the sequence, 'They would have been able to read the codes because they too had done those things. It seemed equally certain that my neighbours had no such fund of personal experience to help them find their way around the film' (311).

Stokes' love for French film was then closely connected to a deep investment in French culture and to a belief that watching these films could provide him with a knowledge and cultural prestige that would differentiate him from his fellow citizens of Leytonstone, who no doubt made quite different cinematic choices. This belief in the quality of French film and the cultural distinction it is able to provide is a theme we can see threading throughout this story of French cinema's place in Britain. If we cast our minds back to those early pioneers at the Film Society, we will recall their belief in film as art and their dedication to sourcing the 'best' of Continental cinema. This underlying belief in the 'quality' of French cinema, closely aligned to those Anglo-Saxon assumptions about French cultural prestige so fiercely decried by Bill Marshall (Marshall 1999: 263), has endured throughout. Attempts to popularise French cinema and perceived crises in French production may at times have led certain commentators to question the status of the Gallic product, but overall the notion that French cinema connotes 'quality' and cultural prestige has remained at the heart of British perceptions of the cross-channel product.

Writing in *Sight and Sound* in June 2005, Nick James described French films as 'the gold standard for art cinema in the UK' going on to assert that 'without a regular flow of distinctive work from France there would be little sense of an alternative cinema to Hollywood' (James 2005: 14). As we have discussed elsewhere (Mazdon and Wheatley 2008), his comments are perhaps a little surprising, given the British prominence, only two years later, of French films such as *Tell No One* and *La Vie en Rose*, films which are firmly positioned within the conventions of mainstream commercial cinema (the thriller, the biopic) and as such do little to further the cause of art cinema.[1] Indeed, James himself acknowledges that the films which he perceives as challenging the mainstream (Bruno Dumont's *Twentynine Palms* and Olivier Assayas' *Clean*, for example) are not 'necessarily popular with the majority': they were roundly beaten at the British box office by Jean-Pierre Jeunet's World War One love story, *A Very Long Engagement* and *The Chorus*, a nostalgic remake of a 1940s movie, *La Cage aux Rossignols*, celebrating the power of music to transform the lives of a group of young boys. Of particular note is James' avowal that *Sight and Sound* itself has at times been guilty of lambasting these 'challenging' films while simultaneously holding them up as a benchmark against which 'unadventurous' British cinema can be defined (20). Here he voices a longstanding British critical discourse which, as this book has revealed, champions 'art' cinema and turns to the 'Continent' as a model while at the same time dismissing the 'pretention' and the overt intellectualism both at times are perceived to display.

So rather than see French cinema as the saviour of the British art house, it would appear to be more accurate to describe it as the stalwart of foreign-language distribution in the United Kingdom, the cinema which

21. *Tell No One* (Guillaume Canet, 2006).
Image courtesy of the BFI stills department.

22. *La Vie en Rose* (Oliver Dahan, 2007).
Image courtesy of the BFI stills department.

has been a constant presence at film societies and specialist theatres and which has an enduring appeal for middle-class audiences looking for something a little more challenging, a little more distinctive than the products of Hollywood, a cinematic experience which is 'safely exotic' (Mazdon and Wheatley 2008: 39). Recall once more those early screenings at the Film Society in the 1930s where, a number of avant-garde programmes aside, French cinema was largely appreciated for its quality: strong production values, solid scripts and rich performances. To a great extent these expectations persist today (consider once again the huge success of *The Artist*). While French cinema may at times have been seen to challenge convention (the New Wave and the more recent 'New Extremism') or attract cult audiences (the *cinéma du look* whose iconic poster images adorned student bedrooms across the country in the late 1980s), for the most part it has represented the middle of the road for foreign-language exhibition in the United Kingdom. Audiences on the lookout for challenging foreign fare now turn towards other 'world' cinemas, in particular the films of Asia, the Middle East, or Eastern Europe.

The longevity of these perceptions is nicely illustrated by the success of Christophe Barratier's *The Chorus* which made £133,000 on its opening

23. Jean Dujardin and Bérénice Bejo in *The Artist* (Michel Hazanavicius, 2011). Image courtesy of the BFI stills department.

weekend in the United Kingdom in March 2005 and went on to top the tables for French releases in Britain that year. Back in 1946, as British audiences began to get a taste of recent French film-making after the dark days of the war, *La Cage aux Rossignols*, source for Barratier's remake, was similarly appreciated. Writing in *Sight and Sound* in 1946, Roger Manvell praised the film's 'humanism', which he compared to other recent French releases and re-releases *Farrebique* and *La Femme du Boulanger* (Manvell 1946: 154). This focus on the film's 'humanism' again reminds us of those expectations and/or stereotypes which have dominated British responses to and reception of French film: strong dramas, powerful character acting, a grounding in the 'real'.

Manvel's mention of *La Femme du Boulanger* provides us with another example of the endurance of particular attitudes towards French film as cinematic treatments of the work of Pagnol have long proved popular with British audiences. Claude Berri's adaptations of the 1980s were immensely popular as they embodied and reinforced notions of an idyllic if impoverished rural France, notions later echoed in a whole series of representations ranging from Peter Mayle's best-selling account of his life in the Luberon, *A Year in Provence*, to a Stella Artois advertising campaign. And such affection for this gritty yet simultaneously picture postcard version of French life has a long and enduring history as Jean Queval revealed in *Sight and Sound* in 1953 when he noted British love for the

24. *Amélie* (Jean-Pierre Jeunet, 2001).
Image courtesy of the BFI stills department.

films of Pagnol which were, in his opinion, 'vastly over-estimated in Hollywood and Hampstead for obvious reasons of exoticism' (Queval 1953: 106). As British audiences fell in love with Audrey Tautou's gamine Amélie and her adventures in a kitsch Montmartre, we were reminded once again of this love for films which are recognisably and yet unthreateningly French: much-loved locations, familiar genres and forms and perhaps a recognisable star. These are the movies which seem to appeal to those cinema-goers with a taste for the films of France. As the relative failure of more challenging 'art-house' fare and populist products such as the *Taxi* series, which do little more than ape Hollywood, reveals, attempts to move beyond these clearly defined and quite limited tastes more often than not fail to succeed.

So what is the future for French cinema in Britain in the twenty-first century? At the end of the 1980s, Andi Engel saw new possibilities for its promulgation in the VHS market; without a doubt more recent developments in technology, notably the advent of DVD and BluRay, and video on demand downloaded from the internet on to personal computers or mobile phones, would seem to offer a far wider range of possibilities for the consumption of French film with potential audiences no longer reliant on a handful of distributors and exhibitors. The arrival of specialist French movie channel *Cinémoi* in 2009 established a dedicated forum for the screening of a variety of French films to viewers willing to pay an additional subscription. Initiatives set in place by the now defunct U.K. Film Council also seemed promising: the Prints and Advertising Fund had an annual budget of £4 million to support the distribution and marketing of 'specialised' films (including foreign-language works); the 2005 launch of the Digital Screen Network aimed to install state of the art digital projection facilities in 240 screens in 210 cinemas, including multiplexes and independents, with the cinemas guaranteeing a number of specialised film screenings in return (Patterson 2008). The publicly funded Independent Cinema Office also supports the British presence of non-mainstream cinema, currently programming seventeen cinemas, and with a stated aim to 'increase the audiences for specialist film and to make a variety of work available to them' (Patterson 2008: 31). The proliferation of film festivals is also encouraging as it provides an alternative distribution forum for films, including French films, which may never otherwise achieve British distribution. Richard Mowe, director of the French Film Festival, now in its twentieth year, claims that 'the horizons of British cinephiles have expanded dramatically over the past couple of decades. They're now incredibly discerning punters – very aware of what's out there, and very aware festivals are going to be their only realistic chance of seeing a really good range of French [. . .] films' (Henley 2011).

Yet despite these indubitably positive developments, the language that surrounds these films is telling: 'specialised', 'non-mainstream', 'alternative': these are still the terms that are used to refer to much French-language film in the U.K. A two-tier system is still very much in place. Mowe's comments perhaps go to the heart of the matter. The festivals are the 'only realistic chance of seeing a good range of French films': general distribution remains narrow and festival audiences are restricted due to the specificities of location and temporality. The U.K. Film Council was axed in 2010 by the newly installed coalition government, rendering highly precarious the development of those initiatives which had seemed so promising for foreign-language film. *Cinémoi*'s impact is limited by its own somewhat constraining definitions (once more French cinema seems to be 'ghettoised', made into a thoroughly specialised product) and its subscription-based audience. And even DVD is arguably something of a poisoned chalice: the huge profits it potentially engenders lead some distributors to limit cinematic release to just a few days, a means to acquiring the rights to the far more lucrative small-screen product. It is worth noting the relatively small place accorded to Unifrance in this book which speaks volumes about French cinema's always already restricted presence in the U.K. While Unifrance is dedicated to the international promotion of French cinema its activities in Britain have remained limited due to the agency's own perceptions of the barren nature of the U.K. market.

Britain's independent screens which would seem to offer the potential for cinematic choice and diversity are, as Hannah Patterson reveals, programmed by a small group of people leading instead to a rather worrying uniformity (Patterson 2008: 31). The relationship between Artificial Eye and Curzon has become closer since the turn of the century, culminating in a full-scale merger between the two companies in 2008. The Curzon's programmer, Claire Binns, not only books films for all five Curzon sites but also the City Screen group, better known as the Picturehouse Cinemas, as well as another thirty or so independent venues (31). Binns makes no bones about her remit, which she states is to 'make sure the cinemas I book are successful and show the kinds of films we're asked to play. That tends to be cultural cinema, but everyone has budgets to meet so you have to deliver a mix that includes commercially successful films' (31). This means opening weekends are now as crucial for art house as for Hollywood: if a film does badly at the weekend it is swiftly removed from theatres. Tom Abell, director of small distributor Peccadillo Pictures, gives a rather pessimistic response to this state of affairs, 'The arthouse circuit is now operated on the Hollywood model so it becomes very difficult for the smaller distributors to get their films into the right cinemas. The fact that City Screen now books so much and books the same thing everywhere means a lot of the variety has vanished. So it's much harder to find a screen for our films because movies like *Lady Chatterley* will be playing everywhere' (32).

This rather monopolistic state of affairs was the subject of a *Sight and Sound* panel discussion that took place in Summer 2008, at which the authors of this book were present and at which Binns herself was invited to speak. The debate, which continued in the pages of the magazine over the course of the following three months, recalled a much earlier opposition between cinephilia and commerce. Nick James' accusation that Binns' 'sole criterion is profit' (2008: 5), and that City Screen and the Curzon's superior buying power left a limited selection of films available for smaller outlets, echoes, to a certain extent, Elsie Cohen's despair at the bidding wars provoked by the Curzon's first owner, the Marquis de Casa Maury, almost eighty years ago. A certain snobbery appears to persist which positions those members of the specialised exhibition industry interested in profit as vulgar and philistine, while 'true' cinephiles eschew such concerns. This is the position reflected in a letter written by Mark Cosgrove, programmer of the Bristol Watershed, and published in the September issue of that year. Cosgrove blamed City Screen for the 'narrow' choice of 'medium-scale arthouse films with crossover potential' available in London, and demanded support for the 'commercially less viable but culturally significant' film (2008: 96).

So should we despair at the merger between Britain's major art-house distributor and London's foremost specialist chain and its reduced opportunities for smaller distributors and narrowing of cinematic diversity? Or on the other hand, should we see the marriage of Artificial Eye and Curzon as a rather more felicitous combination of Roger Wingate's bums on seats commercialism and Pam and Andi Engel's whatever it takes utilitarianism? In an irate letter to *Sight and Sound*, Binns took pains to point out that the financial strengths of the firms she worked for allowed her to throw her weight behind certain niche films (2008: 96), thus situating herself and the cinemas she programmes as the natural extension of the policy that Artificial Eye's founder inaugurated, in which those medium-scale films are shown precisely in order to fund the exhibition of what Engel himself termed 'more difficult films'.

It would seem that to a great extent it is a case of *plus ça change, plus c'est la même chose*. Spaces for French film in the United Kingdom remain limited and the range on offer, as in the 1930s, is determined by a select group of individuals. Summarising the findings of that investigation into the state of specialist distribution in the 2000s, Nick James concludes that 'one newspaper reviewer has the power the make or break a specialist film (stand up the *Guardian*'s Peter Bradshaw); a film like *Heartbeat Detector* can go great guns in London and utterly flop elsewhere; you can put a digital screen into any number of multiplexes but people who like specialist cinema still don't want to go a multiplex' (2008: 5) Within this context, the French films which achieve prominence are the heritage films and visions of Frenchness which appeal to middle-class Francophile tastes (or those, like *The Artist*, which mask their Frenchness entirely). It is striking that Tom Abell should cite Pascale Ferran's *Lady Chatterley* (2006) as an example of the type of French film which would exclude others from independent screens (and it is worth noting here that the film in question is distributed by Artificial Eye). The film is of course based upon Lawrence's novel and thus provides a reassuring degree of familiarity to British audiences. Yet with its lush cinematography and stunning landscapes and its tasteful depictions of sexuality, it absolutely conforms to British expectations of a 'classy French movie' (Wheatley 2010: 92).

We began this book by describing the creation of a place for 'Continental' cinema in Britain in the 1930s. To enjoy French film by the end of that decade was to appreciate quality and good taste – attributes which those audiences who flocked to see the Pagnol adaptations of the 1980s, the heritage film of the 1990s and Jean-Pierre Jeunet's artfully kitsch *Amélie* would, we suspect, claim to share. As we move forward into the twenty-first century the future of French cinema in Britain is far from certain. The possibilities offered by new technologies and new forms of filmic consumption are encouraging and yet, as we have seen, it would be foolhardy indeed to ignore the commercial and cultural forces which continue to curtail cinematic diversity. 'French' cinema is a far more multifarious object than British distribution and exhibition patterns have tended to suggest: it is the heritage drama, the *policier*, the challenging art-house picture and the Hollywood style rom-com. To understand and accept this diversity and to enable its full presence in the British context could only enrich audience experience and cinematic culture on both sides of the Channel.

Note

1. It should of course be noted that terms such as 'art' and 'art-house' cinema are far from self-evident and to a great extent dependent upon specific contexts. The spaces accorded to foreign cinema in the U.K. and responses to these films clearly play an important role in constructing and defining these terms.

Bibliography

Binns, C. 2008. 'Fair Representation', letter to *Sight and Sound* 18(8): 96.
Cosgrove, M. 2008. 'The Bigger Picture', letter to *Sight and Sound* 18(9): 96.
Henley, J. 2011. 'Foreign Cinema is Expanding Our Horizons', *Guardian*, 3 March.
James, N. 2005. 'French Cinema: The Anti-Hollywood', *Sight and Sound* 15(8), August: 14–20.
James, N. 2008. 'The Specialist', *Sight and Sound* 18(7), July: 5.
Manvell, R. 1946. 'Continental and British Films of the Quarter', *Sight and Sound* 15(60), Winter: 153–56.
Marshall, B. 1999. 'Minor Leapfrogs', *French Cultural Studies* 10(255): 255–64.
Mazdon, L. and C. Wheatley. 2008. 'Intimate Connections', *Sight and Sound*, 18(5), May: 38–40.
Patterson, H. 2008. 'Dealer's Choice?', *Sight and Sound*, 18(4), April: 30–33.
Queval, J. 1953. 'French Film Since the War', *Sight and Sound* 22(3): 38–40.
Stokes, J. 1999. 'London E11/Paris 6e: espèces de rêves', *French Cultural Studies*: 307–20.
Wheatley, C. 2010. 'The Language of Love ? How the French Sold *Lady Chatterley's Lover* (Back) to British Audiences', in L. Mazdon and C. Wheatley (eds), *Je t'aime, moi non plus: Franco-British Cinematic Relations*. Oxford, Berghahn, pp. 81–100.

Filmography

A bout de souffle / Breathless (1960, Jean-Luc Godard)
Les Amants (1958, Louis Malle)
L'Artiste / The Artist (2011, Michel Hazanavicius)
La Cage aux Rossignols (1945, Jean Dréville)
Les Choristes / The Chorus (2004, Christophe Barratier)

Clean (2004, Olivier Assayas)
Les Cousins (1959, Claude Chabrol)
Le Fabuleux Destin d'Amélie Poulain / Amélie (2001, Jean-Pierre Jeunet)
Farrebique (1946, Georges Rouquier)
La Femme du Boulanger (1938, Marcel Pagnol)
Hiroshima mon amour (1959, Alain Resnais)
Lady Chatterley (2006, Pascale Ferran)
Un Long Dimanche de fiançaillles / A Very Long Engagement (2004, Jean-Pierre Jeunet)
La Môme / La Vie en Rose (2007, Olivier Dahan)
Ne le dis à personne / Tell No One (2006, Guillaume Canet)
Les 400 Coups / The 400 Blows (1959, François Truffaut)
La Question humaine / Heartbeat Detector (2007, Nicolas Klotz)
Taxi (1998, Gérard Pirès)
Tirez sur le pianiste / Shoot the Pianist (1960, François Truffaut)
Twentynine Palms (2003, Bruno Dumont)

INDEX

Abell, Tom 218, 219
Les Abysses (Nikos Papatakis film) 116
Academy cinema 97, 166, 168, 181–2, 192
  New Wave in 112, 119, 121, 124, 125
  sound, changing cultures and advent of 1, 11, 19, 28, 30–32, 38, 42–3, 44, 45, 46–7
  wartime cinema 53, 55, 60, 61, 72, 75–6
Ackland, Rodney 61
Adair, Gilbert 1, 184–5
Adjani, Isabelle 155, 200
Aimée, Anouk 129
Akerman, Chantal 203
Alerte en Méditerranée (Léo Joannon film) 65
Allégret, Marc 44
Alpert, Hollis 110, 132, 135n2
Alphaville (Jean-Luc Godard film) 105
Amanda Films 149, 171n9
Les Amants (Louis Malle film) 107, 108, 128, 135n2, 211, 212
Amélie (Jean-Pierre Jeunet film) 9, 11, 216, 219
L'Amour à Vingt ans (François Truffaut film) 118
Amphitryon (Reinhold Schünzel film) 65
Anderson, Lindsay 107, 121, 131–2, 165
  Truffaut and, relationship between 131–2
Andrews, Nigel 147, 158, 194
Android (Aaron Lipstadt film) 189

Angélique series (Bernard Borderie films) 145, 159–60, 168, 170n5
Annabella (Suzanne Carpentier) 23, 33
Another Time, Another Place (Michael Radford film) 187
Anstey, Edgar 117
Antoine, André 192
Antonioni, Michelangelo 123, 125, 128, 142
Apocalypto (Mel Gibson film) 10
L'Appartement (Gilles Mimouni film) 205
Ardagh, John 120, 128
Arkadin 116, 118–19, 121, 135n6
Arletty (Léonie Bathiat) 33
The Army of the Shadows (Jean-Pierre Melville film) 123, 146
Arnell, Vaughan 196
art film culture 21–2
art-house cinema 158, 166, 183, 185, 204, 205, 216, 218–20
  accessibility of 72
  art-house hits 127–8, 168
  changing perceptions (1970-82) 165–8, 168–9
  culture of, break with past 182
  culture of, demise of 2, 141–2, 203
  London scene 180–81
  New Wave, draw for 120–21
  specialized films in 125–6
  status of, threat to 100
  subtitled audience, preference for 13
  television rights and 202

Artificial Eye 176, 181, 182, 183, 191, 198, 199, 203, 204, 205, 218, 219
The Artist (Michel Hazanavivius film) 11, 12, 100, 214, 215, 219
Assayas, Olivier 213
Associated British Picture Corporation's ABC circuit 56, 82–3, 124, 153, 185
Astruc, Alexandre 113–14, 124
L'Atalante (Jean Vigo film) 129
audiences of RFTs (BRU survey) 178–9
see also filmgoing audiences
Autant-Lara, Claude 106
Auteuil, Daniel 194
Auty, Chris 185
avant-garde 21, 35, 38, 95, 114, 165, 169, 182, 214
Avatar (James Cameron film) 13
Avions de France (wartime short film) 53
l'Avventura (Michaelangelo Antonioni film) 123

bad taste 159–64
La Baie des Anges (Jacques Demy film) 135n7
Baker, P. 112, 114, 124, 126–7, 130, 136n11
La Balance (Bob Swaim film) 200
Balch, Antony 135n1, 160, 181
Balio, T. 81–2
I Bambini ci Guardano (Vittorio de Sica film) 89
Baratier, Jacques 107
Barberis, René 76
Bardot, Brigitte 91, 95, 96, 114, 121, 128–9, 167, 194
Barkeley, Richard 164, 194
Barker, Felix 152, 155, 159–60, 164, 171n8
Baron, Saskia 201
Barratier, Christophe 214–15
Barrett, Frank 194–5
Barry, Iris 14, 20, 21, 24, 31–2, 33, 34, 36–7, 41, 47, 63
Les Bas-fonds (Jean Renoir film) 64
Basil, Roy 108
Batman (Tim Burton film) 204
The Battle of Algiers (Gilles Pontecorvo film) 165
Bazin, André 108, 132
Bean, Keith 54, 69
Béart, Emmanuelle 194

Le Beau Serge (Claude Chabrol film) 106–7, 108, 131
Beauties of the Night (René Clair film) 87, 92
Beccarie, Claudine 158
Bedroom Mazurka (John Hilbard film) 135–6n10
Beineix, Jean-Jacques 187, 188–9, 190, 193
Bejo, Bérénice 12, 215
Belle de Jour (Luis Buñuel film) 151
Belmondo, Jean-Paul 145, 151, 154, 167
Benton, Anthea 196
Bergman, Ingmar 87, 123, 142
Bergson, P. 193
Bernstein, Sidney L. 34, 37, 47, 69–70
Berri, Claude 187, 192, 193, 194, 195–6, 197, 201, 215
Berry, Jules 54
Besson, Luc 15n3, 100–101, 189, 193, 205
La Bête humaine (Jean Renoir film) 64, 67
Betts, Ernest 23, 117
Betty Blue (Jean-Jacques Beineix film) 190–91
Betz, Mark 170n2
Bicycle Thieves (Vittorio de Sica film) 83
Billon, Pierre 76
Billy Liar (John Schlesinger film) 133
Binns, Claire 218, 219
Birkett, P. 161
Black Orpheus/Orfeu Negro (Marcel Camus film) 108, 109
Blade Runner (Ridley Scott film) 189
Blier, Bertrand 205
The Blood of a Poet (Jean Cocteau film) 39
Blow Out/La Grande Bouffe (Marco Ferreri film) 161–2, 166, 169
Bob le Flambeur (Jean-Pierre Melville film) 135n7
Boisrond, Michel 96
Les Bonnes Femmes (Claude Chabrol film) 120, 127
Bonnie and Clyde (Arthur Penn film) 151
Boorman, John 165
Borderie, Bernard 145, 159–60
Borowczyck, Walerian 165
Borsalino (Jacques Deray film) 145, 151–2

The Bostonians (James Ivory film) 184, 187
Le Boucher (Claude Chabrol film) 150
Boyer, Charles 95, 211
Bradshaw, Peter 219
Breathless/A Bout de Souffle (Jean-Luc Godard film) 2, 105, 119, 127, 135n8, 211
Bresson, Robert 204
Brian, Alan 188–9, 201
Brian, Keith 190
The Bride Wore Black/La Mariée était en noir (François Truffaut film) 121, 122, 145
Brief Encounter (David Lean film) 108, 109
Brien, A. 158
British Board of Film Censors (BBFC) 17, 35, 87, 89, 124, 157, 159, 160–61, 170n4
British cinema in wartime 55–7
British film industry, hard times for 81–3
British Film Institute (BFI) 61, 63, 66, 85–6, 112, 166, 170n6, 179, 180, 183
British films on British screens 186–7
Brosset, Colette 185
Brown, Charles H.V. 90–91
Brown, Geoff 135n8, 197–8
Brunel, Adrian 34
Bryher (Annie Winifred Ellerman) 20–21
Buñuel, Luis 40, 151, 162
Burgess, Antony 203
Butch Cassidy and the Sundance Kid (George Roy Hill film) 151
Butcher's Distribution 160, 170n5, 171n9

La Cage aux Rossignols (Jean Dréville film) 213, 215
Cahiers du Cinéma 107, 131–2
Cameo-Poly Distributors 88, 92, 112, 113, 114–15, 120, 183
Cameo Royal, Charing Cross Road 90, 112, 121
Cameron, James 13
Camille Claudel (Bruno Nuytten film) 200
Camus, Marcel 109, 110, 120
Canard Enchaîné 116
Canet, Guillaume 213

'canonisation' 7, 42, 51, 65–6, 67, 86
Carax, Leos 193, 205
Carné, Marcel 44, 61, 68, 110, 120, 169
Un Carnet de bal (Julien Duvivier film) 18, 61, 65, 66
Carnival in Flanders/La Kermesse Héroïque (Jacques Feyder film) 45, 46, 59, 61, 65
Carol, Martine 91, 95
Carpenter, John 189
Carthew, Anthony 90
Casa Maury, Pedro J.I.M.R.Mones, Marques de 44, 45, 46, 55, 218
Castell, D. 145
Cavalcanti, Alberto 25, 40
Centre National de la Cinématographie (CNC) 53, 94, 109, 134
Le Cercle Rouge (Jean Pierre Melville film) 145, 147–8, 150
Cette Sacrée Gamine (Michel Boisrond film) 96
Chabrol, Claude 105, 106, 108, 110, 118, 120, 132, 133, 142, 150, 164, 167, 201, 204
changing perceptions (1970–82) 141–71
  art houses 165–8, 168–9
  bad taste 159–64
  dubbed features, unpopularity of 149–55
  Eady levy 143
  end of French New Wave 142–6
  European tide 142–6
  French cultural policy, changes in 144
  literary adaptations and heritage films 168–9
  National Film Finance Corporation 143
  pornographic cinema in France 144–5
  quota regulations 143–4, 152, 156
  second features on circuits 146–9
  sexy cinema 155–9
  soft-core porn, scandals surrounding 160–62
Chanvel, Ambassador Jean 109, 135n4
Chaumeil, Pascal 197
The Cheat/Le Roman d'un Tricheur (Sacha Guitry film) 29, 55, 61
Chetham, John 74–5
China (Michaelangelo Antonioni film) 166
Chinatown (Roman Polanski film) 157
La Chinoise (Jean Luc-Godard film) 106

Chivers, Michael 149
Chnouf (Henri Decoin film) 89, 101n3, 124
The Chorus (Christophe Barratier film) 213, 214–15
Chrisafis, Angelique 2
Christian-Jaque (Christian Maudet) 72
Christie, Agatha 1
Christie, Ian 157, 159, 178, 180, 188, 190
Christie, Julie 133
Chronicle of Anna Magdalena Bach (film by Jean-Marie Straub and Danièlle Huillet) 165
Cinecenta 171n9, 183
Cinema TV Today 157
Cinémaction 134
Cinémathèque française 63
Cinematograph Films Council 143
Cinémoi TV 217
Citizen Kane (Orson Welles film) 65
City Limits 186
Claire's Knee (Eric Rohmer film) 201
Classic cinemas 92, 112, 146, 157, 183
Clauir, René 22, 23, 25, 32, 40, 43, 44, 53, 68, 85, 92, 110, 135n6, 169
Clavering, Sir Albert 92, 112, 126, 130
Clayton, Jack 132, 165
Clean (Olivier Assayas film) 213
Clément, René 110
Clinch, Minty 191
Cloche, Maurice 74
Close Up 20–21, 23, 42, 43
Clouzot, Henri-Georges 96–9, 100, 110
Cocks, Jay 147
Cocteau, Jean 39, 40, 71, 72
Cohen, Elsie 14, 19, 28, 32, 33, 42–3, 45, 46, 47, 55, 62, 181, 218
Cold Comfort Farm (Gibbons, S.) 41
Coleman, John 121, 130, 157, 189
Combs, Richard 164
Coming Home (Hal Ashby film) 179
Comité de l'Industrie Cinématographique Européene (European Cinematographer's Committee) 143
Comité d'Organisation de L'Industrie Cinématographique (COIC) 53
commercial cinema
 entrenchment of, resistance to 20–21
 power of 19–20

The Contemporary Cinema (Houston, P.) 128
Contemporary Films 112, 113, 116, 118–19, 124, 152, 160, 165–6, 171n9, 200
Contempt (Jean-Luc Godard film) 2
'Continental' cinema 31, 38, 42, 47, 52, 57–8, 61, 66, 87, 89, 168, 181, 212, 219
 Continental circuit release 95–101
 perceptual shift towards 90–93
 selling French film on British market 93–5
Continental Film Review 91, 92–3, 95, 100, 101, 159
Cook, C. 68, 88
Cooper, Charles 112, 118–19, 124, 135n6, 160, 200
Cooper, Kitty and Charles 166
Coppola, Francis Ford 148, 180
co-productions 10, 93, 97, 107, 142–3, 145, 170n2, 202
Cosgrove, Mark 218
Cosmo, Glasgow 47, 61, 65
Cousin Cousine (Jean-Charles Tacchella film) 145, 164, 171n8, 194
Les Cousins (Claude Chabrol film) 108, 110, 135n2, 211
Coxhead, E. 42
Cravenne, Robert 93
Crewe, Quentin 117
La Crise est finie (Robert Siodmak film) 43
Cristo Proibito (Curzio Malaparte film) 89
criticism
 critical regard for French cinema 68–9
 public taste and critical opinion, disparity between 69–77
 shifts in (1982-2002) 184–6
The Critics (BBC) 117
Crocodile Dundee (Peter Fairnan film) 194
Crow, D. 82
Crowe, Russell 195
Cuba (Richard Lester film) 179
cult film 114–17
cultural snobbery 11, 198, 218
Curzon cinemas 13, 28, 38, 44–7, 55, 74, 94, 151, 161, 162, 164, 167, 168, 218–19

filmgoing audiences (1982-2002) 182–3, 186–7, 192, 193–4, 195, 200, 205
New Wave in 109, 110–11, 112, 121, 125, 128–30
Curzon Film Distributors 71–2
Cyrano de Bergerac (Jean-Paul Rappeneau film) 168, 203–4, 205

Dahan, Oliver 214
Daily Cinema 114
Daily Express 98, 128, 159, 188
Daily Herald 117
Daily Mail 17–18, 20, 28, 117, 128, 157, 158, 163, 170n7, 191
Daily Mirror 96–7, 190
Daily Record 111
Daily Sketch 36, 151
Daily Telegraph 115, 121, 128, 146, 156–7, 164, 188
Daily Worker 108, 121
Dalle, Béatrice 190–91
The Dames of the Bois de Boulogne (Robert Bresson film) 1, 6
Dangerous Moves (Richard Dembo film) 181
Danson, Ted 197
Dark Star (John Carpenter film) 189
Darville Films 171n9
Dassin, Jules 96, 184
David Golder (Julien Duvivier film) 32
Davies, Russell 155, 162
Davis, Stuart 29
Davy, Jean-François 157
Dawson, Jan 14, 154–5, 181
The Day After (Nicholas Meyer film) 189
Day for Night/La Nuit américaine (François Truffaut film) 153–4, 168
Daybreak/Le Jour se Lève (Marcel Carné film) 18, 61, 64, 67, 68–9
de Lane Lea, Major W. 87
de Sica, Vittorio 85
de Toth, André 127
Dearest Love/Le Souffle au Coeur (Louis Malle film) 162–4
Death in a French Garden/Péril en la demeure (Michel Deville film) 191–2
Decoin, Henri 89–90
Degand, C. 143
Dehn, Paul 117

Delannoy, Jean 71, 72
Dellow, R. 74
Delluc, Louis 34
Delon, Alain 145, 146, 148, 151, 160, 167
Deneuve, Catherine 146, 151, 154
Denning Films 38
Dent, Arthur 121
Depardieu, Gérard 194, 203, 204
Le Départ (Jerzy Skolimowski film) 167
D'Estaing, President Giscard 144, 156
Les Deux Timides (René Clair film) 25, 29
Deville, Michel 135n6, 191, 192
Dewe Matthews, T. 87
Le Diable au corps (Claude Autant-Lara film) 89
Dickinson, Thorold 27, 33, 39, 57, 62
Dignam, Virginia 148, 159, 162
Dirty Money/Un Flic (Jean-Pierre Melville film) 145, 146–7, 151, 152
distribution for New Wave films 111–14
Diva (Jean-Jacques Beineix film) 180, 187–8, 188–90, 191, 198, 206n3
Dixon, Campbell 108, 110
D'Morais, Joe 199–200, 202, 205
Dobson, Frank 34
Docherty, David 175–8, 179, 198
The Doctor in the Nude/Traitement de Choc (Alain Jessua film) 160
La Dolce Vita (Federico Fellini film) 127
Donald, James 23
À Double Tour (Claude Chabrol film) 167
La Douceur d'aimer (René Hervil film) 42
The Draughtsman's Contract (Peter Greenaway film) 187
Drazin, Charles 56, 57, 61, 63, 70, 77n1
Dréhy, Robert 185
Dreyer, Carl 25
dubbing 6, 10, 11, 13, 15n4, 26–7, 67, 75, 86–7, 96, 126, 135n7
 changing perceptions of French cinema (1970-82) and 147–8, 149–50, 151, 153, 154, 155, 168
 dubbed features, unpopularity of 149–55
Dublin Evening Press 109
Duffy, Kenneth 28–9
Dujardin, Jean 12, 215
Dulac, Germaine 35

Dumont, Bruno 213
Dunkley, Robert 195
Dupin, Christophe 132
Duras, Marguerite 179, 202
Duvivier, Julien 44, 45, 53, 61, 68, 73
Dyer, Ernest 59–60, 67–8
Dyer, Peter John 127

Eady levy 143
Easy Rider (Dennis Hopper film) 151, 180
Les Echos 110
L'Eclipse (Michelangelo Antonioni film) 134, 151
Ecstasy (Gustav Machaty film) 39
Eisenstein, Sergei 32, 40
Ekberg, Anita 127
Elliot, Tony 185
Ellis, John 58, 62, 186, 202
Emmanuelle (Just Jaeckin film) 135–6n10, 144–5, 156–7, 158–9, 169
The Empty Table (Masaki Kobayashi film) 181
En Rade (Alberto Cavalcanti film) 29
The End of St. Petersburg (Vsevolod Pudovkin film) 36
End of the Dialogue/Phela-ndaba (Anonomous film, 1974) 166
L'Enfance Nue (Maurice Pialat film) 167
Les Enfants du Paradis (Marcel Carné film) 2, 3
Les Enfants Terribles (Jean-Pierre Melville film) 4, 146
Engel, Andi 14, 176, 181, 182, 186, 193, 201–2, 203, 204–5, 216, 219
Engel, Pam 203, 205, 219
England, Leonard 86
The Entertainment Film in National Life (Broadcasting Research Unit) 175–6
Entrée des artistes (Marc Allégret film) 55
Epstein, Jean 25
The Erasers (Robbe-Grillet, A.) 115
Errol, P. 151
E.T. (Steven Spielberg film) 180
European tide 142–6
The Europeans (James Ivory film) 187
Eve (Joseph Losey film) 132
Evening News 128, 152, 159, 171n8
Evening Standard 20, 68, 70–71, 90, 99, 135n4, 184

Event magazine 186
Everyman cinema 38, 43–4, 47, 55, 75, 154–5, 183, 201
exhibition and regional film theatres (RFTs) 178–80
Exhibition (Jean-François Davy film) 157–8, 159, 162
exoticism 22
experimental films 31–2
L'Express 105
Eyles, Allen 75, 135–6n10

Fahrenheit 451 (François Truffaut film) 121
Fairfax-Jones, James 43–4
The Fall of the House of Usher (Jean Epstein film) 29
Farrebique (Georges Rouquier film) 215
Fassbinder, Rainer Werner 142
Fellini, Federico 87, 127, 128
La Femme du Boulanger (Marcel Pagnol film) 61, 65, 68, 215
Une Femme est une Femme (Jean-Luc Godard film) 135n7, 149
Une Femme Mariée (Jean-Luc Godard film) 121, 125
Femmes de Paris (Jean Loubignac film) 124, 185
Fernandel 91, 101, 185, 211
Ferran, Pascale 219
Ferreri, Marco 162
Feyder, Jacques 25, 46, 55, 59, 61
Fielding, Alan 188
The Fiends/Les Diaboliques (Henri-Georges Clouzot film) 92, 96, 98, 99, 101n4
The Fifth Element (Luc Besson film) 15n3
film-as-art 21
end of an era for? 47
Film (BBC TV) 203
Le Film Français 205
film industry in crisis 176–8
Film Societies 84, 91
changing cultures and advent of sound 31, 34–41, 42, 47
wartime cinema 59–63
The Film Till Now (Rotha, P.) 20, 24–5, 29, 32
filmgoing audiences (1982-2002) 175–206
audiences of RFTs (BRU survey) 178–9

British films on British screens 186–7
criticism, shifts in 184–6
cross-fertilization of audiences 179
exhibition and regional film theatres (RFTs) 178–80
failed French films on British screens 198–203
film industry in crisis 176–8
hit French films on British screens 187–96
London scene 180–84
perspective from France 196–8
programming 179–80
Films and Filming 95, 108–9, 122, 126, 149–50, 160, 166, 167, 168, 170n5, 171n9, 175
Films de France 94, 112–13
Films Illustrated 152
La Fin du Jour (Julien Duvivier film) 68
Financial Times 97, 115, 151
Finis Terrae (Jean Epstein film) 29
Flaud, Jacques 94, 109
Flesh (Andy Warhol film) 161
Followell, Duncan 157
For Pete's Sake (Peter Yates film) 146
Forbes, Jill 159
Ford, John 18, 85
Forman, Denis 63
Forsyth, Bill 165
Forsythe Hardy, H. 57–8, 60, 64
The Fourteenth of July (René Clair film) 32
La France Continue (wartime short film) 53
Franju, Georges 109
Fraser, Ingram 93–4, 95–6, 113
French, Philip 184
French Can Can (Jean Renoir film) 92
French cinema
critical regard for 68–9
dual position in Britain of 74–7
filmgoing audiences (1982-2002) 196–8
'French Revival' at NFT 107
hit French films on British screens 187–96
'Hollywoodisation' of 100–101, 107
pornographic cinema in France 144–5
realism of 67–8
talkies on British screens 29–33
wartime cinema 51–4
wartime cinema in Britain and 57–9

see also changing perceptions of French cinema (1970-82)
French cultural policy, changes in 144
French Cultural Studies 211
Friedberg, Anne 20–21
From Russia with Love (Terence Young film) 127

Gabin, Jean 33, 89, 148
La Gai Savoir (Jean-Luc Godard film) 106, 165
Gainsbourg, Charlotte 200
Gala Group 112, 113–14, 114–15
The Game of Love (Claude Autant-Lara film) 113
Gance, Abel 25
Gant, C. 195
Gaumont British Picture Corporation 29, 56, 82
General Cinema Theatres 71–2
The German Cinema in Great Britain after 1945 (Lembach, J.) 91
Gibbons, Stella 41
Gibbs, Patrick 115, 121, 128, 162, 164
Gigi (Vincente Minelli film) 135n4
Gillard, D. 151
Gillett, John 165, 166
Girardot, Annie 160
Girl About Town magazine 191
The Girl with the Dragon Tattoo (David Fincher film) 13
Giroud, Françoise 105
Glasgow Herald 188
And God Created Woman (Roger Vadim film) 90
Godard, Jean-Luc 105, 119–20, 121, 122, 125, 127, 133, 142, 185, 201, 205
The Godfather (Francis Ford Coppola film) 148
Goha (Jacques Baratier film) 107
Goldschmidt, Eric 66, 76–7
Golon, Anne and Serge (Sergeanne) 145
Gomery, D. 22
Goodman, Ezra 56
Goodmayes, M. 87
Grafton, M. 87
Graham, Peter 122, 126
La Grande Illusion (Jean Renoir film) 45, 64, 65
Granger, Derek 97–8

Greater London Council (GLC) 157, 158, 159, 161, 170n4
Green Card (Peter Weir film) 203
The Green Mare's Nest/Le Jument Verte (Claude Autant-Lara film) 106, 117
The Green Ray/Le Rayon Vert (Eric Rohmer film) 200–201
Greenaway, Peter 165
Greene, Graham 68
Gregory's Girl (Bill Forsyth film) 182, 187
Grousset, Didier 190
Guardian 2, 5, 110, 116, 119, 129, 147–8, 151, 184, 219
Guitry, Sacha 61
Guttenberg, Steve 197
Guy, Michel 144

Hackett, H. 54
Hake, Sabine 32
Hakim, Eric 30, 31, 42, 43
Halliwell, Leslie 100
Hampstead and Highgate Express 183
Haneke, Michael 116, 197
A Hard Day's Night (Richard Lester film) 132
Hardy, Thomas 193
Harmsworth, Madeleine 151
Harper, S. and Porter, V. 90
Harris, Mai 28
Hart, R., Dally, P. and Whitaker, S. 182, 185, 187
Hart, Romaine 14, 181, 182–3, 185, 186, 187, 188, 189, 193
Hart-Williams, Nick 165, 166
Hartley, Hal 205
Harvey, Miss J.M. 34, 38
Hawks, Howard 18
Hayward, Susan 144, 157, 166
Hazanavicius, Michel 11, 12, 215
H.D. (Hilda Doolittle) 20
Heal, S. 190
Heartbeat Detector (Nicolas Klotz film) 219
Heartbreaker (Pascal Chaumeil film) 197
Heat and Dust (James Ivory film) 184
Heaven Fell that Night/Les Bijoutiers de la Clair de Lune (Roger Vadim film) 95
Henley, J. 217
Hensel, Frank 63

Hibbin, Nina 121
Hidden/Caché (Michael Haneke film) 116, 197
Hill, Derek 107, 165–6
Hinxman, Margaret 17–18, 89, 147, 154, 157, 158, 162
Hiroshima, Mon Amour (Alain Resnais film) 105, 108, 111–12, 113, 114, 118, 128, 211
Hitchcock, Alfred 18, 43, 47, 98, 189
Hitler, Adolf 46, 53
Hobson, Harold 118
Hoellering, George 55, 166, 181
Hollingsworth, A. 110
Hollywood films 1–2, 5, 9, 10–11, 13, 14, 84, 86–7, 97, 118, 123, 179, 180, 202, 203, 218
  antidotes to, welcome for 189–90, 212–13, 214
  dominance of 143, 145, 196
  emergence of 'New Hollywood' 159–60
  heritage films and differentiation from 197–8
  'Hollywoodisation' of French cinema 100–101, 107
  sound, changing cultures and advent of 18, 19, 20, 22, 25, 26, 31, 32, 33
  spectaculars from, upsurge of (1970–82) 141–2
  technological innovation in 186
  turbulent times 81, 83, 90, 93
  wartime cinema 51, 54, 56–7, 58, 65, 68, 70–71
Holmes, Su 82, 91
Un Homme et une Femme (Claude Lelouch film) 129, 130, 152, 188
Un Homme qui me plaît (Claude Lelouch film) 167
Hotel du Nord (Marcel Carné film) 55, 64
Houston, Penelope 14, 123, 126, 128, 129, 131, 132–3, 134, 141–2, 151, 157, 184
Howden, Peter 55, 186
Hudson, Christopher 162
Huillet, Danièlle 165, 182
Hunnings, Neville 144, 160–61, 170n3, 170n4
Huston, John 97
Hutchinson, T. 194

I Mongoli (film by André de Toth and Leopoldo Savona) 127
Igor (Anthony Leondis animation) 10
Independent 194, 205
India Song (Marguerite Duras film) 179, 202
Infidelity/Altri Tempi (Alessandro Blasetti film) 100
Inglourious Basterds (Quentin Tarantino film) 10
Inside North Viet Nam (Felix Green documentary) 166
International Federation of Film Archives (FIAF) 63
International Film Distributors 94
International Film Theatre 112, 113
Into the Blue/Paris Méditerranée (Joe May film) 29
Irish Press 109
Isaacs, Jeremy 186
Isles of Sinners/Dieu a Besoin des Hommes (Jean Delannoy film) 100
Italian Straw Hat/Un Chapeau de Paille d'Italie (René Clair film) 25, 29

Jacey cinemas 74, 112, 157
Jaekin, Just 144–5, 156–7
James, Nick 190, 212–13, 218, 219
Jancsó, Miklós 166
Jarman, Derek 165
Jarosy, Ivo 166
Jealousy (Robbe-Grillet, A.) 115, 118
Jean de Florette (Claude Berri film) 2, 9, 168, 192–6, 197, 199, 201, 203
Jean de la Lune (Jean Choux film) 42
Jenkinson, Philip 168
Jessel, Ian R. 150
Jessua, Alain 160
Jeunet, Jean-Pierre 213, 216, 219
John Calder Publishers 115
Johnson, Celia 109–10
Johnson, Douglas 155–6
Johnston, Sheila 135n8
Johnstone, I. 189, 192
Jour de Fête (Jacques Tati film) 83
Juggernaut (Richard Lester film) 157
Jules et Jim (François Truffaut film) 2, 105, 121

Kameradschaft (Georg Pabst film) 32
Kamikaze (Didier Grousset film) 190, 199–200

Kanal (Erden Kiral film) 166
The Keepers/La Tête Contre Les Murs (Georges Franju film) 109
Kine Weekly 93–4, 113
Kinematograph Weekly 28, 90, 91, 95–6
Kingsley, David 125–6, 127, 136n11
Kinugasa, Teinosuke 40
Kirkhope, Tony 179
Kirwan, Patrick 68, 70–71, 72
The Kiss (Rodin sculpture) 108
Knight Without Armour (Jacques Feyder film) 55
Korosawa, Akira 87
Kristel, Sylvia 156
Kutner, Philip 94–5, 160

Lady Chatterley (Pascale Ferran film) 218, 219
Lai, Francis 130
Lambert, Gavin 131, 132
Lancaster, Burt 151
Landru (Claude Chabrol film) 118
Lang, Fritz 18, 40
Lang, Jack 196, 197, 198
Langlois, Henri 63
Larsson, Stieg 13
Lassally, Walter 86–7, 88–9
The Last Battle (Luc Besson film) 189–90
The Last Chance (Leopold Lindtberg film) 66, 71
The Last Metro (François Truffaut film) 200
Last Tango in Paris (Bernando Bertolucci film) 152
Last Year in Marienbad/L'Année Dernière à Marienbad (Alain Resnais film) 114, 115, 116–17, 118, 120, 123, 126, 145
anticipation surrounding arrival of 117–20
Lawrence, D.H. 219
Léaud, Jean-Pierre 109, 111
La Lectrice (Michel Deville film) 192, 200
L'Effort Franco-Britannique (Anon, 1940) 53
Lejeune, Caroline 19, 20, 22, 37–8, 44, 65, 72
Lelouch, Claude 129, 145, 164, 188
Lembach, Joachim 10, 11, 14, 15n2, 91, 100

The Leopard/Il Gattopardo (Luchino Cisconti film) 151, 152
Lermon, Sue 201
Lester, Richard 132
Let's Go to the Pictures (Barry, I.) 20, 31–2
Levy, Raoul 95
Lewin, David 128
Lewis, J. 157
L'Herbier, Marcel 25
Les Liaisons Dangereuses (Rogen Vadim film) 114
Libération 109
Lift to the Scaffold/L'Ascenseur au Chauffaud (Louis Malle film) 128
The Light Across the Street (Georges Lacombe film) 92
Lindtberg, Leopold 71
Lipstadt, Aaron 189
Listener 115–16, 117, 184
Lister, Moira 113
literary adaptations and heritage films 168–9
Lloyd, Harold 25
London Evening Standard 20, 152, 155
London Film Institute Society 39, 63
London Film Society 35, 60–61
London Polytechnic 112
London scene, filmgoing audiences (1982-2002) 180–84
Longford, Frank Pakenham, Lord 160–61
Losey, Joseph 132
Love Eternal/L'Éternel Retour (Jean Delannoy film) 71, 72, 74
Love on a Pillow/Le Repos du Guerrier (Roger Vadim film) 114
Love Story (Arthus Hiller film) 130
Lubitsch, Ernst 40
Lucas, George 180
Ludemann, Ralph 205
Lulli, Folco 97
Lye, Len 60

M (Fritz Lang film) 18
Machaty, Gustav 39
McLeod, P. 190
Macpherson, Kenneth 20–21
McSnarry, D. 128
Madame Sans Gêne (Léonce Perret film) 24
Maedchen in Uniform (film by Leontine Sagan and Carl Froelich) 27, 32

La Main Chaude (Gérard Oury film) 113
Mainline Pictures (Hart's Screen Group) 181, 188, 190–91, 198, 200, 206n3
Makavejev, Dusan 165
Making It/Les Valseuses (Bertrand Blier film) 161, 162, 166, 169
Malcolm, Derek 151, 153, 156, 158, 162, 164, 184, 189, 192, 193, 194, 202, 203–4
Malle, Louis 107, 110, 120, 121, 124, 128–9, 133, 145, 162–3
Malraux, André 132
Maltby, R. 81
Mamselle Striptease (Marc Allégret film) 124
Man Ray 35
Manchester Guardian 20, 89–90, 101
Manon des Sources (Claude Berri film) 187–8, 190, 192, 193, 194, 195–6, 201
Manon (Henri-Georges Clouzot film) 89
Manvell, Roger 67, 71, 74, 215
The March of the Penguins (Luc Jacquet animation) 10
Marcorelles, Louis 108, 131, 132
La Marine Française (wartime short film) 53
Marius (Alexander Korda film) 27
marketing 2, 28–9, 44, 55, 89, 90, 101n2, 111, 113, 114, 124, 127–8, 133, 134, 143, 156, 188, 217
Marlowe, David 84–5
Die Marquise von O (Eric Rohmer film) 168
The Marriage of Maria Braun (Rainer Werner Fassbinder film) 180
La Marseillaise (Jean Renoir film) 64
Marshall, Bill 8, 212
Maupassant, Guy de 113–14
Mayle, Peter 195, 215
Mayne, Richard 195, 201
Mazdon, L. and Wheatley, C. 9, 212–13, 214
Mazdon, Lucy 196, 197, 198
Melville, Jean-Pierre 146–8, 204–5
Memories of Underdevelopment (Tomàs Gutiérrez Alea film) 166
Le Mépris (Jean-Luc Godard film) 185
Mercier, Michèle 160
Midnight Cowboy (John Schlesinger film) 151

Millar, Gavin 115–16, 184
Miller, Claude 200, 205
Miller, Hugh 20, 34
Le Million (René Clair film) 23, 65
Mimouni, Gilles 205
Miracle Films 90, 160, 171n9
Mississippi Mermaid/La Sirène du Mississippi (François Truffaut film) 154–5, 168
Les Mistons (François Truffaut film) 106–7, 108, 131–2
Mizoguchi, Kenji 87
Moderato Cantabile (Peter Brook film) 127
Molinaro, Edouard 110
Momentum Pictures' exit poll survey 13
Mon Oncle d'Amérique (Alain Resnais film) 200
Mon Oncle (Jacques Tati film) 106, 126
Le Monde 116, 144
Mondo Cane (film by Paolo Cavara, Gualtierro Jiacopetti and Franco Prosperi) 125
Monsieur Vincent (Maurice Cloche film) 74
Montagu, Ivor 14, 20, 33, 34, 47, 62
Montand, Yves 97, 98–9, 194
Monthly Film Bulletin 135n3, 184
The Moon in the Gutter (Jean-Jacques Beineix film) 190
Moore, B. 22
Moreau, Jeanne 128–9, 132, 167
Morgan, Michelle 211
Morning Star 148, 159, 162
Morris, Phyllis 37
Morrison, Captain H.G. 44
Morrison, David 175–8, 179
La Mort du Cygne (Jean Benoit-Lévy film) 55, 65
Mortimer, Penelope 160
Le Mouton à Cinq Pattes (Henri Verneuil film) 185
Movie magazine 184
Mowe, Richard 217
Moynihan, John 135n4
Mr Deeds Gowes to Town (Frank Capra film) 65
Mr Wonderbird/La Bergère et le ramoneur (Paul Grimault film) 92
Mulvey, Laura 165
Muriel (Alain Resnais film) 117, 120–21, 126, 134

Murphy, Robert 82, 176, 180, 181, 182
Murphy, Stephen 125, 161
Mycroft, Walter 20, 21, 34
A Mysterious Affair of Style (Adair, G.) 1

Nana (Jean Renoir film) 37
Napoleon Buonaparte 162
National Film Finance Corporation 143
National Film Theatre (NFT) 85, 107, 113, 120–21, 124, 125, 131
'national' tastes in film 24–6
La Neige était sale (Luis Stavslasky film) 124
Néry, Jean 110, 126
New Realm Films 171n9
New Statesman 76, 117, 121, 130, 131, 146, 157, 189–90
New Wave 105–35
   Anderson and Truffaut, relationship between 131–2
   anticipation surrounding arrival of *Marienbad* 117–20
   backlash against 120–22, 133
   cult film 114–17
   disillusionment with 127–8
   distribution 111–14
   dubious fortunes of 123–6
   end of French New Wave 142–6
   first recognition of 106–11
   'French Revival' at NFT 107
   legacies 130–33, 134
   low tide for 126–30
   origins of 105–6
   retrospective image 106, 133–4
   standing in retrospect 133–4
   stir caused by first films 107–8
   style without substance 129–30
News Chronicle 108, 135n1
Nice-Matin 110
The Night Porter (Liliana Caviani film) 157
Nimoy, Leonard 197, 198
Noel, Magali 89
Norris, Sue 183
Nothing but Time/Rien que les heures (Alberto Cavalcanti film) 29
A Nous la liberté (René Clair film) 32
Nouvel Observateur 129
Nowell-Smith, Geoffrey 106, 107, 108, 112, 113, 118, 126, 132
Ma Nuit Chez Maud (Eric Rohmer film) 168

Nurse, Keith 188
Nyman, Kenneth A. 30–31

Oakley, C.A. 65
Observer 2, 9, 19, 20, 37–8, 44, 65, 149, 151, 155, 162, 184
Observer Review 116
Occupe-toi d'Amélie (Claude Autant-Lara film) 89
Odeon cinemas 44, 56, 82, 98, 99, 123, 146, 155, 185, 188, 203
Odeon Printworks, Manchester 13
The Odessa File (Ronald Neame film) 157
Ophüls, Max 40, 87
Oppidian 157–8
Oshima, Nagisa 165
Les Otages (Raymond Bernard film) 55, 65
Outside London 125

Pagnol, Marcel 61, 169, 192–3, 194, 196, 198, 215–16, 219
Painlevé, Jean 40
Palance, Jack 127
Pallanca, William 112–13, 118–19, 127, 135n6, 149–50
Papatakis, Nico 116
Les Parapluies de Cherbourg (Jacques Demy film) 105
Parente, William 188, 194
Paris Nous Appartient (Jacques Rivette film) 105, 108, 116, 117
Paris Pullman 112, 116, 125, 183
Parrish, Robert 147
Partie de Campagne (Jean Renoir film) 52
Passion (Jean-Luc Godard film) 200
The Passion of the Christ (Mel Gibson film) 10
Pat Garrett and Billy the Kid (Sam Peckinpah film) 146
Patterson, Hannah 217, 218
Pauline at the Beach (Eric Rohmer firm) 201
Pearson, Gabriel 117
Pearson, George 62
Peckinpah, Sam 146
People 117, 159
Pépé le Moko (Julien Duvivier film) 45, 65, 73, 200
Perry, Simon 178, 187

Perspectives 1970: CNC Bulletin d'information (91) 134
Petit Club Français 63
Le Petit Soldat (Jean-Luc Godard film) 119, 127
La Petite Voleuse (Claude Miller film) 200
Petley, Julian 179, 183, 198–200, 201–2
Pham, P. 205
Phelps, Guy 180–81
Philippe, Gérard 95
Pialat, Maurice 167, 204
Picture Post 91
Picturegoer 22, 66, 84, 87, 96
Pierrot le Fou (Jean-Luc Godard film) 105, 127, 134
Planet Films 171n9
Plant, Sir Arnold (and Plant Committee, 1950) 82–3
Platt-Mills, Barney 165
Playboy 110, 157
The Ploughman's Lunch (Richard Eyre film) 187
Pokorny, Michael 17
Polanski, Roman 151, 193
Pontecorvo, Gilles 165
pornographic cinema in France 144–5
Porter, Henry 2, 9
Porter, Vincent 18, 27, 29, 31, 36, 38, 42, 45, 143–4, 145–6
Powell, Dilys 58, 88, 108, 117–18, 120, 147, 157, 184
Price, Peter 60
Price, Stanley 149, 151
programming 27, 42, 55, 74, 75, 175, 179–80, 181, 182, 183, 186, 198, 217
Prostitute (Tony Garnett film) 182, 187
The Proud Ones/Le Cheval d'orgueil (Claude Chabrol film) 201
Prouse, Derek 117, 118
Proust, Marcel 203
The Public Enemy (William A. Wellman film) 151
public taste and critical opinion, disparity between 69–77
Pudovkin, Vsevolod 20, 32, 36
Pulleine, Tim 179, 185, 186, 191, 198
The Pumpkin Eater (Jack Clayton film) 132

Quai des brumes (Marcel Carné film) 64
Les Quatre Cents Coups (François Truffaut

film) 105, 106, 108–9, 110–11, 132, 211
Queenan, Joe 105–6, 133
The Queen's Necklace (film by Tony Lekain and Gaston Ravel) 28
Queval, Jean 215–16
Quigley, Isabel 117, 119, 120
Quinn, James 112, 125
Quota Act (UK) 30–31, 56
quota regulations 25, 30–31, 56, 71, 143–4, 152, 156

Radio Times 168
Raft, George 151
Raimu (Jules Muraire) 33, 68
Ramuntcho (René Barberis film) 76
Rank, J. Arthur 71
Rank Film Distribution 56, 70–71, 72, 74, 82, 89, 114, 124, 146, 176, 180, 182
Rappeneau, Jean-Paul 203–4
Raven, Susan 156
Raylor, John Russell 121
Rayns, Tony 146
Razzia sur la Chnouf (Henri Decoin film) 89, 101n3, 124
regional film theatres (RFTs) 125, 178–80, 181, 186, 206n2
Reichsfilm archive 63
Reisz, Karel 131, 165
Renoir, Jean 25, 37, 44, 52, 53, 67, 68, 87, 108, 110, 167, 169, 175
repertory and revivals 64–6
Repulsion (Roman Polanski film) 151
Resnais, Alain 105, 108, 114, 116, 118, 120, 126, 128, 133, 145, 175, 200
The Return of Martin Guerre (Daniel Vigne film) 184
Reunion Film 38
Rhode, Eric 115
Richards, Jeffrey 55–6, 59
Richardson, Tony 165
Du Rififi chez les Hommes (Jules Dassin film) 96, 99, 145, 148, 200
Rive, Kenneth 92, 111, 112, 114, 118–19, 125–6, 135–6n10, 135n6, 161, 163, 200, 201
Rivette, Jacques 108, 116
Robbe-Grillet, Alain 115–16, 118
Robinson, David 32, 34, 36, 39–40, 41, 106–7, 108, 115, 119–20, 121, 124, 135n9, 147, 151–2, 157, 184, 192, 195
Rocha, Glauber de Andrade 165
Rochant, Eric 205
Rodin, Auguste 108
Rohmer, Eric 133, 164, 168, 200–201, 204
Le Roi des resquilleurs (Pierre Colombier film) 42
Rolling Stone magazine 200
La Ronde (Max Ophüls film) 87, 92, 94, 129, 180, 185
A Room with A View (James Ivory film) 129, 184, 187, 193
Rossellini, Roberto 87, 108
Rotha, Paul 20, 24–6, 27, 29, 32
Roud, Richard 107, 129, 131, 132, 133, 147–8
The Round-Up/Szegénylegények (Miklós Jancsó film) 166
Roxy, Westbourne Grove 112
Ruiz, Raul 203
The Rules of the Game (Jean Renoir film) 2
Russell-Taylor, John 47, 121, 147, 152

Sainsbury, Peter 165
The Samourai (Jean-Pierre Melville film) 147, 150
Samson, J. 34
Sartre, Jean-Paul 116
Saturday Review 110, 135n2
Savalas, Terry 147
Savona, Leopoldo 127
Schlesinger, John 165
Schlondorff, Volker 203
Scorsese, Martin 180
Scotsman 188
Scott, Ridley 189
The Seashell and the Clergyman (Germaine Dulac film) 35
second features on circuits 146–9
Sedgwick, John 17
Segal, Clancy 158–9
Selleck, Tom 197
Selwyn-Lloyd, Selwyn 135n4
Sennett, Mack 25
A Sense of Loss (Max Ophüls film) 166
Sequence magazine 131, 184
Serreau, Coline 197, 198
Seventeen (Annelise Meineche film) 135–6n10, 152

Sexton, Jamie 19, 20, 21, 32, 35, 36, 37, 41
sexy cinema 155–9
Shail, Robert 165
Shaw, T. 161
Shelley, Norman 29
Shoe Shine (Vittorio de Sica film) 66
Shoot the Pianist/Tirez sur la pianiste (François Truffaut film) 120, 121, 127, 211
Shorter, Eric 146, 163
The Sicilian Plan/Le Clan des Siciliens (Henri Verneuil film) 145, 148–9, 150, 151
Siclier, Jacques 119, 131, 132
Sight and Sound 215–16, 218, 219
  changing perceptions (1970-82) 141, 143, 144, 160, 165, 166
  cultural change and advent of sound 18, 19, 23, 30, 32, 47
  film culture of the 1950s 83, 84, 86, 88–9, 100
  gold standard for art cinema, French films as 212–13
  New Wave 108–9, 116, 119, 121, 123, 124–5, 127, 131, 132
  video and French film 175, 178, 184
  wartime cinema 52, 53–4, 67, 71, 74
Signoret, Simone 95
silent cinema, exportability of 24
Silken Skin/La Peau Douce (François Truffaut film) 121, 122
Siodmak, Robert 43
Slow Motion (Jean-Luc Godard film) 200
Smith, R.D. 97
soft-core porn, scandals surrounding 160–62
sound, changing cultures and advent of 17–48
  Academy cinema 1, 11, 19, 28, 30–32, 38, 42–3, 44, 45, 46–7
  advent of sound 22–6
  art film culture 21–2
  avant-garde 21
  beginning to take film seriously 18–22
  commercial power of cinema 19–20
  entrenchment of commercial cinema, resistance to 20–21
  Everyman cinema 38, 43–4, 47
  exoticism 22
  experimental films 31–2

film-as-art 21
film-as-art, end of an era for? 47
Film Societies 31, 34–41, 42, 47
French talkies on British screens 29–33
  marketing 28–9
  'national' tastes in film 24–6
  pioneers, afictionados and 33–4
  problems of sound, finding solutions for 26–9
  silent cinema, exportability of 24
  specialised cinemas 31–2, 42–6
  subtitling, art of 27–8
specialised film culture (1950-59) 83–7
Spectator 20, 72, 117, 157, 158, 162
Spielberg, Steven 180
Stalin, Josef 52
Star 108
Stardust (Michael Apted film) 157
Stavisky (Alain Resnais film) 145
Stephenson, Ralph 112
Sternberg, Josef von 18
Stimpson, Mansel 191–2
Stokes, John 211–12
Stolen Kisses/Baisers Volés (François Truffaut film) 154
Stone, Barbara and David 182
The Story of Adele H. (François Truffaut film) 155–6
Stratford Express 211–12
Straub, Jean-Marie 165, 182
Strausfeld, Peter 46, 75, 76, 181
Street, Sarah 97
Streisand, Barbra 146
Studio One 45, 68, 112, 157
style without substance, New Wave criticism 129–30
subtitling 6, 10, 15n4, 26–8, 67, 71, 96, 149, 151, 155, 168, 203
  art of 27–8
Subway (Luc Besson film) 190
Summers, Sue 112, 182–4, 186
Sun 151
Sunday Express 56, 121, 151, 164
Sunday Mirror 151
Sunday People 158
Sunday Telegraph 121, 147, 195, 201
Sunday Times 58, 88, 108, 117–18, 147, 156, 157, 182–3, 184, 188, 192, 194
Sutherland, A. 187
Swaim, Bob 200

Swann in Love (Volker Schlöndorff film) 203
Symphonie Fantastique (Christian-Jaque film) 72, 74

Tacchella, Jean-Charles 145, 164
Taken (Pierre Morel film) 10
Tales of Ugetsu (Kenji Mizoguchi film) 89
Target Films 150, 171n9
Tati, Jacques 96, 106, 167, 189
Tautou, Audrey 216
Taxi (Gérard Pirès film) 75, 216
Taylor. A.J.P. 17
Un Tel Père et fils (Julien Duvivier film) 53
Tell No One (Guillaume Canet film) 212–13
Le Temps Moderne (Sartre, J.-P.) 116
La Terra Trema (Luchino Visconti film) 185
La Terre (André Antoine film) 192
Tess (Roman Polanski film) 193
That's Entertainment (Jack Haley, Jr. film) 157
Thaw, John 195
Thérèse Raquin (Jacques Feyder film) 29
Thinkell, Arthur 147, 150, 162
37,2 Degrés le Matin (Jean-Jacques Beineix film) 190–91
Thomas, Yvonne 23–4, 27
Thomson, David 141
Three Men and a Baby (Leonard Nimoy film) 197
The Threepenny Opera (Georg Pabst film) 27
Time 129, 147
Time and Tide 68, 120
Time Out 185–6, 187, 191, 197
Times 23, 115, 120, 121, 129, 130, 135n8, 147, 164, 184
Times Literary Supplement 155–6, 201
titling (and retitling) 6, 126, 147
Tobis Film Distributors 38
Today's Cinema 90, 112
Tom Jones (Tony Richardson film) 132
Tombs, R. and Tombs, I. 63
Totterdall, A. 190
A Town Called Hell (Robert Parrish film) 147
Tracey, Michael 175–8, 179

Trans-Europe Express (Alain Robbe-Grillet film) 135n9
The Tree of Wooden Clogs (Ermanno Olmi film) 180
Trevelyan, John 124, 135n9, 161
Tribune 97, 107
Trintignant, Jean-Louis 129
Trop Belle pour toi (Betrand Blier film) 204
Truffaut, François 105, 106, 109, 110, 111, 120, 121–2, 126–7, 133, 145, 153–5, 155–6, 164, 167, 200
  Anderson and, relationship between 131–2
Tunbridge Wells 146, 169n1
Turner, Adrian 152–3, 154
Turner, Robin 121
Twentynine Palms (Bruno Dumont film) 213
Tyneside Film Society 59
Tyneside Film Theatre 179

Ugetsu Monogatari (Kenji Mizoguchi film) 89
UK Film Council 2, 13, 14, 77, 217
Under the Roofs of Paris/Sous les toits de Paris (René Clair film) 23, 64, 65
Unifrance 5, 93–4, 95, 110, 126, 190, 217
Union Internationale de l'Exploitation Cinématographique (International Exhibitors Union) 143
Unknown Soldier (Advin Laine film) 166
Usher, Shaun 190, 191

Vadim, Roger 90, 95
Van Eyck, Peter 97
Vanel, Charles 97, 98–9
Vaughn, Olwen 14, 61, 62, 63
Vautrin (Pierre Billon film) 76
Vedres, Nicole 73
Ventura, Ray 95
Verdi, Giuseppe 196
Vertov, Dziga 40
A Very Long Engagement (Jean-Pierre Jeunet film) 213
Vesselo, Arthur 52, 66–7
video technologies 7, 170n4, 176, 177–8, 203–5, 206n3, 216–17
Une Vie (Alexandre Astruc film) 113–14, 124

La Vie en Rose (Oliver Dahan film) 212–13, 214
Vie Privée (Louis Malle film) 121
Vigo, Jean 39–40, 43–4, 60, 204
Vincendeau, Ginette 26–7
Visconti, Luchino 128, 152
Visions 202–3
Les Visiteurs (Jean-Marie Poiré film) 75, 204
Viva Maria! (Louis Malle film) 128–9, 167, 168
Vivre sa Vie (Jean-Luc Godard film) 121
Vogue 20
von Trier, Lars 134
The Voyeur (Robbe-Grillet, A.) 115
Vue Cinema, Hull 13

The Wages of Fear/Le Salaire de la peur (Henri-Georges Clouzot film) 96, 97, 98, 99, 100, 145, 147
Walker, Alexander 121, 130, 154, 155, 164, 184, 189, 192–3, 194, 196, 197, 198
Walsh, Maurice 153
Walsh, Michael 163
The Wanderer (Jean-Gabriel Albicocco film) 181
Warhol, Andy 161, 165
wartime cinema 51–77
　Academy cinema 53, 55, 60, 61, 72, 75–6
　British cinema 55–7
　'canonisation' 51, 65–6, 67
　critical regard for French cinema 68–9
　dual position of French cinema in Britain 74–7
　Film Societies 59–63
　foriign films, special nature of 66–9
　French cinema 51–4
　French cinema in Britain 57–9
　public taste and critical opinion, disparity between 69–77

realism of French cinema 67–8
　repertory and revivals 64–6
　'selective' nature of French films shown 66–7
Watts, Stephen 56
We From Kronstadt (Efim Dzigan film) 18
Webster, P. 156
Weekend 105
Weightman, John 116
Welles, Orson 189
Westfront 1918 (Georg Pabst film) 32
What's On 193
Wheatley, C. 101n2, 135n5, 219
Whitebait, William 68
Whitehouse, Mary 161, 163
Whitley, Reg 96–7
Wickes, David 194
Wilcox, John 89
The Wild One/L'Enfant Sauvage (François Truffaut film) 124, 154
Williams, Professor Bernard 170n4
Wilson, Cecil 147, 160, 161, 163
Wilson, Norman 62, 84, 86
Wingate, H.H. 71–2, 129
Wingate, Roger 72, 130, 183–4, 186, 187, 192, 193, 219
Winnington, Richard 68
Wistrich, Enid 170n4
Wolf, Julia 11, 14, 27–8, 71
Wollen, Peter 165
Wordsworth, Araminta 147, 162–3
Wright, Basil 44

X-certification 87–90, 92, 96, 100, 112, 113–14, 127, 144, 160, 164

A Year in Provence (Mayle, P.) 195, 215
Yentob, Alan 199
Yerrill, D.A. 67, 70
Youthful Sinners/Les Tricheurs 120

Zéro de Conduite (Jean Vigo film) 39–40, 43–4

CPSIA information can be obtained
at www.ICGtesting.com
Printed in the USA
JSHW032339080421
13393JS00007B/155